LIVING ART

LIVING ART

INDIVIDUAL AND COLLECTIVE CREATIVITY:
BECOMING PAUL-ÉMILE BORDUAS

JEAN-PHILIPPE WARREN

TRANSLATED BY STEVEN URQUHART

PREFACE BY RAY ELLENWOOD

Publishers of Singular
Fiction, Poetry, Nonfiction, Translation, Drama and Graphic Books

Library and Archives Canada Cataloguing in Publication

Warren, Jean-Philippe, 1970- [Art vivant, autour de Paul-Émile Borduas. English]
Living art : individual and collective creativity : becoming Paul-Émile Borduas / Jean-
Philippe Warren ; translated by Steven Urquhart ; preface by Ray Ellenwood.

Translation of: L'art vivant, autour de Paul-Émile Borduas.
Includes bibliographical references.
Issued in print and electronic formats.
ISBN 978-1-55096-716-6 (softcover).--ISBN 978-1-55096-717-3 (EPUB).--
ISBN 978-1-55096-718-0 (Kindle).--ISBN 978-1-55096-719-7 (PDF)

1. Borduas, Paul-Émile, 1905-1960. 2. Painters--Québec (Province)--
Biography. 3. Automatism (Art movement)--Québec (Province).
I. Urquhart, Steven, 1974-, translator II. Title.
III. Title: Art vivant, autour de Paul-Émile Borduas. English.

ND249.B6W3713 2017   759.11'4   C2017-906152-6
                                         C2017-906153-4

We gratefully acknowledge the Canada Council for the Arts,
the Canada Council for the Arts translation program,
the Government of Canada, the Ontario Arts Council,
and the Ontario Media Development Corporation
for their support toward our publishing activities.

Canadian sales representation:
The Canadian Manda Group, 664 Annette Street,
Toronto ON M6S 2C8   www.mandagroup.com   416 516 0911

North American and international distribution, and U.S. sales:
Independent Publishers Group, 814 North Franklin Street,
Chicago IL 60610   www.ipgbook.com   toll free: 1 800 888 4741

For Apolline and Léan

For Tristan and Fiona

Contents

WHY YOU SHOULD READ THIS BOOK

A marvellous world is in the making
that will completely destroy the execrable isolation
of Christianity; an isolation of the
soul refusing the universe.

— PAUL-ÉMILE BORDUAS[1]

Paul-Émile Borduas and the Montreal group called the Automatists
are recognized as major figures in the history of modernism in the
province of Quebec and in Canada as a whole. The painters of the
group were among the first in North America to experiment with
non-figurative painting, contemporaneously with the Abstract
Expressionists in the United States, and some came to be quickly associated with Lyrical Abstraction in Europe. They are among the most
internationally well-recognized Canadian painters, but they have also
shaped the physical aspect of Montreal through their art and sculpture
in public spaces of the city, including the subway. But the Automatists
were also an interdisciplinary group including writers, theatre people,
dancers/choreographers, photographers, and designers who have had
a broad impact on the cultural history of their province. One of their
most important collective acts was to publish a manifesto in the great
tradition of European avant-garde movements of the first half of
the twentieth century, criticizing their society and presenting their
work as a call for social and artistic transformation. The manifesto was
entitled *Refus global*, it was published in August 1948, and it caused

---

[1] Letter from Paul-Émile Borduas to Noël Lajoie, Paris, November 29, 1956, in
Écrits II (Montreal: Les Presses de l'Université de Montréal, 1997), p.875.

such a strongly negative official and public response that the lives of the signatories were dramatically affected.

The history of Borduas and the Automatist movement has been widely documented in Quebec through a host of exhibitions, catalogues, biographies, chronologies, monographs, journals, letters, films and articles over the past fifty years. Unfortunately, not much of this material has been made available in English. There have been a few exhibitions such as *The Automatist Revolution*, curated by Roald Nasgaard, first shown at the Varley Gallery of Markham in 2009 before travelling to the Albright-Knox in Buffalo and then, with a pause, returning to Canada through Edmonton, Grande Prairie and Saskatoon. That exhibition and its catalogue (Douglas & McIntyre, 2009) helped spread the word. There was Marc Czarnecki's *Surrealism and Quebec Literature* (University of Toronto Press, 1984), the translation of André G. Bourassa's important book, and more recently the publication of Peter Feldstein's translation of François-Marc Gagnon's *Paul-Émile Borduas: A Critical Biography* (McGill-Queen's University Press, 2013), an update of the original French version published in 1978, always considered a primary source of information on the painter. Exile Editions have done their part, as a glance at their booklist will show.[2] But these are only a small sampling, barely a taste. That is why Steven Urquhart's translation of Jean-Philippe Warren's *L'art vivant: Autour de Paul-Émile Borduas* is so welcome, so necessary, particularly because it takes pains to place the group in its social and artistic context, explaining the intricacies of a society in which the publication of a relatively modest manifesto (similar to others published in Europe, especially France, in the period between the two world wars) should cause such a strong official and public reaction that Borduas, author of the lead manifesto in the document, a respected artist and

---

[2] Publisher's note: In addition to a number of articles relevant to Borduas and Automatism in *Exile, A Literary Quarterly* (now *ELQ* magazine), Exile Editions has published Ray Ellenwood's English translation of *Refus global* (*Total Refusal*, revised edition, 2009) and his *Egregore, A History of the Montreal Automatist Movement* (1992).

teacher, should find himself out of a job, estranged from his wife, and effectively shunned by even the progressive Catholic milieu in which he had moved.

The negative reaction to Borduas' manifesto in Quebec was primarily due to the fact that it was seen as an attack on the Church. Later readings view it the same way, except that now the anticlericalism of *Refus global* is usually regarded positively, as a courageous reaction against a highly conservative institution, part of an early phase of the broader social movement in Quebec often called the Quiet Revolution. But as Jean-Philippe Warren points out, looking back to 1948, Borduas' position appears surprising, even paradoxical, given the fact that he was raised and educated in a Catholic environment, studied religious art in Quebec and France as a young man, worked in his early years as a church decorator with his mentor, the highly spiritual Ozias Leduc, and later fought for "living art" against academicism and conservatism along with artists and critics who were men of the cloth. It is this apparent contradiction that Warren sets out to explore, by giving a detailed account of the painter's intellectual milieu, including the impact of such internationally known and highly influential Catholic intellectuals as philosophers Jacques Maritain and Henri Bergson, and the Dominican monk, artist, critic and educator, Marie-Alain Couturier.

It is true that *Refus global* is often read out of context, especially in English Canada and by commentators who want to present the manifesto as a highly revolutionary document, as if Borduas and the Automatist group suddenly sprang up as isolated figures in a hostile, sternly conservative environment. Jean-Philippe Warren works to bring nuance to that picture. He shows the power of the Church at the time, its impact on education and public taste, its tendency to reject vehemently any avant-garde tendencies in art. Certainly nothing so detailed has been available in English as Warren's account of the sclerotic attitudes in the two rival institutions responsible for art education in Montreal in the mid-1940s: the École des Beaux-Arts and the

École du Meuble. Borduas worked at the latter, and Warren carefully documents, through reference to an impressive array of published texts, letters, interviews and newspaper articles, the tensions between and within the schools, resulting in student and faculty objections to what Borduas called "a pedagogy of repression" and to the actions of small-minded administrators. This is particularly well done in the third section, "The Charge of the Expormidable Painter." But Warren is just as detailed in showing that there were progressives within the Church and among Catholic intellectuals, doing their part to reform official policies and attitudes. Marie-Alain Couturier, for example, whom Borduas met in France before the war at the *Ateliers d'art sacré* run by Maurice Denis, became a strong and public agitator later on, in Montreal, against the conservatism of the École des Beaux-Arts while working to promote, encourage and explain young, experimental artists. Warren also situates Borduas within a broad movement to reform the teaching of art, with a heavy emphasis on the importance of children's art, so important for him as a model of freedom and spontaneity. Among the friends and colleagues who collaborated with him in this regard was Brother Jérome, a monk who had a career as a painter and encouraged young students such as Jean-Paul Mousseau (who later signed *Refus global*) to seek out Borduas. And from my point of view, some of the most interesting observations Warren makes concern a kind of vocabulary shared by the Automatists and Catholic intellectuals, having to do with the need for a "vertiginous descent into oneself," with the need to eschew "intention" in favour of "necessity." Both groups used the words "surrational" and "surrationalism" in their own ways. And although Warren insists that he is not an art critic, that his emphasis is on sociology and the history of ideas, he does a very good job of commenting on the almost mystical quality of Borduas' emphasis on the materiality of painting, as he quotes him writing about the "song" of a painting that comes from a vibration imprinted on matter by human sensibility, transforming matter into a living thing. Therein lies all the mystery of a work of art: bringing inert matter to life (see section titled "A Pure and Living Art"). Warren argues that the revolution proposed by the Automatists was, in the final analysis, spiritual in its wish to transform human sensibility. That is where he sees the main connection with some progressive Catholic thinkers and artists.

So what caused the strong reaction to *Refus global* and the rift between Borduas and his former allies? As Warren explains in the final chapter, none of the examples of Automatist theory or painting or literature in the document would have been enough to cause any truly important shock. What really mattered were the social and cultural questions raised in Borduas' lead manifesto, the call for "resplendent anarchy" the expressed urge to be done with *le goupillon et la tuque*, (the holy water and the tuque), with old-fashioned, sentimental Catholicism and nationalism. Warren argues, probably rightly so, that the Automatists were naive to think that nothing would come of their actions. But the suggestion "they should have known what would happen" doesn't necessarily justify the conduct of Borduas' erstwhile friends and allies. As much as I admire this book, I would betray my own research if I didn't object that Mr. Warren paints a somewhat rosy picture of the people he calls the "personalist Christians," concentrating on what they had in common with Borduas and underplaying what might have caused him to write the kind of sentiment I have quoted as an epigraph. It is fine to show how the Automatists appreciated the early support of Couturier, but no less important to understand why they rejected it later. Many Catholic intellectuals who supported Borduas' criticisms of Quebec society could not tolerate his criticisms of the Church, so they either kept silent and declined to support him, or spoke out actively against him. Among them were Gérard Pelletier (later an important figure in the Liberal government of Pierre Trudeau) and Jacques Dubuc who as journalists conducted a "debate" with the "young Surrealists" in the pages of *Le Devoir* (see "The Charge of the Expormidable Painter"). Warren presents them as basically reasonable; I find them sanctimonious, pompous and paternalistic, especially when they suggest that the young followers of Borduas (Jean-Paul Riopelle among them) aren't likely to have much of a future. But most unsavory, in my opinion, was Robert Élie, an early and close friend, author of the first book on Borduas, who wrote an unctuous critique entitled "*Au delà du refus*" (Beyond Refusal) in *la Revue dominicaine* some months after *Refus global* was published and who later, according to recent research, may have collaborated with the painter's widow to discourage the showing of Borduas' work in Europe after his death.

I could go on expressing objections to certain details, as one can always do with a provocative book, but despite any reservations I might have, I consider it essential reading for anyone who is curious about the complexities of the struggle for modernism in Quebec and about the avant-garde in Canadian art.

Ray Ellenwood
Toronto, 2017

THE THRESHOLD

Paul-Émile Borduas is a monumental figure in twentieth-century Quebec, whose life and works are inextricably linked to the emergence of the French-Canadian community in the 1940s and 1950s. Indeed, by delving into Borduas' successes and failures as well as his hopes and doubts, it is possible to understand this group's attempt during these years to find a new voice and express previously unspoken and divergent collective aspirations. This being said, Borduas' career remains somewhat puzzling and difficult to understand for many contemporary scholars. This is in large part due to the fact that within his biography, we find the enigma of a society that had to betray itself in order to assure its future. To shed light on this important idea, I propose then to revisit both the intellectual and artistic journey of this exiled painter, once described by art critic Jean Éthier-Blais as being at the "center of our contradictions." In short, I hope with this book to add another, but far from definitive stroke to the portrait of this complex figure who ultimately struggled with many of the questions being raised at an effervescent and turbulent time in Quebec's history.

The central topic of this book is Paul-Émile Borduas. However, the reader will not find in the following pages an exhaustive analysis of the *Refus global* (Total Refusal) manifesto, nor a close study of Borduas' gouaches or oil paintings, nor a biographical narrative. Rather, the reader will discover the winding evolutionary path that led Borduas to adopt a certain pictorial approach that constituted a radical break with the prevailing academic tendencies of his time. How could abstract art, which was initially considered decadent, suddenly appear acceptable in the eyes of a man who was destined at the outset to pursue a career decorating churches? How did Borduas end up embracing Automatism, a method of creation that more or less gives free reign to the impulses of the subconscious after having bathed in the conservative pedagogy of the Montreal's École des Beaux-Arts? These are the questions that I will attempt, in part, to answer in the following chapters.

I am not an art historian, nor do I claim to offer a treatise on abstract art in Quebec. Rather, I am interested in the development of Borduas' mindset as an intellectual, not in his various periods of creation as a painter. To grasp the unfolding of his thoughts on art, I consider the evolution of his ideas. Furthermore, since I am interested in the origins of abstract art in Quebec, I hardly mention the *Refus global* manifesto. Not only does this polemical text speak little about the art of painting, but it marks the end of a long process, the origins of which I want to retrace precisely. Besides, I believe that many commentators have projected the manifesto's ideas on the years preceding the publication of *Refus global*, thus entrenching a retrospective reading of the past that twists the fumbling and experiments of artists in the 1940s and gives the adventure of Automatism in Quebec a teleological coherence that it never actually had.

During my research, I consulted Borduas' writings extensively. The three important volumes of his texts and correspondence show the richness of the questions he asked and the range of his intellectual interests. At twenty-seven, he stood before an attentive Monsignor Olivier Maurault, expressing his fears regarding the erring philosophical character of conversations held at the École des Beaux-Arts. As a partisan of spontaneous acts, Borduas, who was later called "the master from Saint-Hilaire," gladly spoke about contemporary art theories with his friends and colleagues. With his lively and practical intelligence, he gained a reputation for being a fine orator and skilful critic. People said that he spent as much time thinking about as his canvases as he spent painting them.[1] "We used to talk about spontaneous creation," said public intellectual and art critic Robert Élie, "but it must be noted that numerous forays in the realm of logic precede works coming into being. Borduas was passionate about the play of ideas and, during a conversation or class, he liked getting technicalities straight."[2] There is a wealth of material for those seeking to uncover the reasons behind Borduas' decision to embrace non-figurative art.

Upon reading what he wrote and the literature that was produced on his works during his life, it becomes clear that although Borduas left the Catholic Church very early, his words resonated with progressive Catholics in the 1940s. Far from enhancing the image of a misunderstood and solitary artist, analyzing the body of work produced by the avant-garde milieu in Montreal shows that the tangent followed by the young Borduas was not a complete break with the ideology of his generation's critical intellectuals. This realization inspired me to write an essay on Borduas that would attempt to retrace the points of convergence and divergence between the painter and certain Catholic thinkers. Furthermore, I have attempted to show the fruitful nature of the dialogue he maintained with some of his colleagues and how it helped him, as a painter, to define and refine his understanding of modern art.

Obviously, the dialogue between Borduas and Catholic thinkers was never entirely serene. On the contrary, it was constantly plagued by great tension, which resulted from weighty disagreements concerning the true nature of artistic works. This became even more important over time as Borduas delved further into the practice of Automatism. However, the question that begs to be asked is not who was right with respect to these misunderstandings and uncertainties, but rather how Borduas could believe, just after being dismissed from the École du Meuble in 1948, that Father Louis-Marie Régis, a Dominican, would continue to support his new philosophy; or, conversely, how Brother Jérôme, a member of the Holy Cross Congregation, might think that signing *Refus global* was perfectly acceptable.

The issue at hand for me is the same one that I have been examining since the publication of my first critical works on Fernand

Dumont and Gérard Pelletier, namely the Catholic origins of the Quiet Revolution.[3] This time the approach is different, since I am studying a man who was quick to break with the Catholicism of his childhood and who tried to replace it with a radically different ethic. The objective of this book is not, however, to examine Borduas' entire works in terms of the moral, cultural and religious revival that was transforming the province of Quebec at the time. Although Borduas never really renounced his faith (no more than he ever confirmed it) until the outbreak of the war, although Jesuit Father François Hertel was able to declare peremptorily that "until his discovery of the Surrealists, Borduas only really read magazines of devotion,"[4] and although his first Surrealist gouaches bear traces of the sacred art tradition that he had been schooled in,[5] it would be dubious at best to search for any direct link between the Catholic *aggiornamento* and Automatism and to go so far as to claim that Automatism was, as Jean Éthier-Blais has postulated, nothing more than a new expression of an ancient faith. "The magic circle of Borduas' childhood, adolescence and early adulthood was made up of Ozias Leduc, Mgr. Olivier Maurault, Maurice Denis and sacred art theorists. One could even go so far as to talk of a Saint-Hilaire School of thought, where mysticism, a diffuse religiosity, and a deep need to rise above the lack of culture, were primordial elements. Until the end of his life, Borduas evolved within these intellectual and psychological categories; he will empty them of their past contents, but the old framework will not change."[6] As seductive as it may appear, in my opinion this interpretation seems too simplistic. It prevents us from grasping the spectacular nature of the Automatist revolution. Obviously, the Borduas of *Refus global* took exception to dominant clerical ideologies, something that his own contemporaries widely acknowledged. Without ever wanting to impose his atheism on anyone, by the end of the 1940s Borduas thought that Christianity was an impediment to true art and to living a full life.

The goal of this book is not to have the reader believe that the Automatists were unwitting Christians and that their works contain an unconscious prayer, but simply to highlight certain overlapping points within the thoughts of progressive Catholic intellectuals and avant-garde painters of the time. The overall evolution of spiritual sensibility in the country might have seemed, at least for a short while, to be moving in the same direction as Borduas' pictorial quest. And, it is consequently from within an upheaval in the expression of faith that the union between Catholic thinkers and avant-garde artists was made manifest. But, this fragile agreement, riddled with misunderstandings, would soon end up breaking into a thousand pieces. Robert Élie was correct to write: "There is no such thing as spontaneous generations, but after a long evolution, sometimes events speed up and a threshold is crossed, and life finds itself transformed."[7] The present essay follows the path leading to this threshold.[8]

Four pitfalls threaten to compromise the study of the trajectory that Borduas followed in the 1940s. First, I will concede that it is often deceptive to scrutinize the world of ideas in order to understand how an artist works. Le Douanier Rousseau is still famous for his poor artistic judgment, even while showing that he had an eye for producing marvels. One must not trust overly rigid equivalencies between a painter's discourse and his actual practices. Here, then, it is not a matter of revealing within Borduas' work a more or less true reflection of his philosophical principles. His canvases speak for themselves and understanding the author's aesthetic theories neither adds to, nor detracts from any pleasure that we get from contemplating them.

Second, no contemporary witnesses left notes as copious as did Borduas, Fernand Leduc ("the theorist of the group"[9]), Claude Gauvreau (the soul of the movement[10]), or even Robert Élie. The problem is that these individuals are not all equally representative of the diverse tendencies stirring within the avant-garde movement. From outside, the Automatists seemed a tight-knit, united and cohesive group, while in reality they were divided among an array of dissonant interpretations. No doubt, the same mindset animated it, but its expressions were varied, as proved by the dissolution of the group after the publication of *Refus global*. Any analysis is unavoidably biased according to the documentary sources available, but one must nevertheless be careful not to confound Fernand Leduc's words with those of Jean-Paul Riopelle or of Marcelle Ferron.

Third, by focusing my attention on Borduas, I acknowledge having gravitated toward painting in my analysis to the detriment of other forms of artistic expression that the Automatists practiced, including design (Madeleine Arbour), theatre (Muriel Guilbault), poetry (Thérèse Renaud, Claude Gauvreau), dance (Françoise Lespérance, Françoise Sullivan, who was also a painter) and photography (Maurice Perron). The contribution of women suffered particularly from my choice: they did not write as much as the men and practiced genres other than painting. There is an excellent book on these female artists, which I urge the reader to consult for a complementary analysis.[11]

A final potential pitfall of current historical analysis stems from the ever too literal interpretation of Borduas' texts. While attempting to better grasp how Borduas' personal experiences were being appropriated and reinterpreted by religious figures, one must remain vigilant not to confuse, for example, "the faith in his works" with "Christian faith" and lose sight of the rhetoric that is part and parcel of all critical thought. The metaphoric and polysemous nature of numerous terms (all one has to do is think about the word "esprit" or "transcendence") threatens to spread confusion and obscure important differences in a deceptive equivalency. Such a semantic shift is particularly dangerous when moving from critical commentary to the real sense of Borduas' pictorial experience. On numerous occasions, Borduas and a few of his contemporaries thought they were speaking about the same things, although they were bringing up different realities using a common vocabulary. To avoid these issues, historical introductions, scholarly notes, and critical commentaries by André-G. Bourassa, Jean Fisette and Gilles Lapointe in Paul-Émile Borduas' three volumes of complete writings are very useful. For the chronology, one must trust François-Marc Gagnon's Borduas biography, as well as his *Chronicle of the Quebec Automatist Movement.* Another indispensable work is Ray Ellenwood's *Egregore: A History of the Montreal Automatist Movement.*

This book is divided into four parts. In the first segment, I study how a new collective sentiment, that of existential anxiety, contributed to art's emancipation from nationalist and clerical fetters. The denunciation of the "holy water and the French-Canadian tuque!" did indeed first target Saint-Sulpice and the folkloric art of the interwar period. In the 1940s, while working away at a true aesthetic revolution, Catholic artists searching for a new universalism were forced to take a stand in favour of abstract art.

In the second part, I show how, for this very reason, Catholic art critics gradually acknowledged the need to engage in a threefold break: first, with bourgeois society, considered too conformist and trivial. Secondly, with the mimetic representation of the material world, in the sense that it was important for the artist to express his own sensitivities by drawing from the depths of his own being. And finally, with reason itself, for as Father Marie-Alain Couturier noted – in a passage that Borduas would not have denied – the play of lines and colours spread by the painter over the canvas was extracted from "a dark part of our being where the soul and body seem to actually fuse their powers into a primitive unit that is much too simple and elementary to be the subject of rational knowledge and objectively used."[12] These three ruptures were going to push certain painters to acknowledge the canvas itself as being the ultimate goal of their pictorial investigations. It was in the paint, spread out all over the canvas, that they would eventually arrive at an ideal reconciliation between exploring the cosmos and soul-searching.

In the third part, I highlight the pedagogical principles that caused virulent opposition between fine arts partisans and the champions of Surrealism. The vehement criticism of the "tricks" of the *Bôzards* (a pun on beaux-arts, and a derogatory referral to the practitioners of the classical fine arts) was only equalled by the vigorous praise for children's drawings. Young pupils' creativity and candour will from this moment onward be considered superior to the array of ready-made formulas being diffused in the province's schools. Adopting what several observers considered a Rousseauist, not to say a libertarian, attitude toward his teaching at the École du Meuble, Paul-Émile Borduas was subject to the wrath of those who could not admit that a teacher's duty was to guide pupils without trying to tame them. The scandal caused by the form of education practiced by Borduas and certain progressive Catholics (including Brother Jérôme) was the direct reflection of the conservative milieu's resistance in Quebec to a new way of painting, which had definitively broken away from traditional realism.

Yet, as the fourth and last part of this book shows, it was indeed the publication of *Refus global* that caused Borduas' ultimate marginalization. While the most progressive Catholics of the time accepted abstract art, and even Automatist and Surrealist art, and favourably welcomed open and alternative teaching methods, they could not accept the cry of revolt against God and religion expressed in the manifesto. From then on, the many misconceptions that had allowed Borduas and enlightened Catholics to get along (they thought they saw in his painting the same quest for transcendence driving them) fell to pieces. *Refus global*, therefore, may have seemed to appear out of nowhere, whereas, in reality, it had in part arisen from an on-going discussion with several Christian intellectuals.

OUR ANXIETY

Art's domain is that of adventure, of questioning.
　　　　　　　　　—MARIE-ALAIN COUTURIER

An impressive amount of literature (literary studies, discourse analyses, chronologies, critical essays) has already documented Automatism's genesis. Many papers and conferences have revisited Borduas' writings to understand the social and ideological context in which he lived, especially by studying local and foreign networks in New York and Paris. For example, François-Marc Gagnon published a meticulous biography and a detailed chronicle of the Automatist movement, while Esther Trépanier showed in her innovative work how "the triumph of abstraction is just the end of a period of transition from which Quebec, no more than any other, was spared."[1] Other researchers, like Ray Ellenwood, Jean Fisette and Gilles Lapointe have enriched our understanding of the intellectual roots of Automatism.[2] This imposing collection of studies has shed great light on the numerous motives that drove a generation of artists to embrace non-figurative art in the 1940s.

Until now, two main hypotheses have been proposed to understand Borduas' path toward abstract art. On the one hand, and quite correctly, certain authors have insisted on Surrealism's central influence. "I suspect there is nobody who is closer to understanding us than [André] Breton," Borduas wrote in a letter to Jean-Paul Riopelle, dating back to February 1947. "He's the one to whom I owe the little bit of order that's in my head."[3] On the other hand, researchers have highlighted the contributions of English-speaking Montreal artists (including numerous Jewish painters) to the general evolution of

Catholic thought based on a rereading of Saint Thomas Aquinas, Maritain opened doors for the literary and aesthetic avant-garde and authorized still timorous French Canadians to appropriate trends that were then renewing in Europe the understanding of art and its relationship to society. "It was in *collège* that we read *Primauté du spirituel* (Primacy of the Spiritual), *Trois réformateurs* (Three Reformers), *Art et Scolastique* (Art and Scholastics) and where we were convinced by the extent of his human warmth, which is that of charity. [...] He [Maritain] re-established contact between Catholic thought and the avant-garde in all areas."[11] It is not by chance then, that Jacques de Tonnancour, just when he was being expelled from Montreal's École des Beaux-Arts in 1940, based his dissident convictions on his reading of *Art et Scolastique*.[12] But, in addition to Maritain, it is also important to mention a group of thinkers overseas, the first being Henri Bergson, whose essays were the subject of wild discussions in Quebec, as they counterbalanced, by means of their defence of intuition, the Cartesianism prevalent in classical *collèges*. The province's artists particularly appreciated *L'évolution créatrice* (Creative Evolution) and *La Pensée et le Mouvant* (The Creative Mind),[13] two books that restored respectability to personal experience, favoured manual activities over purely cerebral ones, and defined art as a vital impetus. In effect, Bergson believed that spiritual energy already inhabited matter and that the work of an artist consisted of being in communion with the sacrosanct by exploring new forms of art.

In addition to receiving works and journals from Europe, the adversaries of Quebec's conservative ideology were encouraged by numerous French Catholics who visited the province in the 1930s and 1940s. "The enormous progress recently accomplished by our literature, coincided with the more frequent presence in Canada of several masters of French and European thought."[14] The great overseas travellers were not content to simply circulate new ideas and make previously unheard intellectual trends known. They dared, at times, to severely criticize the cultural climate that reigned in Quebec. They were particularly shocked by the clergy's stranglehold on temporal affairs and feared that this grip would bring about a violent anticlerical backlash. Starting in 1934, the theologian Marie-Dominique Chenu warned his Quebec friends about a "decisive crisis" among the French-Canadian elite, a crisis that "could cause a wave of anticlericalism, capable of washing away the seemingly solid edifice of university teaching and Catholic culture."[15] Upon returning from a trip to Canada, Maritain wrote to Émmanuel Mounier that he had "encountered obscurantism first hand" and that the journal *Esprit*, founded and directed by Mounier, had an important role to play in opening up a religion that had become too rigid.[16] Father Paul Doncoeur condemned the religious practices of French Canadians and reproached them for a lack of humanity and a detestable pharisaism.[17] From Dom Bellot to Henri Charlier and Étienne Gilson to Henri Ghéon, French visitors were scandalized by a clerical institution that placed genuflexion and reciting the Our Father above authentic manifestations of faith.

ANTICLERICALISM FROM WITHIN

The new interpretation of Catholicism supported by progressive intellectuals – which can be conventionally labelled "personalism"[18] – proved to be highly critical of spiritual and cultural conformism. At the heart of the incisive attacks against aging institutions was the conviction that faith could no longer be blindly adhered to, as in the days when it was part of a confused hodgepodge of traditions. Habit, in the admirable words of Charles Péguy, was impervious to grace. For this reason, those who were called the "adventurers of the absolute" questioned the routine teachings of Christianity. Georges Bernanos affirmed that true belief is similar to the poetry of a small child; Émmanuel Mounier challenged the closed hearts of bigots and Julien Green demanded that baptism be renewed every day. "Catholics," Péguy famously wrote, "are truly unbearable in their mystical assertiveness. They imagine that the natural state of the Christian is a peaceful one, peace through intelligence, peace in intelligence. What characterizes the mystic, on the contrary, is an insurmountable anxiety."[19] Losing the reassurance that established dogmas used to convey, the revealed truth espoused the unpredictability of history. The authenticity of faith no longer came from servile obedience to ecclesiastical authorities, nor from the hieratic practice of religious rites. On the contrary, it was believed that faith was even more rich and fertile when it allowed itself to be penetrated by uncertainty. The career of Henri Daniel-Rops – "the uncontested master of today's youth"[20] according to a French-Canadian student – began in 1926 with the publication of a book intended to be a vast public success. Confronted by the weakening of old truths and the general collapse of the political and economic system, Daniel-Rops tried to convince the reader in an essay simply entitled *"Notre inquiétude"* (Our Anxiety) that human existence is an adventure and that faith is a constant calling into question.[21] He took stock of "this inner questioning which is first and foremost perpetual dissatisfaction, indefatigable demand."

He added: "We are not permitted to either take refuge in the past or to abandon our quest."[22] In his eyes, faith must remain open to doubt and to tragedy.

For French-Canadian Catholics, this European discourse was becoming more and more convincing. For example, the young Gilles Héault, an avid reader of Péguy, like so many of his friends, reiterated Daniel-Rops' remarks almost word for word: "The first movement was always a movement of love and faith, of risk and abandon brought forth by questioning. The desperate man, the dis-illusioned man, incapable of finding any joy in life, or pleasure in his actions, is not worried. Only those who believe deeply in something are ridden with this worry, which surpasses all pessimism and all optimism, and is found in a blank space yet to be discovered."[23] From then on, faith demanded that the believer take risks, make a giant leap into the unknown. It was not enough for the believer to live in the calm serenity of his soul: he had to be worried for his sal-vation and for himself. He had to be incessantly in search of himself, because any adherence to Christianity worthy of its name necessar-ily involved anguish and trepidation. Since God could not be pur-chased like a piece of merchandise, it was often said that Christians could not be as certain of salvation, as one is of possessing an object. In other words, it was not enough to claim to be Catholic to actually be one; belonging to some church could never make up for vibrant and lived faith. The believer could only be sure of his own uncer-tainty. His questioning was precisely the proof of the sincerity of his convictions.

On this basis, progressive Catholics set about completely restoring the dogma of the Catholic Church: Revelation was not offered to humankind in one block, but rather it revealed itself throughout his-tory. Sainthood was not achieved by fleeing from the world and all its temptations; it was learned through hard-fought battles for greater justice and freedom here on earth. Science and technology were not innately bad; they needed to be conquered and mastered to become instruments of divine glory. All these were manifestations of a revolution that incited the believer to attach more importance to what were called the "signs of the times," an expression that made reference to historical events, telling trends of the future, and unprecedented situations. It was necessary to embrace the new and to live faith by virtue of a relentless confrontation with the world. Loyal to a certain Christian existentialism,[24] progressive Catholics echoed themes such as the dramatic dimension of human existence, personal conversion, social engagement, or dialogue, in an original world view based on the need to question everything. It was not about preserving Christian institutions, but rather about building a Christian-inspired society from within, which in turn forced the laity into implicit, direct and intense collaboration in the different spheres where their actions were taking place.

Therein lay the groundwork for a total questioning of traditions, authorities and knowledge in the name of a more fluid and open definition of the world and faith. In the 1930s, the Catholic religion seemed to many observers to be folded in on its dogmas. The Catholic faith had lost the charisma of its origins and was content to sermonize and afflict the faithful. It was frightened of everything: of luxury, of pleasure, of desire, of Jews, of Masons, of temptation. *Refus global* would declare "blue fear – red fear – white fear: links in our chain." Borduas proved himself to be unforgiving in his criticism of religion. For him, the Catholic Church had lost its magical aspect and passionate vigour, and had fallen back on rigorist and utilitarian values. Unable to renew itself, the Church stifled all efforts made by the faithful to reconnect with the prophetic force of the primitive Church. "The Church is developing a defence mechanism against life, which it no longer controls. [...] Contact with the object of desire, whether it is human contact, or of the physical, mysterious or magical kind no longer exists for the people. Instead of a troubling operation, people have another dead object on their hands. The emphasis is placed on reassuring techniques."[25] As a result, *Refus global* condemned what it called "a small and humble people clutching the skirts of priests" and "shielded from the perilous evolution of thought going on all around us."[26]

It would be wrong to believe that the father of Automatism was the only one on the banks of the Saint Lawrence River criticizing a religion contaminated by rigid moral standards and Jansenism. Many progressive Catholics were also convinced that the ecclesiastical institution had become prisoner to stifling structures. They deplored seeing the philosophy of life being reduced to a handful of debilitating lessons taken out of scholastic manuals, having the passionate search for the truth replaced with lowbrow certitudes and watching their faith turn into ritualistic practices and pathetic devotion. Claude Gauvreau tells of his *collège* educators making reproachful remarks to him, not because of his impious attitude, but, on the contrary, for having repeatedly denounced the unacceptable abdication of faith itself: "Far from smoothing over disagreements with my teachers, my reputation as a very sincere Christian greatly highlighted them – because I was disgusted by all this spinelessness and all this truly anti-Christian bargaining. If I was expelled from the Collège Saint-Marie during my year in Philosophy II, I can say that it was because I was Christian."[27] In a rather spectacular roundabout way, the radical criticism of religious institutions served the interests of the Church as a believing community. Personalism represented in this way was an "anticlericalism from within," since the criticism of the Roman Catholic Church was made in the name of the authentic Christian tradition itself. Believers attacked the Catholic hierarchy, most especially for not sufficiently embodying the virtues of hope and charity. Borduas was right to criticize a journalist "for using the epithet ANTI-CLERICAL as a scarecrow, when religious officials with universally recognized knowledge and intelligence were of the opinion that anticlericalism favours the clergy's salvation."[28] Many laypeople, but also some clerics – the Dominican Georges-Henri Lévesque and the Jesuit, François Hertel, for example – did not hesitate to condemn a religion that was a mere façade and the subsequent mutilation of the soul resulting from this.

Beyond the Catholic Church, French-Canadian society on the whole seemed to teach resignation and obedience. The family, as much as the *collèges*, seemed to have put out the fire in young people, extinguished their dreams, limited exploration, and closed off infinite possibilities. In all the spheres of life, French Canada had replaced passion with routine. In philosophy, teachers got students used to thinking using a Thomist catechism that made any sort of existential questioning disappear within a scholastic compendium. In literature, it was the same thing: works were adulterated to the point of being reduced to meaningless platitudes. Textbooks were purged of almost all provocative material and students would look in vain for names like Charles Baudelaire, Marcel Proust, André Gide or Arthur Rimbaud. The education being provided in French-Canadian establishments was in dire straits, as adolescents on their academic journey only ever met with rules telling them what not to do. There was no place for doubt or dreaming. For progressive Christians, there was no need to look elsewhere to explain the lack of fervour in French-Canadian people. "The real cause of this lack, as with all the others, is the fear of living."[29] Indeed, doubt was condemned by a school manual, as "doubt is a worry that pushes one to search and then to think."[30] And in this way, they lamented, French-Canadian youth were dying out little by little, slowly, and sadly, due to excessive conformity and faint-heartedness. Due to an inability to freely investigate the world, and a lack of desire, young people simply disengaged.

For this reason, existentialist Christians hoped that the culture of liberty in Quebec would grow. Rather than cave into the paternalistic religious elite and blindly venerate the grand authoritative figure-heads in traditional societies (the father, the boss, the priest, the Pope, God), they wanted to see liberty restored, knowing that nothing great is possible without it. The abyss separating them from conservative Catholics and all those obsessed with issues related to order, doctrine, authority, and revelation was obvious. Indeed, between the authoritarianism of traditional Christianity (Thomist catechism in philosophy, episcopal hierarchy in the Church, ultramontane obedience in politics, submission to ancestral traditions in the realm of culture) and the invitation to undertake an all-consuming search for new meanings, the difference could not have been any more striking. A new state of mind had pervaded the province. It encouraged social reforms based on a tragic sense of existence, which was at once the engine of a virulent anticlericalism and proof of the spiritual awakening of humanity. In a limited and monotonous world, a world in which the preaching and teaching of morality had often taken on dark overtones, it was henceforth necessary to become fully engaged in a passionate personal quest. "It [the young generation] is looking for solutions by espousing a more intense spiritual life. Young people dream of devotion and sainthood and, too often, all they are offered is an ideal of false renunciation and pseudo-elegant capitulation. They cannot accept this, because they feel that achieving true grandeur demands entirely distinct kinds of sacrifices."[31] In short, a new urge toward Christian perfection animated the spiritual world of reformist Christians.

Stirred by such sentiments, certain elements of the French-Canadian population did not take long to condemn all that impeded the spontaneous movement of life. In a general and harsh way, they inevitably came to the point of criticizing systems that confined people to a cultural universe that was too reassuring. The denunciation of the reign of fear, and conversely, the promotion of a climate of questioning constituted an effective means of struggling from within Christianity against the older generation who, according to some, had reduced Christian spiritual life to soulless rituals. "Contrary to these dead people, youths are more and more worried on the spiritual front. You can ridicule this feeling of anxiety all you want, but one thing is certain: this sentiment exists and it is growing."[32] It is in this sense that it could be said: "The rise of religious questioning must be considered the most important fact of the last twenty years [1930-1950]. This on its own utterly explains the movement toward spiritual liberation currently reorienting the intellectuals' attitude."[33] Whether this affirmation made by Maurice Blain entails a slight (or considerable) exaggeration by no means denies the corrosive power of worry as a sentiment. The charges against dogmatism were growing into a general condemnation of the social order. Everything, absolutely everything that threatened to subdue worry as a sentiment and consequently the power of dreams and passion, was subject to the criticism of progressive Catholics. To experience transcendence, without which a person would be denying his or her potential, and to feel this anxiety which constituted the measure of a real life, an individual had to take sides with the opponents of fossilized traditions, bring down the barriers of a stifling religious milieu, break with servile actions, conservatisms and lies. Faith was no longer, and never again would be a calming assurance, but rather a risky wager.

In Father Couturier's Footsteps

There is only one step between such a religious posture and modernist discourses on living art that emerged in Quebec in the 1930s. There are close links between the revival of religious thought and how progressive Catholic art critics view aesthetics.[34] Recognition of abstract art was being encouraged by the appearance of a religious ethic taking the side of history and incarnation. Redefining faith in this way was going to end up creating a favourable perception of non-figurative art, at least in certain enlightened circles in Quebec in the 1940s, since many intellectuals perceived the liberation of painting as a concomitant spiritual liberation.

For example, the painter and sculptor Henri Charlier, who was invited to spend several months in Canada, put the members of *Jeunesse étudiante catholique (JEC)* (Catholic Student Youth) in contact with the Christian revival movement during a general study week held at Collège Notre Dame, in July 1937. For works of art to have a religious character, they had to carry an element of risk, according to Charlier. Exploring the purity of the material created an opportunity to discover the intimate secret contained within things. Engaging in a personal, intrepid and inventive quest, the painter demanded that forms and colours give an approximation of what lay beyond. Faithfully depicting reality was only good for cowardly and weak souls. One had to dig and search through the real in an uncertain and perilous manner. Faced with this discourse, which forced them to engage their entire personality, the young members of the *Jeunesse étudiante catholique* who were listening to Charlier felt like they were reborn. "Christian life was no longer this mandatory, boring and respectable, sad and bitter existence. We had now heard the song of total freedom."[35]

Three years later, the arrival and visit of another French painter, the Dominican Father Marie-Alain Couturier (1897-1954), also proved to be decisive. This former pupil of the *Académie de la Grande*

21

Chaumière, one of Paris' fine arts schools that he had frequented in 1919, turned his interests toward the *Ateliers d'art sacré* (Sacred Art Workshops) where he studied for five years under the direction of Maurice Denis (1870-1943) and George Desvallières (1861-1950). Borduas met him in France, not at the Ateliers (where he had worked extremely hard from November 1928 to May 1930 making stained-glass windows and drawing bucolic countrysides) but rather in the French Department of Meuse, where they had both come to work on decorating a church.

Father Marie-Alain Couturier and Jacques Maritain knew each other well. We see them here standing next to each other during the ordination of the Dominican in July 1930. Soon afterward, however, the disciple would surpass the master, as the priest began to espouse audacious aesthetics, which provoked misunderstandings and backlash. (Archives de la province dominicaine de France.)

"Couturier is a saintly man and a *great* artist,"[36] Borduas wrote in a letter to Mgr. Olivier Maurault. In 1936, Couturier joined Father Raymond Régamey in taking the reins of *L'Art sacré*, a journal that was going to crusade against the most mediocre of works produced by so-called Christian artists.[37] Later, when the war forced him to prolong his stay in the United States, Couturier had the chance to admire some of the great private American collections, among which he discovered some unsuspected treasures by Picasso and Matisse. After viewing them only once, he understood their pricelessness. Along with Fernand Léger, Amédée Ozenfant, Henri Focillon and Ossip Zadkine, he was part of a project (unfortunately abandoned) to create a French Institute of Modern Art in New York. By 1945, his energetic speeches and opinions had earned him the reputation in certain circles of being "the most important regenerator of modern sacred art in France."[38]

Couturier, through his stances, overturned a significant number of aesthetic and religious premises in Quebec during his intermittent stays there between 1940 and 1945. An unabashed personalist, he exhorted French Canadians not to succumb to the temptation of "abandoning adventure and its risks" for the beaten path of tradition. He insisted that true artists had learned to live in the shadows and conveyed their soul's torment in their work. "It takes an effort of pure intuition to assure the birth and development of a work of art, a total abandonment to a certain obscure sense of the absolute. And, to tell the truth, there needs to be an absolute risk, which implies a state of constant insecurity for the artist. This is psychologically very difficult, often even anguishing, as it is entirely foreign to the stable order of certitudes that rule over and guarantee all other human activities."[39] According to Couturier's philosophy, impatience, agitation, insecurity, life, truth and vitality were all part of an indivisible whole.

His book *Art et Catholicisme* (Art and Catholicism), which was finally printed in April of 1941, caused serious upheaval in the province's close-knit circles.[40] His remarkable public lectures, including *"Décadence du sens artistique dans le monde moderne"* (Decadence of the Artistic Sense in the Modern World), *"Le divorce actuel entre le public et les artistes"* (The Current Divorce Between the Public and Artists), *"La notion d'un art indépendant"* (The Notion of an Independent Art), *"L'art et la démocratie"* (Art and Democracy), helped young students such as the Gauvreau brothers, Claude and Pierre, to break with old preconceived ideas and to discover "the general problems of contemporary art."[41] "The problem of [living] creation in literature and music became obvious first to readers and listeners; in painting, we finally acknowledged it three years ago, when [in 1940] Father Couturier came and gave talks here that were unequivocal, radical and, I would even say, revolutionary for the weak who became afraid and who still seek to legitimize their fright."[42] During his stays in Canada, Couturier organized an ephemeral group of independent painters called *Les Sagittaires*, organized radio interviews about so-called modern art, taught for a few months at the École du Meuble, presided at the Séminaire de Joliette over the opening of an exhibition that brought together, among others, painters such as John Lyman, Alfred Pellan and Borduas. He also organized an exhibition of religious crafts at the École du Meuble and another for the group of *Indépendants* in Quebec and Montreal, in addition to expending his inexhaustible energy on numerous other projects.

It would hardly be an exaggeration to agree with Élie that: "None of the foreign writers that the war had brought far from their homeland, and that America had welcomed, exercised a greater influence and wanted to be our true friend more than Father Marie-Alain Couturier. [...] Father Couturier arrived at a time when the liberation movement was underway and his attentive friendship was a great help to all those who wished to break with an official line of thought that was fed by nothing more than empty words."[43] His public discussions with Parizeau, Gagnon, and Borduas further supported the revival of arts in Quebec, a movement already in the works before his arrival, but that lacked confidence and coherence before then. "I hope," wrote the Dominican to Borduas, "that together we will do a good job and that our common efforts, our exchanged ideas, will little by little bring about some results!"[44] This wish was largely granted. After the eventful time that Father Couturier spent in the country, Borduas noted: "The ice has been broken."[45]

TO HELL WITH HOLY WATER AND THE FRENCH-CANADIAN TUQUE!

The lessons learned from Father Couturier and other great thinkers of the Catholic revival would not be forgotten. Gradually, the artistic endeavours of painters in Quebec became shaped by a greater acceptance of their misgivings, and Borduas would follow suit. Had Jacques Dubuc not been impressed upon first visiting Borduas' art studio by a life "shaped by the boldness of questioning?" In summary, Dubuc noted: "The painter must not subjugate himself to his vision: the person must not let himself dissolve in a work of art like a conclusion yields to its premise. Rather, art must grow within the person himself like the most beautiful fruit of human questioning."[46] Robert Élie, who reiterated this commentary in his own words, linked Borduas to the lengthy baroque tradition by showing his determination to confront his inner demons without worrying about what people would say. "The modern artist, with perhaps more anxiety, goes back to an experiment that has been tried a thousand times and, in this way, earns his place in living history."[47]

Borduas confirmed that the artist's gift could not fully develop without anguish, saying that the perilous path of the invisible involved hurdles. "I studied technique for technique's sake," wrote Borduas while talking about his first pictorial phase. "[...] I studied everything, coldly, without enthusiasm, because I felt no anxiety, was guided, monitored, coddled and risked nothing. [...] My life was vain, hollow, useless, and sterile; the more I learned, the less rich I became."[48] Later, abandoning arbitrary rules and relentlessly condemning desertions and cowardly acts, Borduas aspired to constantly discover the strange, the disconcerting and the unforeseen. He wanted to become like those poets who were "resistant [...] to the dulling repetition of a convulsive quality" and who were tormented by "harrowing anxieties."[49] For this avid reader of Soren Kierkegaard's *Sickness Unto Death* and *The Concept of Anxiety*,[50] so-called "modern" art only pushed to the extreme the attempt to discover the unknown by means of an irreplaceable and irreproducible, wholly original gesture; it represented a vertigo, a gamble, a disinterested and delirious act. It shattered reassuring illusions and demanded that the artist take responsibility for himself, for the world, and for the course of history.[51] "We are risking everything," one can read in the *Refus global* manifesto, "for our total refusal."

Progressive Christians who frequented avant-garde painters adopted such a philosophy to cultivate a fundamental state of torment. According to them, it was a matter of being anxious, not about futilities, but rather for their salvation and that of the world. To question was not respectable if it did not stem from misgivings concerning the ultimate ends of human existence, which provided artists with a critical stance. Because they seemed to be inhabited by a creative breath more than anyone else, the artists were also more capable of approaching the unfathomable and starting a conversation with the inexpressible. In the midst of the tumult of urban life, a work of art would give rise to a moment of contemplation. It would make it possible to hear a slight murmur or even make silence almost audible, as when we set out to listen to the world. There would be something providential given to human beings in the artistic act, something to elevate nature and the soul, but pushed to the extreme in a kind of contemplative fury. Poetic inspiration would be as close as possible to divine inspiration. Seen in this way, artistic expression, deeply personal and yet the fruit of a creative intuition that transcends the artist himself, would establish a mysterious yet precious relationship with religious life. Something would unite the poet and the saint, each on a quest for an occult harmony, both haunted by an absence.

Several art critics during the interwar period adopted this discourse. Quoting Jacques Maritain's *"Réponse à Jean Cocteau,"* in which Maritain maintains that "art itself spontaneously goes toward God," Robert Élie affirmed in 1935 that: "Beauty is one of the names of the divine: it transcends everything; because wherever the integrity of being exists, beauty finds itself like the true and the good." From this, he radically concluded: "To deform art is, therefore, another way of betraying the spirit."[52] In his eyes, anything that got in the way of the expansion of aesthetic inspiration was guilty of halting personal development and realization. From the singular point of view of the personalist critique, and not from the creative act itself, there seemed to be a perfect reciprocal relationship between the aesthetic quest and the adventure called faith. Everything that had been said about harmful restrictions weighing on the believer, such as hierarchies, dictates and directives, enveloping him in a stifling morality, could be applied *mutatis mutandis* to art. When a society censured its artists, it was ultimately the spirit that was dealt a blow and suffered. Élie could thus boldly accuse French-Canadian painting of basking in scholarly conventions and do so while feeling he was doing a service to art and religion. In his opinion, the clichés that had replaced experimentation and attempts to actively confront the world actually diminished painting and spirituality. For Élie, this was and remained the same quest for the absolute and the same search for a deeper questioning. Like the Church and society, art needed to open itself up to doubt, to turn toward mystery, and let itself be swept away by an insatiable passion.

In the first part of the twentieth century, as we learn from the harsh debates surrounding the magazine *Le Nigog*, the cultural elite in Quebec had generally refused to accept art for art's sake. For them, a work of art before all else was destined to serve religion and the country: "Art for art's sake, nothing is more false, more stupid and more ridiculous than this theory."[53] Members of the traditional elite argued that one could not deny that artists live in a certain place, that they address a particular audience and that they impart an implicit message in their work. In this way, artists, like everyone else, like the head of a family or a politician, were subject to strict duties. If humanity's most noble aspirations were to be respected, the obligation of idealizing and perfecting reality had to be conceded. Works that exuded elevated sentiments and that did not detract from moral goodness were considered to be timeless. And what exactly were these sentiments and supreme values that artists had to respect? According to general opinion, they were none other than French-Canadian nationalism and the Catholic religion. The throne and the altar were idols that commanded the devotion of artists. "The ideas of God and of country, are they not like a hearth that gives off all the warmth and richness that human existence has to offer? Are they not the most precious of emotional realities, of those that generate superiority, so much so that they seem to be the supreme law of our prosperity in terms of the material and spiritual order of things?"[54] In this climate, how could art be anything other than the reflection of the tradition of the land and religious beliefs? The most beautiful paintings, for most art lovers at the time, were ones that depicted a bucolic countryside or featured a pious person. "Man is not an abstraction. He is dependent on the things that surround him, ethnic influences, forlorn or recent memories. They provoke reactions, both mental and racial, and form the principal substance of an artistic work."[55] According to this creed, if artists ignored their spiritual and cultural obligations, they were bound to degenerate and end up producing horrors. Artists thrived when they adopted a didactic posture and produced beautiful, apologetic, and propagandistic images for art lovers.

Although it did not please advocates of the back-to-the land movement, a growing number of Catholic art critics, following the lead of Alexandra Cingria (the iconoclastic author of *La Décadence de l'art sacré*, in 1918), realized that this moralizing attitude had a negative influence on the Church's artistic production. By valuing generic characteristics of subjects and commonplace images, Catholic art had lost sight of the universal essentials. Proselytism had killed art. In convents and churches, visitors could only discover insipid statuettes and poorly painted frescos, which did not allow Christian heroism to shine forth. Instead of trying to show the noble and humble image of sainthood, a tight-laced straightjacket of prescriptions forced artists to use a series of inept clichés. In *Art et Scolastique*, Maritain was saddened by the ugliness of religious art being produced in France. Because of their lack of finesse, for him, these works, destined to decorate European sites of worship, were in extremely bad taste and had been done by artists who were badly in need of adequate training. Therefore, Maritain said that he wanted to "free churches of the creations that had been vomited up from the depths of religious mercantilism."[56] Father Marie-Alain Couturier, a painter himself, was also struck early on by the Catholic European clergy's poor attitude toward art. "When ecclesiastical authorities are left to work according to their own devices the result is usually ghastly."[57] For him, everything that had been done over the past hundred years was "pretentious" and "soulless." There was nothing but "rubbish," "misfortunes," and works of "common mediocrity."

Upon seeing the nonsense adorning sites of worship in Quebec during his visit there in the winter of 1940, Couturier was only further convinced. Do not look for any remotely inspiring works in churches in Trois-Rivières or Montreal, he warned. More or less everywhere, you will see paltry icons varnished in sentimentality, pretty pastel plasterworks, and finally, all the trappings of "merchandise whose pretentiousness and false luxury flatter people's most common and lowly instincts."[58] Portraits of Christ, of Saint Theresa and of the Sacred Heart decorating the walls were pretty-pretty, unexciting, and meaningless. In Quebec, the most lucid of art critics agreed with Maritain and Couturier. They, too, would have liked to purge French-Canadian churches of their sickly sweet and sanctimonious works, which were a disgrace to art and religion. "The R.P. Couturier said in a public lecture given in Montreal that if one were to come across these Christ figures or Saint Theresa's tarted-up in this way in the streets, everyone would laugh in their face. Why do we tolerate the Church being disgraced in this way? True faithfulness cannot put up with this."[59]

Borduas was particularly sensitive to this degeneration, as he had been approached by Ozias Leduc to follow in his footsteps and undertake a career as a church decorator. Several years after Borduas' return from Paris in 1930, this project was no longer mentioned. The reason was that, on the one hand, the Great Depression was killing all church construction and renovation projects; priests did not have the financial means to assume such vast endeavours. And, on the other hand, most priests' artistic taste did not go beyond rosy-cheeked angels and bleeding sacred-hearts from the Italian tradition, which continued to dominate churches in the city and countryside.[60] Rare were the religious leaders who resisted this saccharine fashion, which transformed any biblical scene into one out of the Tuscan countryside. As such, there were very few artists who were able to go beyond such pictorial Italianisms. Even Ozias Leduc was never able to fully express himself in the contracts he had signed with religious groups and church builders. Although he always refused to cover French-Canadian churches in Mediterranean skies and dress the Madonna like a friendly bourgeois woman, he never seemed to show off the full extent of his talents when painting for the clergy. Besides the works he did on commission, he produced a small number of very personal paintings, which showed a certain humanity that could not be fully detected in the coldness of his frescos. Removed from the artificial platitudes decorating Quebec's churches, it was as if he created a dream world that was truly his own.[61]

On the national art side of things, the situation was worse, if that were even possible. Under the direction of Charles Maillard, the École des Beaux-Arts in Montreal had agreed to incorporate a patriotic element into its program that, with Abbot Lionel Groulx at the helm, imposed itself on Montreal's intelligentsia. To Maillard, a Frenchman born in Algiers but who had been living in Montreal for a long time, it seemed reasonable to promote a vision of art that served the spiritual interests of the nation. "Art must be national before being human."[62] Maillard wanted the plastic arts to exude a family-like quality and to be rooted in the homeland's soil. His ideals brought him to admire pretty, pastoral sketches done by regionalists. He attempted to capture the picturesque aspect of the French-Canadian countryside, the grey sun of the Ile d'Orléans, the shimmering colours of the Sainte-Famille church, the beautiful red barns in the Charlevoix region, and the solid carts pulled by strong horses of the Canadian breed. In short, he cultivated a local touch and the charm of the land. "I asked pupils to take inspiration from the French-Canadian countryside and to deal with subjects taken from Canadian history."[63] Without cracking a smile, he stated that it was possible to create a "typically French-Canadian baby Jesus."[64] No one but the director of the École des Beaux-Arts was better at promoting the tyranny of the represented subject.

The entrenchment of art in the national soil meant identifying with the long line of artists who had helped create this realist tradition. A journalist summarized this approvingly, saying: "To rediscover the inspiration of our first craftsmen and develop a regional body of art corresponding to the country's soul, that reflects its constitution and highlights our own special view of the world, Mr. Maillard feared that our artists might lose themselves by adventuring too far into an art that was too advanced."[65] The director of the École des Beaux-Arts attempted to maintain minimal contact with his counterparts abroad on the pretext that cosmopolitan influences could endanger the morality of young artists.

Far from his homeland and washed up on unknown shores, did the exiled French-Canadian artist not risk losing his Catholic soul and patriotic fervour? In the preamble to its 1927 report, the Board of Directors of the École des Beaux-Arts took a stance in favour of "French-Canadian art that would borrow as little as possible from foreign and exotic cultures and would avoid baroque ideas propounded by certain groups seeking to explore problematic art, having more provocative potential than artistic merit."[66] Giving himself over to xenophobic and anti-Semitic tendencies, Charles Maillard openly feared the pernicious influence of Jews and socialists and, in this way, cut himself off from the most innovative artists of the century in Paris and New York, as well as in Montreal. As such, in his struggle "against

In the eyes of avant-garde painters, Charles Maillard represented the perfect embodiment of the stubborn and old-fashioned academic professor. For the director of Montreal's École des Beaux-Arts, art, rooted in the fertile soil of French Canada, was to serve patriotic and religious propaganda. (Charles Maillard, painted by himself, 1912, oil on canvas, 147.7 x 91.8 cm. Musée des beaux-arts de Montréal. Donated in memory of Nellie Maillard-David, the artist's only daughter. Photo MBAM, Brian Merrett.)

American art influenced by Jews and tied to Bolshevik propaganda," he insisted that "[The École des Beaux-Arts] will keep its foothold on sensible ground and continue to invite young people to remain Canadian."[67] To participate in this modern "farce," mocking the timeless laws of art and national ideals, would have been nothing short of laying the groundwork for "chaos and anarchy."

Just as they had targeted so-called Catholic art, avant-garde circles criticized the idea of a national artistic tradition.[68] For modern artists, it was only normal that a young country would want to celebrate its countryside and its particularities and envisage painting exclusively from a regionalist perspective. But Canada was no longer at this stage; therefore, it had to liberate itself from an outdated artistic canon. Jacques de Tonnancour jeered at what he called an "incubator of feeble-minded chickens" (by which he meant the École des Beaux-Arts) founded on the promotion of folklore and the rejection of foreign trends. "The fine courses of hollow words! Beware of external influences!"[69] Tonnancour could not have cared less about regionalist art, which degenerated too often into trinkets for tourists. Drawings of farmers in fields or joyous winter scenes had nothing universal about them, exuded nothing of the absolute, and bore witness to an inferior form of expression. When an artist sets about dealing with national styles by adopting local ways due to laziness or weakness, the purpose of the vocation is compromised, irrevocably preventing the development of talent. Even the Group of Seven, according to Tonnancour, despite the undeniable talent of certain members, was not able to go beyond a superficial freedom in its treatment of subjects. The Group refused to plunge into the heart of what makes up a human being and had thus contented itself with simply rearranging colours and shapes in its depiction of nature. Art critics such as Tonnancour were severe with anything that came close to an art subordinate to the nationalistic creed. Adopting the rallying cry, "The spiritual first and foremost!" that Maritain had first coined, critics no longer agreed to favour politics over what was human.

Ironically, it is in part due to chauvinism that French-Canadian traditionalists ended up accepting that the most shocking representatives from the "École de Paris" – the Matisses, Renoirs, Dufys, Modiglianis, Bonnards, Picassos, Légers – should be considered talented artists. At the time, actors, poets, musicians and painters, whether they were on the left or right of the political spectrum, and whether they were churchmen or anticlerical thinkers, only swore by trends that were fashionable in the motherland. "France, generous and ardent in its pursuit of what is truly important, of eternal truths, and the absolute"[70] remained the centre of attraction for French Canadians who prided themselves on being able to wield a pen or a brush. As long as it was coming from the Hexagon (France), all artistic movements had a good chance of resonating on the banks of the Saint Lawrence River. "France is the universal of art."[71] Of course at this time, the most admired French art was so-called modern art. Nationalists could not turn a blind eye to the glorious achievements of their motherland, and therefore the most hardened ones found it difficult not to salute French artists even when they were producing works that went against their own most deeply-ingrained feelings. This is where we find a not-so-banal paradox: French-Canadian nationalism became an obstacle to converting to a universalist doctrine of art, as much as it favoured it. "In art, we do not want to see any manifestation of racial or national chauvinism. However, when we, as French Canadians, find ourselves in the presence of beautiful French works, let's not be afraid, if we truly want to protect the French spirit here, to confirm our enthusiasm. This would be missing out on an occasion to repel the Anglo-Saxon and American mentality that is infiltrating our society."[72] The marginalization of the conservative way of thinking, which was already noticeable during the war, would become even more pronounced at the end of the hostilities, with the collapse of Pétainism and the end of the movement led by Charles Maurras. Léon Daudet had been discredited, Robert Brasillach executed. From then on, it was the socialist, existentialist and personalist intellectuals forging the path of progress. For example, Hertel, who had formerly been a close ally of Lionel Groulx, was trying to make friends with Fernand Léger, Gabriel Marcel and Robert Aron, when he visited France in 1947. He was reading Albert Camus' latest novel and attended a screening of Marcel Carné's *Enfants du paradis* (Children of Paradise). Comparing Paris and Montreal, he stated that "decidedly, in Canada, things were quite dull."[73] As for Éloi de Grandmont, a former student of the École des Beaux-Arts, he was involved in discussions with Jean-Paul Sartre, frequented La Bolée and nightclubs, wandered the Grands Boulevards and visited non-figurative painting exhibitions.[74]

It is in this vast movement of rejecting all art subordinated to nationalistic and clerical doctrines that Borduas' production must be interpreted. He could not accept Zhdanovism, regardless of the political ideal it served. His universalism was "integral humanism." His whole being revolted against the bigotry of parish priests and the École des Beaux-Arts' national chauvinism.[75] By opposing aesthetic rants made by Maillard, who was still obsessed with the fantasy that painting should serve the national cause, Borduas had the impression that he was serving not art through his country, but his country through art. His anti-nationalism – which did not prevent him from accepting the idea that an artist comes from a place, subtly permeating his style – opposed a vision of art, which was aimed at the general and not the universal, the picturesque and not the unique, the nation and religion and not the human aspect. Consequently, his condemnation of clerico-nationalism in art was fierce and irrevocable. He wanted once and for all to be done with "the holy water and the French-Canadian tuque."

This no doubt explains in part why some members of the Quebec avant-garde distrusted naive art (Simone-Mary Bouchard's, for example), in which they never showed a true interest.[76] Although they marvelled at more ancient periods, they could never come to recognize what, for them, looked even remotely like folklore. Gilles Hénault was supposed to write a "judicious and fanciful study" for *Éditions de l'Arbre* entitled "*Primitifs canadiens*" but revealingly this study never came out in print.[77] This distrust also applied to Mexican and American art of the 1930s (Diego Rivera, José Orozco, Thomas Hart Benton), which participated in an enterprise of social education, and also to Soviet art, which was far too propagandist and apologetic. Pierre Gélinas, the director of the Communist journal *Combat* and grand inquisitor of the "so-called revolutionaries of the canvas, who positioned themselves against the movement favouring human progress across the economic, political and social fronts,"[78] professed opinions that shocked non-figurative painters to the extent that they opposed the transformation of art into an ideological message, whether it be evangelical, patriotic or Stalinist. Upon returning from a festival in Prague, Mousseau asked himself: "How can a work of plastic arts, which is the fruit of a slow internal elaboration of a personal train of thought and of an even more strictly personal unconscious, how can such a work comply to the point of becoming the bullhorn for direct political action exerted over people?"[79] There was no way he could not prefer the Automatist works to the Soviet serial productions that dominated Communist artist exhibitions at the time.

During the interwar period, certain Catholic intellectuals gradually moved away from the most obtuse forms of proselytism and nationalism. Father Couturier, for example, who was a royalist and had supported Charles Maurras, became one of the most ferocious critics of the Vichy regime. By replacing Maurras's "Politics first and foremost!" with Jacques Maritain's "The spiritual first and foremost," Couturier imagined himself as better serving the interests of Catholicism. In his opinion, Christian painters had to reach for the heavens with all the resources of their art, while disengaging themselves from spatial and temporal contingencies. They had to be one with a truth not of this world. This quest for the Christian universal supposed an ever-increasing detachment from the observed object. By abandoning subjects that were too situated – too specific – by emancipating itself from the appeal for the picturesque, art was propelled toward more ethereal spheres.[80] The simplicity of a painting enabled one to experience spirituality in a more direct and clear manner. By avoiding overly commonplace and trivial details, art could, with greater certainty, come closer to God. It was at this defining moment that the meeting between sacred art and abstract art took place.

ABSOLUTE AND ABSTRACTION

Henri Bremond, one the most cited art theorists of his time, provoked a heated debate in 1926 by declaring that poetry was something pure, which drew its strength from the mysterious emotions it stirred in its readers. Five logical consequences result from this premise, according to Bremond: that a poetical essence traverses all works regardless of their genre, their origin or their style, and that true poetry was thus universal; that poetic enchantment is beyond the reach of immediately making sense, and a sonnet by Gérard de Nerval could be magnificent even if it remained obscure; that rational knowledge is incapable of accounting for the value of a poem; that the poem echoed magical formulae, ellipses and spells as the state of the poet's soul was inaccessible to ordinary consciousness; finally, that this magic, this "reminder from within," ultimately resembled a prayer. If the poem was a descent into the depths of being, it was also an ascent toward mysticism for Bremond. Reacting to the interpretation of poetics by Nicolas Boileau, (the seventeenth-century French poet and critic who made reason and clarity the most important qualities of a poem), Bremond intended to rehabilitate oneiric invocation. He summarized his aims by declaring: "[A poem] owes its strictly poetic character to the presence, the radiance, the transformative and unifying action of a mysterious reality that we call pure poetry."[81] The musicality that Bremond appreciated in a poem remained largely ornamental, yet it cleared the intellectual horizon and in this way announced the upheavals to come.

In Maritain's critical work, *Frontières de la poésie* (Frontiers of Poetry), also published in 1926, he took up defending pure art, on the condition that it involved searching for what is human and that it continued to probe, as Baudelaire and Rimbaud had done, the sources of the soul. With respect to the art of painting, his thoughts were of the same nature. He felt that Picasso was a genius for having broadened human consciousness. By promoting its own mystery, Picasso's work had seized upon a more noble reality, a more spiritual one than raw matter. "But not only do things become transfigured in passing from his eye to his hand; at the same time another mystery is inferred: it is the painter's soul and flesh endeavouring to substitute themselves for the objects he paints, to drive out their substance, to enter into and offer themselves under the appearances of those trifling things painted on a canvas, and which live there with a life other than their own."[82] Maritain found this share of mystery in the poet's inspiration; it had nothing to do with rational reasoning. The torment of existence, which he identified as being the essence of poetry, haunted a space other than the one occupied by rationality and positivist reality.

According to Maritain, the fundamental pictorial experience always spilled over into the rational domain and opened the door to the absolute by means of visions and previously unseen symbols. It was quite different from the theatre of shadows and appearances defining Naturalism, which had, through an excess of pride, enclosed human existence in mundane realities. "When visiting a museum, one moves from the rooms featuring primitive works to the ones where oil paintings and a much more visible material science triumph. The foot steps onto the floor, but the soul falls into the abyss. [...] In the sixteenth century, the lie becomes part of the art of painting, which began appreciating science for itself. It sought to recreate nature and make us believe that we were standing in front of a scene or a person and not in front of a tableau."[83] Naturalism lost itself in the representation of vulgar pleasures and sensual emotions. Shapes and colours were no longer blended into the light and no longer permitted the miracle of creation to spring forth in a poetic arrangement.

Maritain subsequently demanded that contemporary artists renew their ties with spiritual truths. For him, art expressed a presence; it hinted at a superior reality, designated a space that escaped the ordinary data of life, be it logic or physical reality. The mysteries remained objective in the sense that they pointed toward a superior rationality, but one that was organic and no longer mechanical, alive and no longer formal. The aesthetic terms heralded during the interwar period – new realism, Surrealism, surreal realism, idea-based realism, transcendental realism, poetic realism, surnaturalism, extra-realism – all speak to the necessity of capturing in the immediate experience of nature "the reflection of the invisible order," the intuition of something that is "more than real," which the followers of Thomism (just like Surrealists who shared similar preoccupations connected to this time period) called "surrational."[84]

This is what Ozias Leduc realized. Leduc's importance with respect to Borduas' career is well known. After hiring Borduas as an apprentice, Leduc gave him his first painting and art history lessons. He looked after Borduas' training by giving him practical advice, guiding him on a personal level, giving direction to his education and by offering him the opportunity to decorate churches with him, including Sherbrooke's Archdiocese Chapel, the Rougemont Church, the Baptistery of Notre Dame and the Chapel of the Dames du Sacré-Coeur. "I owe him for having enabled me to make the leap from the spiritual and pictorial atmosphere of the Renaissance to the power of dreams, which opens the door to the future."[85] What is important to note here is that Leduc's work took its inspiration from European symbolist aesthetics, just as the writers of Le Nigog had done (Leduc illustrated the cover page of the magazine). He aimed at contesting the suffocating traditionalist currents in Quebec. "Deeply spiritual, Ozias Leduc, rises above the religion of the time through his art. His paintings neither teach, nor reveal. They define a spiritual dynamic. The pretext for this is a Christ-like gesture."[86] Leduc's intimate paintings bear witness to both the torment experienced by the artist and his own sentiments. His admirers were correct to say that they saw in his paintings the dream of an artist, more than any particular object. A tree, a face or a house, these realities were not important in themselves and disappeared from the frame, leaving only a vague impression, a diffuse sentiment and a fleeting idea. To give birth to perfection in a painting, Leduc sought out the absolute by shaking up the shapes and colours in his pictures, as if they were the embers of a fire. In his search for beauty, he fittingly spoke of "tormenting" the raw material.[87] In the boundless pursuit of invisible signs, artists had to accept losing themselves.

For a long time, Borduas sought to follow the path set out by his master, Ozias Leduc. "Rather foolishly," he asserted in 1953, "for many long years, both enthusiastically and ignorantly, I tried to be like him in his much too beautiful way of painting." (Ozias Leduc in his workshop. Société d'histoire de Beloeil–Mont-Saint-Hilaire, Fonds Michel-Clerk.)

When Leduc met Maurice Denis, who was visiting Quebec, he quickly understood that the Ateliers d'art sacré, which Denis ran, were the perfect training ground for his young disciple, Paul-Émile Borduas. It was not by chance that Father Couturier had himself studied at the Ateliers d'art sacré.[88] Maurice Denis, who was a fervent admirer of Gauguin and Cézanne, went much further than Maritain in his abandonment of personal will and intelligence. For this religious man, what the canvas had to transmit was not an impartial image of the world, but rather the tenacious impression of the intrinsically symbolic nature of the world and beings. For him, the mind was a less noble faculty than the heart, since it was only by listening to his heart that the artist could save something of the beauty of creation and bear witness to God's existence. "Instead of a system of cold, banal, and fixed allegories and hieroglyphics, instead of any old, undefined, sappy conventions, instead of a hypocritical and sickly-sweet image, instead of applying historical painting to religion, Christian artists must give us a living art, one found within their own depths, and speak from the heart."[89] This is where the ferocious criticism of naturalism and academicism came from. "Such an art [of the heart] forces us to make an effort to be sincere, which implies radically excluding what is accepted and academic. Representing and symbolizing our emotions, translating religious sentiment through fine art is to work on our inner and intimate core. It involves unearthing the mysteries of our inner life, a clear image of our faith."[90] With this understanding, Denis believed that one had to recommit to emotions, to personal experiences, which alone could translate a believer's spirituality. It was important not to be afraid of descending into the half-light of one's being in an attempt to rediscover the primordial impetus of faith. In his haste to define "an art that was sensitive to the heart," and that could come close to "a mystical state or at least be analogous to a mystical vision," Denis suggested, quoting Bergson, putting to sleep "the active or rather resistant powers of our personality and bringing ourselves in this way to a perfect state of docility where we can carry out the idea suggested to us, where we commiserate with the expressed sentiment." He called for the restitution of "muddled memories" and "subconscious forces."[91] This transmutation of human anxiety into images could not produce clean, calm, rational, bourgeois results. One had to expect that the vibrations felt by the soul would burst forth in a chaotic manner. For Georges Desvallières, the other director of the Ateliers d'art sacré, this gave rise to torturous and disturbing images, which reflected his tormented vision of religion.

The imitation of nature bore the brunt of these new preoccupations. It must be said that the growing popularity of photography had a definitive impact on the theory that art was simply a means of replicating reality. With the invention of the camera, the question of copying nature exactly seemed to have been resolved once and for all. Figurative art had no reason to exist, since the external world could be captured on film by anyone, simply by clicking a button. "Who can compete with photography, if he resigns himself to just this? Can we say that servile and insensitive replication, which is within the reach of any resigned robot, is a worthwhile human activity?"[92] The consequence of photography was that the question of impersonally reproducing nature was no longer an issue.[93] Realism, nineteenth-century style, had become a closed case.

But even more fundamentally, realistically imitating physical reality went against the ideal objective of art, as defined by Maritain and Denis, which was to bear one's soul. Instead of looking at the world in a detached way, the artist had to express an emotion, a one-of-a-kind turmoil. If science were the description of the outside world, art was the expression of inner realities. Realist painters faithfully reproduced nature. The most contemporary art of the time, on the other hand, demanded that artists take hold of the subject matter, impressing upon it their indelible mark. Before the war, Borduas' religious paintings paved the way for such a revolution. It was said that his works embodied an intense presence and concealed a veritable mysticism. His portrait of Saint John, the property of Deputy Minister Jean Bruchési, exuded a "stunning, surnatural vitality." "This expression of humanity is immersed in asceticism; it has become divine from within; its spiritual quality shines through from the depths of reality to the delicate skin of a changing face. Works of such eminent religious character should already have their place in our Canadian churches where replicas, camouflage and duplicity have too often been used to serve a God who is nothing but Truth."[94] Borduas was, however, conscious that his creations did not go far enough in terms of exploring the artist's singular sensibilities. He felt impeded in his drive and constrained with respect to his inspiration. His language remained stymied by a series of arbitrary conventions that he felt prevented him from putting forth all that he was.

At the end of the First World War, Georges Desvallières (here in 1930) founded, alongside Maurice Denis, the Ateliers d'art sacré, with the objective of completely renewing religious art in France. Deeply disturbed by the armed conflict that bloodied Europe, Desvallières wanted to reconnect with the drama of the Catholic faith. (Archives de la province dominicaine de France.)

At the end of the 1930s, a major impediment to expression persisted: the norm according to which artists had to paint recognizable figures. For a long time, Catholic art critics had thought that sacred art could not be reduced to abstraction; being irrational, this form of art could not be religious. But they soon realized that intuition favoured a divine union, much more than codes and the rules of fine art. For the believer, the figure of Christ was beyond reason; it could only be apprehended by the grace of prayer. For Catholics, it was in each person's most intimate depths that the believer could find God, who was irreducible to Cartesian formulas. What is more, multiple examples demonstrated the ineptitude of charges levelled against abstract art. For example: architecture did not mimic forms existing in nature and yet could serve as a means of singing God's praises. By mysteriously balancing materials and proportions, architects could attain a version of reality that was pure, absolute, and real. The art of painting, a visible art *par excellence*, also strove toward unveiling the invisible. The colours on the canvas, by virtue of their materiality, could conjure up the immateriality of human existence.

In a sudden reversal, abstraction was becoming the quintessential religious art form, whereas realistic art was relegated to an inferior rung. "In this way, it is naturalistic art, it is realistic art which, in itself, is anti-religious, whereas abstract art, having severed all these [sensual] connections, is already participating in a certain spiritual freedom, in a 'detachment,' which predisposes it to this transfer and to the expression of sacred realities."[95] Abstraction embodied a more impalpable and disquieting presence than the prosaic engravings of the inglorious "art pompier," i.e. official academic art.

Avant-garde artists found that the term "abstraction" was inadequate, but they continued using it because it was frequently used; not because they felt that it described their creative intentions. In their opinion, the label – abstract art – more aptly suited academicism, which was not sensitive and not very concrete. On the other hand, they explained that "surrational painting is the most concrete form of painting there is – as it does not hide its reality behind abstract veneers such as definable similarities, resemblances, illusions and normalizations."[96] Borduas admired the purity of form in Klee's work. In 1943, he wrote: "Paul Klee's geometry is not at all abstract, churlish or like some scholarly geometry. On the contrary, it is loaded with the most tangible, divine material. It is full of emotion, of mystery and life."[97] Surrational painting cared nothing for the illusions and tricks of realistic art, which turned painting into nothing more than pretty and inoffensive decoration.

If we are to believe progressive art critics, for at least five centuries Western society preferred an art form that was incompatible with mystical fervour. The evolution toward a more and more sterile realism was especially obvious to Borduas because, early on, he had to deal with the idiocies of church bureaucrats. The Italian Renaissance, which untalented painters identified with as they invaded the French-Canadian countryside, projected a feeble, petrified image of the history of art since the Quattrocento. Churches were filled with ridiculous ornament – mosaics from Florence, Italian marble floors, mass-produced wooden stalls – which transformed these places of prayer into gaudy theaters. Italianism was a deformed caricature of the Renaissance, which, for Borduas, had initiated art's fall from grace by subjecting painting to Neapolitan sentimentalism for centuries. Consequently, it is hardly surprising that Borduas described a vision of history that was marked by the precocious decline of the West in a November 1942 lecture entitled: *"Des mille manières de goûter une oeuvre d'art"* (Thousands of Ways to Savour a Work of Art). In his opinion, the Renaissance had plunged itself into an unpardonable materialism, involving abandoning the pursuit of higher realities and, as such, had halted the creative evolution that nourishes life. Just as Greek art honoured technical skills and codified exercises, the Renaissance denatured the generosity of life and replaced it with a rigid science. "This is the negation of art through the loss of balance and human harmony."[98] By not obeying the laws of its own potential and by compromising itself with official institutions, an era wasted its efforts on meaningless sensualism and rationalism. As early as the thirteenth century – the grand century of Saint Louis – the fatal turning point had occurred, as rationalistic reasoning replaced intuition. "Gradually, acts of faith ceded to calculated acts. […] The spirit of transfiguration succeeded the spirit of observation."[99] To reconnect to the incandescent resources of the invisible world, a formidable change of course had to occur. "Everything has to be redone, everything in all spheres has to be redone from the beginning. Who will have the courage and the strength to do so? […] This destiny will ultimately unfold. More and more heroes will come forth."[100] A new myth was going to arise from the ashes of Western civilization, a myth born of the vision of those poets who had learned to "break ranks with utilitarian predispositions," which for centuries had quashed energy, desire, generosity and passion.

Borduas' 1942 lecture was consistent with the opinion of those Catholics who were struggling against modern naturalism and rationalism. Father Guy Courteau, the chancellor of the Collège du Sacré-Coeur in Sudbury, Ontario interpreted Borduas' words as a call to "reconnect with the spirit of the Middle Ages."[101] For the contributors to the magazine *La Relève*, the establishment of a "new Renaissance," according to the slogan coined by Émmanuel Mounier, also involved returning to the medieval spirit, a move that was seen as the basic condition for the establishment of an organic Christianity. They wanted to redress the course of history, to provoke "the passage from modern rationalism to a surrationalism of the medieval kind,"[102] discarding the bourgeois order of things.

> We are at a turning point in history; we are witness to a world falling apart and the birth of another. The one we see dying (the moribund is not going quietly!) is a world created by the Renaissance, that period when the world saw an excessive development of mechanical science, eventually ending in the worship of matter. The one we see emerging, the one whose precursory signs we can currently distinguish, is a time when spiritual forces

are once again going to assert their primacy over matter. The likes
of Berdiaeff, Maritain and Daniel-Rops have given us a glimpse of
this world.[103]

At the same time, Simone Aubry and Jacques de Tonnancour were
rebelling against art forms that were not inspired by spiritually universal sources. For them, it was important to make religious beauty shine
forth, without submitting to the fine arts rules inherited from the
Renaissance, which had until then blocked its expression. They
opposed art forms that did not go beyond the surface of things and
proposed instead forms that were once again capable of making the
darker sides of human nature the subject matter of pictorial expression. By accepting this immateriality, Aubry and Tonnancour were
able to enthusiastically embrace the style of contemporary painters,
whom they saw as explorers capable of capturing the inscrutable.
Until then, the Christian world in the twentieth century had produced
works that were totally lacking Christian meaning, whereas the pagan
twentieth century was giving birth to truly spiritual art. The sensualism and naturalism of sacred art paled in comparison to the magnificent and mystical painting of revolutionary artists. "Modern painters,
troubled by a level of questioning and anxiety unparalleled in the history of art, reacted against the materialistic and mechanical climate
suffocating us."[104] These innovative artists sought to fight the harmful values of bourgeois civilization and found the sustenance to do so
"by feeding off an anxious and insatiable France, whose quest for the
absolute made it all the more Christian."[105] Avant-garde painters
offered a formidable plastic revival to those in search of the absolute.
It was in the work of these anarchist, bohemian and anticlerical artists
that sincere Catholics had to track down the signs of transcendence.

In the first half of the century, Jacques Maritain believed he had
guaranteed the religious nature of Catholic art based on the artist's
faith and the quality of his spiritual life. To "produce something
Christian," one had to be Christian. Beauty was attained by those,

who as pupils of God, made their painting a sort of oration. Fra Angelico personified the model artist, as he drew inspiration to produce truth and beauty in saintly contemplation. For a long time, Father Couturier also thought that an unbeliever could not produce pious works. However, by the end of the 1930s, he realized that it was simply not enough for works to have been produced by devout artists for them to awaken and give rise to religious sentiments in the faithful. Highly devout painters had produced an incalculable number of mediocre works, while debauched artists had managed to produce masterpieces. Was it necessary to take down the two magnificent murals hanging in the Saint-Sulpice church in Paris simply because Delacroix had not been baptized? The Renoirs, the Gauguins and the Rimbauds had followed the path of scepticism, and affirmed that their works were free from everything, including God and faith. Was this cause to discredit their works?

Couturier understood that a work's beauty had nothing to do with morals or the entreaties of the catechism. He accepted that what these mad, rebellious and libertarian men were searching for had merit. They had broken away in one fell swoop from the strict confines of scholastic aesthetics. "Even in the harsh and perilous acrobatics featured in Picasso's works or in those of a Surrealist writer, there is enough truth to carry toward God a life that would not otherwise be impeded."[106] For him, it was only half ironic that "it was precisely in this same anarchist, impertinent and insubordinate France that this renaissance had begun – and that everything was coming from this country, and not from saintly, hidebound, conformist and virtuous countries."[107] The clergy's frightened reaction to the audacity of these contemporary painters did nothing but confirm the gross incompetence of their initial training. They were unable to see in Picasso, whom Couturier admired and they liked to deride, an immensely talented artist who had taken his art to unparalleled heights. "This man […] even when following the hideous paths of ugliness and bestiality, has gone further than all others, is more powerful than all others, and is more lucid than all others," because he works to "push the autonomy and power of creative endeavour to its most extreme limits."[108] There was a "God for artists" and it was before this God alone that they had to bow down. Nothing more could be asked of artists than to do what their heart told them. Only in this way could they allow art lovers to catch a glimpse of the extraordinary and indescribable calling that lies deeply buried within each person.

According to Couturier, there was not a sacred art on one side and a profane art on the other. Rather, art was only divided between true art and pseudo art. There were no religious and atheist artists, but simply good and bad artists. The bourgeois art of Saint-Sulpice, which favoured visible illusions over unexpected revelations, was the opposite of sacred. "Modern painting is the only one that counts, because it is the only one that is living: all the rest, despite appearances, are dead. The specific form, or if one prefers, the style, of 'modern painting' does not matter much. Whether it is abstract or representative, Cubist or Surrealist, this essentially changes nothing: there is only good and bad painting, and that's all."[109] Father Couturier did not need to know whether Marc Chagall, Fernand Léger, Jacques Lipchitz, Henri Matisse, Le Corbusier or Jan Lurçat were atheists, Communists or Jews; it was enough that they were explorers searching for the absolute. "We knew very well that some of these artists were not good, strictly practicing Christians; that some of them were separated from us, due to political as well as intellectual differences. Trusting in Providence, we said to ourselves that a great artist is always a deeply spiritual person, each in his or her own way...."[110] The need to objectively reproduce reality had vanished, nationalistic and Catholic callings were dismissed, and the only intention remaining was an irrepressible drive toward some elevated questioning. For beauty to shine forth again in the Roman Catholic Church, for spirituality to once again penetrate religious art, for frescos to turn believers' hearts naturally towards God, one needed to explore the mysteries of the world rather than present a comfortable and tidy image of it.

Like many other French-Canadian intellectuals, Maurice Gagnon, Borduas' colleague at the École du Meuble in Montreal, came to accept this unprecedented vision of artistic works. "Art is not first and foremost a form of preaching: otherwise, a saintly artist would always be an excellent painter. A religious work of art must first be a work of art; sentiments of a religious order come forth once per-fection is obtained allowing the qualities of superior soulfulness and spiritual essence to show through."[111] From this point on, Catholic art critics in Quebec accepted works of art whose main purpose was not religious and whose objective was not to proselytize. For them, as for Couturier, there were no longer divisions such as Christian art versus pagan art, nor Communist art versus modern art. There was only one universal art, which unveiled in its universality the incommensurable power of life. They realized that art could better serve the God of Christianity through an atheist brush if the artist sought out the absolute, than if it languished in mediocrity under the brush of a pious painter who lacked real talent. No real emotion whatsoever could ever come from a superficial or saccharine art. Yet, it was precisely emotion that needed to be pursued; not necessarily a religious one, but a dis-concerting, obscured and troubling one, given that this emotion had the greatest chance of generating enriching questions pertaining to the ultimate ends of human existence.

Borduas' non-figurative works were like explorations into the unknown, which opposed a mechanized and rationalized world. Hav-ing contemplated them in 1942 at the Ermitage, Maurice Gagnon could not help but think of André Breton and his need to come into contact with "a surreality that restored thought's original purity."[112] For Gagnon, Borduas' approach revealed something beyond, hidden in dreams, passion and chance; there was something of the divine power of mystics about it. The desires of this Automatist painter revealed something supraterrestrial. "Everything in this form of art depends on nothing other than the artist's personality and that's mar-vellous. Convulsive vision into convulsive beauty, forms are brought to life, stolen from the depth of being, and enter a world without dimensions, a spiritual and concrete reality that overwhelms and ravishes those who can devote their faith to it." Having written this, Gagnon went on to say: "The seduction of the soul by certain poetics is all the more real when the reality that it expresses is elusive and unexpected. Following Rimbaud's lead, Borduas, an obscure poetic force himself, has expressed the inexpressible... And some dare claim that we have lost the sense of mystery. The continuity that can only be found in dreams, as André Breton believes, is entirely turned toward the inside."[113] It would be difficult to better express the unexpected encounter between Automatism and Catholic mysticism in French Canada in the 1940s.

In Gagnon's estimation, Borduas had re-established the "anarchistic" demands of the spirit in a materialistic and bureaucratic society. At a time when industrialized society was sinking into materialism, Borduas helped art to show what an ordinary eye would otherwise remain blind to. In this way, for progressive Catholics, he had helped his compatriots achieve salvation more than the pile of monotonous and dry sermons pronounced by the province's bishops. He had awakened French Canadians from their dogmatic slumber. He directed them to plunge into the darkness of things and to immerse themselves in the movement of life. In light of these conditions, why not ask him to participate in decorating Canadian churches? Didn't Father Couturier – although not without creating a considerable public debate[114] – ask that Fernand Léger complete a mosaic depicting the Virgin Mary to adorn the walls of the Church in Assy? In October 1952, the hanging of Borduas' canvases in the *Foyer de l'art et du livre* (Foyer of Art and Books) in Ottawa had prompted laudatory comments.

On this occasion, a young Dominican Frenchman, Father Pomeler gave a speech in which he said that he hoped French-Canadian churches would make room for avant-garde artists such as Borduas, even though his anticlerical and agnostic stance was well known by then. "In France, right in the middle of working-class suburbs, we have built churches whose pictorial art work and even stained-glass windows are non-figurative. On the way back from work, it is rare not to see workers stopping to look at them in quiet contemplation. These daily workers like their church because it has once again given them the sense of mystery in a uniquely dull and lowly world. And I am sorry [Mr. Borduas] that I do not have a church to build, as I would have immediately entrusted the stained glass and the walls of my church to you."[115] Borduas, the man, was an atheist, Borduas, the thinker, was anticlerical, but this did not really matter. Because the anticlerical Borduas had advanced the art of painting "one step further within its own mystery," Father Pomeler was convinced that the painter had contributed to the spreading of faith in his country. The incommunicable truth of his canvases had seemingly touched something infinite. The truth buried in the cosmos shone through in his oil paintings, which became like incandescent sources of light. For Father Pomeler, as for Gagnon and his fellow male colleagues (there were very few women in this very masculine world), it would have been absurd to ask a witness of the absolute – such as Borduas – for his baptismal certificate or to force him to go to confession.

THE MYSTIC OF AUTOMATISM

The desire to bring Borduas back into the fold of the Catholic Church would appear futile and out of place, if our analysis did not take into account what needs to be called a certain "mystique" of Automatism in Quebec. Although Borduas declared himself an atheist during the 1940s, his line of thinking had in certain respects retained something of a call to participate in the cosmos, which may have appeared to certain observers like a revisiting of the spiritualism prevalent during the interwar period. For Robert Élie, who not only knew the evolution of art in the twentieth century (he was later named director of the École des Beaux-Arts), but who was also one of the rare close friends of the master from Saint-Hilaire, Borduas' painting was wrapped in a vision of life whose foundations remained imminently spiritual in nature.[116]

Borduas left the Catholic Church without any regrets in the 1940s and *Refus global*'s prose leaves no doubt as to his convictions. What happened for this former diligent reader of the Bible to abandon his childhood faith? What existential thoughts brought him to apostasy? Since Borduas wrote little about the renunciation of his faith, I believe it is useful to study the ideas held at this time by François Hertel, who met the Surrealist painter through Maurice Gagnon in 1940. He subsequently struck up a friendship with Borduas (in 1945, he dedicated a poem to him in his volume of poetry, *Cosmos*[117]) before breaking it off shortly before the publication of *Refus global*. Born in 1905 in a small village at the lower part of the Saint Lawrence River, Hertel, a Jesuit, was one of the rare admirers within his religious order of Fernand Léger's painting and Guillaume Apollinaire's poetry. At one point, in the middle of the 1940s, he even envisaged publishing a *Plaidoyer pour l'art moderne* (Defence of Modern Art).[118] Some of Borduas' earliest followers came from the small circle of people who Hertel entertained during weekly evening meetings at his home on Saint-Viateur Street.

Paul-Émile Borduas was a student in the Ateliers d'art sacré from 1928 to 1930. In these workshops, he expanded his capacity to listen to his inner voice while working on his canvases and drawings. "I truly realize now, after hearing it so many times," he confided in 1929, "that artists should not copy nature, but find inspiration in it, even in a study." (Collection of Gail and Stephen A. Jarislowsky Institute for Studies in Canadian Art collection, Concordia University.)

Hertel recounted how he lost his faith at the onset of the war. After having indifferently swallowed the dogmas that *collèges* in the province promoted, he came to realize that human reason was a biased and only partial means of understanding the world. He ended up adopting an attitude of "cosmic humility."

"I exist. The cosmos even more so. It is the cosmos that pushes me toward myself. It is by the cosmos entering me that I become conscious of myself and everything else,"[119] Hertel wrote. He became persuaded that the only transcendental reality was cosmic matter, a substance so ontologically spirit and matter that he invented a concept to describe it – "*espritmatière*" (spirit-matter). He believed the spiritual realm was already present in matter, but the material realm also entailed a spiritual dimension. Exiled in Paris, Hertel continued to inform his line of thinking with respect to art while trying to elaborate a new language that could replace a system of signs that was too restrictive in his opinion. In part, he saw the possibility, with the help of this new vocabulary, of going beyond fixed conventions and accessing a place beyond the objective and symbolic universe. Poetry, the quintessential language of dreams and madness, seemed to open a window to an intuitive, ethereal and universal expressivity. In his mind, the unconscious and the indeterminate constituted privileged means of access to reality, but a reality that was situated beyond reason, learned rules, and ordinary grammar.

By way of these few biographical lines, we can establish a parallel between Hertel and Borduas. Both were in search of a new language (artistic and poetic) and dreamed of a more perfect beginning. They also resembled one another in terms of their support for what must be called an "atheistic monism." "All the Automatists had been monists; which means that for them, warped and sometimes hypocritical dualism that divided things into "matter" and "spirit" while condemning one of these opposing terms, always appeared vain and contrary to reality."[121] Like Hertel, Borduas did not hesitate to speak about the "mysteriously animated matter of the universe"[122] and used the concept of "spirit-matter."[123] For Borduas, the spirit represented "the organic accident" of matter – and vice versa. In truth, this was of no importance, as atheistic monism postulated that people and the cosmos formed a single and same substance and a single and same spirit.[124] Being part of the same essence, matter and spirit were both infinite. To him, there was only "a difference of intensity in the emotive power of minerals and human beings."[125]

At first, Hertel and Borduas probably borrowed a large part of this atheistic monism from French philosopher Henri Bergson, who defined the life force as a fluid, animating the universe in *Creative Evolution*.[126] For Bergson, the movement of life indistinctly inhabited both matter and spirit along the entire length of the natural evolutionary chain. For him, the universe seemed characterized by an irrepressible evolution, by a transformative inspiration that transcended the ages. The cosmos evolved according to a continuous line, which went from inert matter to the spiritual world. Therefore, there was no difference in kind between them, only differences in degrees between the less evolved stages and the most refined human creations. Bergson spoke of a vital impetus that traversed creation from one end to the other, constituting not only the law of the universe, but a primitive energy that can be drawn from, like a freshwater spring. To be at one with this primordial force, to "shed light on the inside of the vital impetus, its meaning, and its destination," Bergson rejected reason's deceptive insights, preferring the pale glow of intuition. For Bergson, intuition remained "fully disinterested" and "was always turned toward the inside." If, he added "it enabled us to seize the continuity of our inner life, if most of us didn't go any farther, a superior intensification would carry it to the roots of our very being, and by doing so, to the principle of life itself in general. Wasn't that precisely the glory of the mystical soul?"[127] Mystics, of course, but Bergson could have also spoken of artist-geniuses, since in his opinion both of them cultivated the ability to dissolve themselves into the continuous flow of creation through more intense contemplation.

Bergson's monism engaged people to be at one with the world, to accomplish what Father Couturier (who did not hide the French philosopher's influence on his thoughts and whose brand of Catholicism was also defined by some as monistic[128]) described in writing as an "alchemy between the inner and outer world."[129] Borduas, in his own way, tried to accomplish this goal.[130] His dream in life was one of a reconciled world. Borduas believed in the need for human beings to "constantly aspire toward the totality [of reality], otherwise one would be denying oneself."[131] He hoped "to take complete possession of the horizon," and "directly taste the imaginable fullness of space" dissolving himself into infinity. With respect to this, Jean Fisette wrote: "The invention of man in this universe, his 'sacred' role is to participate in this infinite process of transformation, to 'participate' not by placing himself on the outside so as to represent the world, but by integrating himself into the cosmos so as to be one with the global process of transformation."[132] Borduas, as a man of his time, sought to fight against the lost unity of being, which had been broken apart by rationality's unabashed victory. By once again taking up the theme of "the loss of human plenitude," which he had already denounced in *"Des mille manières de goûter une oeuvre d'art"* in *Refus global,* he could condemn the extreme separation between reason and subjectivity characterizing society. "Our reason allows us to invade the world, but it is a world in which we have lost our unity. The growing gap between psychological forces and rational ones is almost at the breaking point."[133] There needed to be a reaction: one had to move beyond the dichotomy of life forces. Humanity's future rested on the hopes of a restored harmony. How was one to once again conjugate the divided properties that make up a human being? How could one unite in a new synthetic way the most immediate subjective sentiments with the distant objectivity of the cosmos? How does one mend the tear between subjective and natural necessity? How does one reconnect beings with "cosmic energies?"

Borduas assigned the task of establishing this "inevitably new relationship with the cosmos"[134] to the artist. For him, artistic creation represented the privileged means of expression, capable of reuniting former contradictions between states of wakefulness and sleep, reason and madness, the objective and the subjective, the past and the future, life and death.[135] His fascination with Pierre Mabille's philosophy can be understood by his desire to reconnect with the creative breath of life,[136] as it seems that what first excited Borduas and his followers was precisely this French author's project of bringing together increasingly isolated human faculties. "For me," Mabille stated, "as for the realists of the Middle Ages, there is no fundamental difference between the elements of thought and the phenomena of the world, between the visible and the comprehensible, the perceptible and the imaginable."[137] He added that humankind "must be envisaged, just like any other object or living being, in terms of a place where the transmutation of cosmic energies takes place."[138] With respect to such a statement, we are on familiar ground, since Bergson used similar language at the same time. However, the main difference was that Mabille, unlike Bergson who came to embrace the Catholic faith at the end of his life, identified the source of dualistic evil in convoluted Christian thought, which taught the separation of body and soul, temporal and eternal, heaven and hell, incarnation and transcendence. Nothing was subsequently more important to Mabille than breaking with this Judeo-Christian philosophy, which was an obstacle to full harmony between the human race and the cosmos, while searching for a new philosophy, if not to say a new religion.

It was by studying ancient Hermetics and not Holy scripture that Mabille, a Freemason with a passion for alchemy and astrology, ended up frequenting the French Surrealists. In his mind, these artists were the most likely and capable, due to their esoteric techniques, of salvaging the compromised fullness of being. "We owe it to Surrealism," Mabille wrote, "for exploring such special mental processes which, before this movement, were for the most part the privilege of only priests. Surrealism concentrated on trying to grasp the mechanisms of inspiration, while attempting to develop inspiration in everyone, and free it from the clutches of intelligent consciousness. Secularized in a way, this domain had previously been exclusively religious. Religious groups tried to find ways of placing the faithful, in groups or individually, in a situation that enabled them to welcome the actions of natural forces in the best possible conditions."[139]

Among all existing aesthetic trends, Surrealism had been able to make way for the future by directly addressing the problem of uniting the human faculties that modern life had divided. Through its methods, this school of thought claimed that a "poetic gift" could lead to a "state of grace." The Surrealist artist's testimony aimed at dissolving itself into the cosmos by establishing a necessary correspondence between the macrocosm and the microcosm. "Everything tends to make us believe," Breton confirmed, "that there exists a certain point of the mind at which life and death, the real and the imaginary, past and future, the communicable and the incommunicable, high and low, cease to be perceived as contradictions. Now, search as one may, one will never find any other motivating force in the activities of the Surrealists than the hope of finding and fixing this point."[140] This passage, from Breton's *Second Manifesto*, which Borduas read with a "sense of revelation,"[141] summarized in few words the Surrealists' monistic utopia.

We find this dream of mystic reconciliation in the works of several of Borduas' followers who were attracted to Surrealism, starting with Fernand Leduc. For example, in 1944 Leduc clearly expressed the reasons for his support of Surrealism when he wrote that "life would not be complete without the efficient collaboration between our unconscious and reason" and that the "arduous and necessary" task of men and women at the time was to "strive toward trying to achieve a harmonious agreement between the secret faculties and lucid means."[142] More than Fauvism or Cubism, Surrealism for Leduc promised to build "the first recognizable bridges between the inner and outer world and to force consciousness to go beyond the apparent reality of things and grasp its latent contents. Of all aesthetic concerns, discovering the tangible sign of this new reality is what interests the Surrealist way of thinking the most in its pursuit of a collective myth [...]."[143]

We know that Leduc, once he was settled in Paris after the publication of *Refus global*, was passionate about George Gurdjieff's works, as well as the writings of Piotr Ouspensky, Arthur Adamov and Jacob Boehme. Electrified by spiritualist speculations, as well as numeral and cosmogonic sciences, he became friends with Raymond Abellio. Abellio was a former supporter of automatic writing and of Surrealism, who became an enthusiast of an eclectic esoteric movement made up of Christianity, Hinduism, Kabbalistic aspects and numerology. If we are to believe Leduc, Abellio and Borduas professed the same things with different words. Borduas denied this kinship, not without a certain annoyance, because he thought that Abellio's words remained far too Christian. However, one cannot help but think that the effect Abellio's charm had on Leduc may have been related to past discussions between friends and colleagues during the evenings organized at Borduas' home, which focused on a possible link between energy, space and light.

This call for more intense participation in the universe made it possible for certain Catholic art critics to interpret Borduas' creative gesture in terms of Christian revelation. Fernand Leduc was not the only one to receive Borduas' invitation to participate more fully in the movements of the universe in terms of eschatological mystical philosophy, because Borduas' vocabulary allowed for a certain degree of ambiguity. Jean Fisette argued that "overall, Borduas represent[ed] creation, be it artistic or scientific, like a religious ritual, a privileged way of integrating the individual into the cosmos."[144] In this way, Catholic critics could bring Borduas' works back within the limits of their own spirituality, notwithstanding Borduas' opinion on the matter, and they could do so with relative ease as his works presented themselves in terms of a search for the absolute.

This convergence between artistic searching and the religious quest is best embodied by Pierre Vadeboncoeur. His writing allows us to better understand how Borduas' painting could be recycled within a religious philosophy with which the painter himself entertained irreconcilable disagreements. The first meeting between Vadeboncoeur and Automatist artists was far from congenial. He accused them of slavishly imitating French painters' works and of exuding a nonchalance tinged with dogmatism. "Despite there being several quite beautiful works, their naivety, ridiculous messianism, their pretentiousness and their hackneyed messages made them seem to me, along with their European masters, like perfect examples of people who use their authority, their truths and the prestige of some famous names in order to spout out nonsense that they convince themselves to believe."[145] Vadeboncoeur spoke differently later on, and the motives behind his change of tone show how he saw the creative act as mystical. Vadeboncoeur claimed that the master from Saint-Hilaire, unable to find the spiritual solace he sought in a disincarnated, bigoted and ritualistic Catholic Church, channelled the overflow of absoluteness that he could not contain onto his canvases. He asserted that Borduas, like a revolutionary artist, eschewing false idols of the time, had embarked upon a personalized quest for truth that was spiritual in essence. "Art, which is a truthful act, absolutely teaches this. Art, whose chief characteristic is to denounce all compromise, is composed of absolutely true spiritual acts [...] It is perhaps the only discipline where tremendous freedom exists and, therefore, where radical truth can exist."[146] By refusing to compromise his conscience, Borduas transformed his creations into sacred testimonies to the human condition. For this reason, Vadeboncoeur saw the master from Saint-Hilaire as a sort of secular saint. He would even go so far as to say that he saw an image of divinity in Borduas' works. "Truth gave Borduas some image of God that became his canvases."[147]

This posthumous attempt to bring Borduas back into the fold of the Catholic faith was based on the conviction that a work of art was spiritual not in its apologetic message but in its appeal to the transcendence of the spirit. For Vadeboncoeur, all painters – Christian and agnostic, religious and non-religious – who bore witness to a "taste for risk" by dedicating themselves to the pursuit of the absolute, produced "images of God." By presenting a Catholic way of interpreting modernity, this Quebec essayist allowed himself to reread Borduas in light of his own faith. In this way, he restored part of faith's former glory, a henceforth wavering faith, that appeared increasingly uncertain and insignificant in an ever-changing modern society, and especially in the world of art.

A PURE AND LIVING ART

In works of art, we have only cherished what was intentional, fin-
ished, and skillful in depiction, that which was fixed, impersonal and
dead. What we should have been looking for is spontaneity, generos-
ity, and what is unmistakably personal, and therefore eternally liv-
ing and ever changing.   —PAUL-ÉMILE BORDUAS

In the 1930s, a concept gradually imposed itself in the language of art
criticism: that of living art, as exemplified by the publication in Europe
of the journal *L'Art vivant* (Living Art) between 1925 and 1939. By the
eve of the Second World War, James Wilson Morrice and John
Lyman's creations were qualified as "living works."[1] In 1941, Jacques
de Tonnancour described the École du Meuble as a "teaching centre
for living art."[2] The collection directed by Maurice Gagnon at the
Éditions de l'Arbre from 1943 was called "Living Art." Fernand
Leduc, in the same year saw art as having a mission, that of making the
world shine forth in all its glory. He said that the artist was "above all,
a living, healthy, and normal man who had heard the concert of lively
vibrations being emitted by the elements of the universe. He understood the harmony of the world and had witnessed its temporal possibilities expand to a point where he could do nothing other than burst
into generous and passionate activity." He thus began to etch "his
enthusiasm for life into the subject matter.[3]" Leduc described Borduas
as one of those painters whose "manifestations of life" opposed the
"whimpering of the dying,"[4] while Claude Gauvreau admired in him
a master having understood how to create "the only form of contemporary art that is living."[5] Around the time Borduas was fired from the
École du Meuble, one of his students, Bernard Morisset, praised him,

proclaiming that he had given his students "an impetus for living art."[6] As for Borduas, he wrote: "Art is born from life. It consequently espouses all life's forms and necessities. It is subject to its *total law*."[7]

This living art was firmly opposed to fine arts, that is to say, to a schooling focused on conventions, rules and traditions. The synonyms that avant-garde artists used at the time for the adjective *academic* left no doubt as to their feelings concerning officially codified art: *dead, cold, voluntary, systematic, rational, repetitive, redundant, impersonal, insensitive, calculated*, etc.[8] "False judgments, arbitrary notions, all the prejudices" represented nothing more nor less than death.[9] For this reason, Father Couturier applauded the necessary "derangement of all the senses" brought about by the works of modern artists since Rimbaud. It was no longer a question of imposing external and arbitrary repetition on art. Couturier trusted the natural movement of painting, its own *élan*, its internal dynamics, rather than seeking to imprison paintings in a rigid aesthetic conception, which was outdated anyway. "Father Couturier stressed that artwork is a field that only has rules and principles in and of itself; the law of artwork is none other than its intrinsic beauty, which is its *raison d'être*."[10] Without risk, there could be no freedom, and without freedom, warned Couturier, there could be no authentic expression of the soul.

By being true to himself, the artist could not subjugate himself to external reality, to other people, to codes, to traditions, nor to any restriction imposed on the imagination. Reproducing the distinctive qualities of classic artists (e.g., borrowing from Titian's sumptuous colouring or Botticelli's elegant strokes) was out of the question. Exactly depicting a model resulted in something cold and mechanical, dangerously close to angelism. Living art was entirely different here, no one could predict the artwork's final aspect; rather, it took shape in the moment, being uncontrollable, unpredictable, enigmatic and fallible. Father Couturier formulated a vision of art based on the "freshness of the soul" of the artist, the "candour of the gift of self" and "integrity, unconscious of itself," which, for him, were spiritual signs.[11] Living art attempted to conquer unknown territory and to fabricate mystery, and for this reason, the artist had no other choice but to shatter all conformist views blocking access to an active faith.

The French priest sponsored or supported several exhibitions in the province, such as that of the *Indépendants* (1941, with Borduas, Lyman and Pellan, among others), that of the *Sagittaires* (1943), or that of the religious arts and crafts at the École du Meuble (1941). In each case, the aim was always to find a source of living art that could victoriously oppose the ambient banality, "the tyranny of realism" and old-fashioned politics. However, such a claim was not without turmoil. "Here," wrote Couturier in the summer of 1941, "I was terribly busy, and I have a ton of worries; I'm currently organizing a 'modern painting' exhibition in Quebec City, which is making a real ruckus even before it has begun: I'm being accused of demolishing 'the teaching of fine arts' in the province of Quebec – politics are involved, the government, [but] the bishops not quite yet!"[12] Such an uproar came from the fact that living art, by its very nature, was opposed – as the term itself implies – to death, and that death for the avant-garde painters, had taken on all the forms of memory, habit, and routine that were once so popular with the French-Canadian traditional elite. Lionel Groulx had made the past the "master" of French-Canadian youth ("our master, the past," he would repeat). In contrast to Groulx, the partisans of living art affirmed the necessity of "making the future" the unconditional master of artists.

In his maxims on art published in *Le Quartier latin*, Maurice Gagnon reflected on freedom and love being essential to the creative act, on the incompatibility of aesthetic formulas and originality, on the need to abandon traditions, and on the harmful nature of learned techniques. Besides a refusal of the past ("When one lives in the past and for the past, creation is no longer possible, for the latter is in the future"), he also called for the categorical refusal of academia ("Academia is the ransom of mediocrity"), of intention ("When one plays on intentions, be it those of the painter or [those] of the subject, art is done for"), and of objectivity ("The external subject of a work is an end goal for the mediocre painter, for others it is nothing.)"[13] Accordingly, "Nothing in art turns out to be superior if it does not possess the quality of audacious innovation, of real innovation which brings something definitively new, which the past contained but had not yet discovered. In other words, living art is turned toward the future."[14] Abbot Groulx could not have envisioned a more direct refutation of his traditionalist philosophy.

Evidently, Borduas also claimed the right to seize the moment, to realize "the fullness of today," to "push the possession of oneself and the universe further into the present," to live "with no certainty other than the possession of the present." "It is not the past which is sacred," argued Borduas, "it is the future."[15] For him, an aesthetic tradition that did not nourish creative urges was null and void. To confine oneself to the past was to serve it very poorly, for an artist who stopped creating stopped living. To escape academia's dryness, one had to follow the laws of the universe, which were of a perpetual becoming. "[The spirit] seeks out the absolute and the absolute flees incessantly. The essential truth of life is therefore this continual search."[16] The progress of ideas and tastes demanded an indefatigable filtering, an uninterrupted evolution of sensibility. "Academicism begins when that process stops."[17] Borduas spoke with admiration about men who "resist habit, the dulling of convulsive qualities due to repetition"[18] and who feel the need to continually renew themselves, to break away from routine to explore disconcerting worlds. In 1946, Claude Gauvreau wrote: "An immutable law of art, discovered by observation and not postulated, demands that a work of art, in order to preserve its qualities of harmony and charm, must always be the fruit of a perpetually changing discipline, of a conscious or unconscious line of thinking insatiably evolving, of a generosity founded on intellectual risk always seeking a more integral knowledge."[19] From this point onward, the never-ending and constantly renewed quest for originality was one of the foundations of the aesthetic. Underpinning spiritual life, as much as organic life, was a thirst, unquenchable in its very nature.

Father Couturier (seen here with the Director of the École du Meuble, Jean-Marie Gauvreau and a student) taught that artists are free from all teaching, free from their previous successes, indeed, free from themselves. For the Dominican priest "the absolute individualism" of the artist represented the most "precious treasure." (Collection of the Gail and Stephen A. Jarislowsky Institute for Studies in Canadian Art, Concordia University.)

For avant-garde artists, championing the absolutely new became the ultimate source of legitimacy; breaking with the past was the recognized and celebrated mode of creation. Of course, beauty was one and universal, transcending its ever local and multiple manifestations. But Borduas never wanted to bury all that had been achieved in the past in one definitive and fell swoop. In his courses at the École du Meuble, for example, he insisted on the "unity of the present and the past." He recognized the "moral qualities" of immortal masterpieces, dating from prehistoric cave paintings to the canvases of Rembrandt and Matisse.

During his stay in Paris in June 1947, Fernand Leduc was enthralled by Léger and Picasso's art exhibitions, just as much as he was by those exhibiting Cézanne, Manet and Bonnard, not to mention others he considered equally marvellous, showing Courbet and Delacroix's works.[20] Every civilization holds its own "treasure." However, aesthetic beauty was not at stake here, but rather an unwavering, passionate attitude. Borduas could do nothing but agree with this: technique and subject mattered little. What was wonderful about the works of the past was the corrosive approach of their artists, who strove each time to push the boundaries of sensibility. Despite his passion and his intensity, Van Gogh's work was of a scrupulous probity, devoid of all artifice, focused as he was on the unexpectedness that is contained within a true work of art. His outbursts of passion had overturned everything standing in their way. The bourgeois champions of half-measures and selfish calculations needed to hear the message: the Dutch painter's excesses were precisely the sign of his genius. The artists of the past had never been so powerful as when they broke through the arbitrary trends of their time and cultivated their own uniqueness. What did it mean to *create*, if not to bring newness to the world? Originality, as people were beginning to realize, constituted a value in and of itself. "Already, for some of us, it was inconceivable to perceive the labour of creation except as constant discovery. Looking back was forbidden, as was any fixed method."[21] In other words, true art had to be disruption, revolution and effervescence, or nothing at all.

Variations in the history of art, from antiquity to the Middle Ages and from the Renaissance to the modern era, were all worthy of interest, and observing them legitimized a certain relativism. As Borduas taught the history of art, he noticed that a number of preconceived ideas about the value of a work of art were nothing other than simple conventions (for example, Egyptian art was grandiose despite lacking perspective, and medieval art succeeded in reaching the sublime without perfectly mastering the art of drawing). Phidias, Velázquez and Picasso were incomparably brilliant, with each one capable of taking the aesthetic potentialities of their age to the highest level. There did come a time, however, when a form of art was exhausted; when it had exploited all its resources and could no longer produce anything new. To continue imposing an ancient style on a younger generation was equivalent to encouraging conformity, which was already largely discredited. Critics had come to accept that artistic schools were born, shone, and then faded away. The cycle, from gestation to full development and then decline, seemed inevitable. "Civilizations are akin to plants; they grow, strengthen, blossom and die. Another emerges."[22] Respect for certain creations of the past did not stop Borduas from recognizing that the art of his immediate predecessors had had its day.

An entire cycle had gone by attempting to depict reality with precision and clarity in portraits and still-life paintings. Since the fourteenth century, Western artists had been digging and delving, trying to create an image of the world as accurately as possible. As it was now well delineated, there was nothing more to explore. To carry on was to perpetuate dead and useless knowledge. Most important, it was forgetting what was most lively in an artist – his personality, his unique human qualities – that truly living art should not fear shattering the narrow moulds constraining creative inspiration.

Exuberance and generosity constituted incontestable evidence of artistic vitality. This had always been the case. The first Egyptian artist "moved by an imperious need to offer a testimonial to life, moved by the love of a more perfect knowledge for an ever-renewed possession," had listened to the voice within his heart without worrying about presumed aesthetic principles. He produced "perfect harmony between intelligence and meaning."[23] The contemporary painter had to do as much, once again taking on the adventure of art, but in a new manner – as if it were just beginning.

WE HAVE LOST INSTINCT[24]

Art is the intense pursuit of the expression of inner feelings through-
plastic means alone.   —Advice from Gustave Moreau to
his student George Desvallières

In the preceding chapter I mentioned that, according to avant-garde painters, contemporary life favoured external appearances and that the modern individual, fascinated by trivialities, had lost the ability to respond to essential truths. In their opinion, pure knowledge had been scorned in favour of useful, pragmatic and technical knowledge. An adjustment seemed to be necessary to contend with this caving in to materialism and rationalism. The avant-garde's discourse opposed an external, superficial reality, to an ontological and mystical inner truth. Life, true life, heroic and noble life, lay in the "unknown depths of the self." Thus, individuals were invited to leave the superficial world of objects and "dive into the dark night of being."[25] In a book greatly appreciated by Borduas, Robert Élie wrote: "Life is found in the night. All our victories have disappointed us, all our dawns were nothing but a mirage, but our hope does not grow any less in strength, our hope in a complete renewal of our inner life, in a deci-sive conversion that will allow us to accept all the risks of life and of liberty, without which there could be no living art, no true thought, nor any genuine faith."[26] This reflects *Refus global*'s injunction to break away from the diktats of reason, considered a cold and dry fac-ulty. We also understand Borduas' fascination for the Surrealist school of thought and for its call to free the powers of dreams. In his eyes, meaningful painters came into their own by intensifying their person-ality much more than by subjecting themselves to some aesthetic order. "Since the time of the Impressionists, a path has been cleared for artists to investigate, that of personality."[27] The principles of art should not be foreign to painters, but on the contrary stem from their personal drives. Perhaps art did not sum up the truth, but there was truth in art, and it came from the ability of artists to sacrifice nothing of themselves.

For his part, Jacques Maritain, who recognized the value of dreams and pure feelings, could not envision yielding completely to the appeals of subjectivity. "Even chance is logical in the heart of a poet."[28] However, he had already admitted – and this was taking an enormous step – that contemporary painters had rediscovered a promising approach capable of enriching spirituality by highlighting the primitive and archaic aspects of their art. "In this sense, and although, even from other points of view, contemporary art is poles apart from Christianity, it is much closer to a Christian form of art than to academic art."[29] Jean Bazaine also recognized the contribution of the avant-garde movement which, by turning its back on positivistic realities, had managed to find the material of its subjective explorations in the most unfathomable realm of subjectivity. In particular, he admired the vigour with which the Surrealist movement freed itself from four centuries of sterile rationalism. Later, Bazaine distanced himself from the Surrealists, finding the productions of the immediate pre-war period much too insignificant, calling them "games for vicious little bourgeois," "party tricks for salons" and "decorative creations for hairdressers."[30] However, little by little, a certain number of Catholic art critics revised their judgment of Surrealism and came to accept it as an instrument of artistic knowledge. They conceded that these "modern" painters had been able to uncover, beneath the ice floe of reason, the white water of the soul. They ignored the artifice of *trompe l'oeil*, blocking out the raw vision of things, and started breathing in the vital essence of the universe.

In 1943, Maurice Gagnon devoted an entire chapter to the Surrealist school of thought in the republication of *Peintre moderne* (Modern Painter), which included black and white reproductions of works by André Masson, Marc Chagall, Salvador Dalí and Giorgio de Chirico. He introduced French Surrealist periodicals from the École du Meuble's library to both Borduas and his students. At the same time, Louis-Marcel Raymond and Robert Élie, who had contributed to the periodical *La Relève*, circulated the works of Louis Aragon, André Breton, Paul Éluard and Pierre Reverdy, as well as the reviews *VVV* and *Hémisphères* in their circles.[31] In 1943, Robert Élie offered Borduas a copy of the Comte de Lautréamont's *Maldoror & Complete Works*. Gilles Hénault, previously a disciple of Charles Péguy, considered founding a journal inspired by the Surrealist approach.[32] Henri Laugier, a French doctor and Freemason who temporarily settled in Montreal[33] and who was also the author of the preface to *Histoire de l'art contemporain* published in 1938,[34] entertained his Montreal acquaintances with readings from Breton's works. As for Irène Legendre, a young follower of Amédée Ozenfant, she often shared her enthusiasm for the works of Roberto Matta and Paul Klee. The shifting of aesthetic sensibilities in French Quebec was obvious and widespread.

Together with Jacques de Tonnancour and Julien Hébert, Lucien Morin attended the École des Beaux-Arts in Montreal from 1935 to 1940. There, he evolved toward a form of art that was more personal, more refined, and liberated from the obligation of representing reality. Rejecting psychoanalysis as a methodology, he nonetheless described himself as being receptive to the Surrealists' idea of the spontaneous act. "I begin by sketching shapes on a canvas. These shapes incite other shapes and ultimately make up a picture. […] This harmony is created by the artist's instincts. It is the primary factor that brings a work of art to life.[35] This was indicative of the fact that the personalist approach[36] was attracting more and more young artists and thus, one began witnessing non-premeditated artistic convergences at the time.

Born in 1929, Paul-Marie Lapointe apparently considered becoming a Jesuit. However, he was deterred from this vocation after reading Loti, Proust, Chateaubriand, Lamartine, and especially works by Rimbaud, Éluard and Léon-Paul Fargue. In 1947, he wrote *Le Vierge incendié* (The Virgin Burned) in a feverish mood, without any knowledge of the existence of the Automatist movement. "The high-est form of poetry, just like the highest form of art, is improvisation, which does not curb expression in any way, even though it does draw its excellence from PRE-EXISTING craftsmanship, whether it be that of the creator's subject matter or its material."[37] Thus, during these years, there was a general hope of rebellion, a shared confidence in spontaneous life, which united people who had sometimes followed quite different trajectories.[38]

To grasp how fervently some Catholics rode the Surrealist wave during these years, it is essential to return to Father Couturier's thought, and particularly to study his series of Quebec conference lectures. First given at the École du Meuble in January of 1941, and redelivered in a distinctly more original and substantial form in March of 1942 in New York, his first talk was subject to strong reactions by the people who attended it, and especially by clergymen, who were amazed that the Dominican concluded his presentation by quoting André Gide. In fact, Couturier's entire speech was designed to challenge the conventional ideas of his Montreal audience. The fact that such iconoclastic lectures were being given by a clergyman only added to the provocative quality of his words in the strongly conservative and pious Quebec of the time. What was the editor-in-chief of *Art sacré* saying then in his talks, conversations, courses and writings that was so terrible?

First of all, he insisted upon the gradual divorce between living art and the public since the nineteenth century. Art had become detached from institutes and schools and had come to reside on the fringes of the academic and commercial world. Avant-garde painters, for example, turned their noses up at honours and comforts, refusing to follow popular prejudices, and became fully absorbed in their virtuous, intrepid and solitary quests.

Secondly, Couturier pointed out how art had turned its back on external reality to construct a more abstract world, different from the one offered in everyday life. By emancipating itself from artificial details and realistic depictions, contemporary art was able to rediscover "a common ground of humanity," which was visible in a work by Rembrandt or a Greek mosaic, just as much as in African sculpture or Chinese calligraphy. "All we have to do is reach a certain zone that is deep enough within ourselves, where the wholeness of our being can be remade, and progressively gather all our power, body and soul, sense and intelligence, so that even beyond the boundaries of our individual being, what is most unique and most personal can win over people who are yet unknown to us, people without number, age, race, or homeland – in other words, people who are separated from us by nothing but their stubbornness, their arrogance, their flaws, aspects which are, after all, incidental."[39] Couturier realized that a kitchen water pitcher drawn by Rembrandt did not stir emotions because it perfectly replicated an ordinary pitcher; on the contrary, it was because it had something different, singular and indescribable about it, that had to do with the artist's soul, the light illuminating his works, the fibres of his very being, which he had woven into his works. It was never the beauty of the depicted objects that bedazzled the viewer. Rather, the amazement stemmed from the reality created beyond the representation, from a troubling magic that owed nothing to representational games and could not be contained within the frame.

And, there was more to come. The second break led to another. Thirdly, art had freed itself from the "constraints of intelligence and given way to pure spontaneity." As a result: "More and more, the artist has managed to avoid the control exerted by reason and will; he is now searching within the subconscious, in dream or semiconscious states for what is most peculiar and most difficult to convey."[40] After gaining independence from society and from the outside world, the artist could escape from the trap of reason. The purity of art suddenly meant that it had to be separated from reasoned intelligence. A journalist who felt the same wrote as such, "What is needed is for the public to unleash the power of dreams from the shackles of reason and materialism. Because, as Father Couturier said when he quoted the admirable words of Edgar Poe: "'They who dream by day are cognizant of many things which escape those who dream only by night.'"[41] Couturier came to believe that the ideal form of art was the product of intuition. Above all else, creation relied on "its irrational, involuntary character, its pure spontaneity."[42] The inspiration for the mysterious harmonies that were unveiled in the painter's works could be found in "the obscure depths of the being, precisely where the body and soul seem to combine their powers into one unified primitive state, too simple and elementary to be the object of rational knowledge and therefore available to all."[43] This unified primitive state was not a magma waiting to be cut up, classified, and analysed. It formed the truly subjective part of being; its essential, unique, unalienable and indivisible anchor. "Freedom and reasoning create in every one of us a split personality which is, generally, a nuisance for the contemporary artist. An artist is, in fact, an individual who reduces his being (including the duality of body and soul) to a very simple unit, which allows him to *act*. He who breaks this unity introduces an element of dissociation into the creative process, which, in turn, destroys superior and spontaneous instincts."[44] Borduas would not have challenged the Dominican on this point.

What exactly was Surrealism in this adventure, if not a window open to magic, something "beyond the realm of signs"? In his talk, Father Couturier proclaimed, "The magician brings to light realities, heralding a world in which people collectively experience a new unity and intimate connections, which are much different than those our eyes and the necessities of life have shown us." What Surrealism offered, under these conditions, was the "total recuperation of [the] physical strength [of the individual] by means of what is none other than a vertiginous descent into [oneself], the systematic illumination of hidden places, and the progressive darkening of others."[45] Couturier was proposing a new understanding of the person, emerging from an "overabundance of contemplation," where shapes no longer espoused abstracted ideas, but rather people's palpable realities. This art was neither irrational nor antirational, but rather, to use Couturier's term, "preter-rational," (or if one prefers Borduas' adjective, "surrational.")

It is this validation – which Maritain would never have endorsed – of dreams, desire, passion and the subconscious that drove Father Couturier to recognize the value of the Surrealists who now formed an influential group in New York.[46] More than anyone, Breton's disciples had understood that it was essential to "make way for magic," "make way for love." They protected the sources of the inner world instead of containing their flow with principles and habits. By striking down the old demons of reason and will, André Masson and Max Ernst, in Couturier's eyes, had enabled the exploration of a region that was essential for human consciousness to thrive, and, unlike the much more cerebral Cubists, had favoured the "depths of being." Thanks to Surrealism, the "non-preconceived" act would reassert itself vis-à-vis the intentional act. Generous, spontaneous and unconstrained, this way of creating would no longer be guided by demanding rules. It was by diving into the fertile source of one's self, by exploring the enigmatic and perilous region that lies beneath abstract signs and empirical reality, a region where subterranean powers reveal themselves, that art had a greater chance of attaining truth and the universal. "The Reverend Father Couturier observed that the Surrealists' experiments offer at times rather troubling elements, but he nonetheless believes that they are rich with possibilities and open new paths to explore."[47] In 1941, Father Couturier often visited Salvador Dalí in New York, and despite certain reservations, saw him as having genius that was far superior to that of Catholic painters. "In painting, there is a certain 'magical' aspect that I had never quite understood before, but that is as essential as the musical aspect."[48] He was beginning to realize that painters like Dalí, by means of their prescience and probity were ultimately "the true witnesses, the only witnesses to mystery." For this reason, his plea in favour of liberty in the face of societal restriction and mundane realities ended up developing into a defence of subjectivity, which was so dear to Surrealism.

> It is thus important to the integrity of a piece of art that pure spontaneity, and I was almost going to say, absolute "autonomy," exist from its inception. Surrealist writers and painters have had the courage and honour to bring about this emancipation, and thus to bring to fruition this long and dangerous initiative of liberation. Artistic activity, already rescued from the tyranny of the external world, was released in this way from the sometimes brutal control of reason and will. And I am by no means saying that this third rupture will give nothing but reassuring results: neither the works of Dalí, nor of Ernst or Masson are entirely reassuring. However, I would like to reiterate that this break stemmed from a solid truth and maintained an essential freedom. [...] This extreme claim, this need to express the most singular and pure part of ourselves, far from forbidding the ascension to humanity's common ground, which I spoke about a short while ago, is on the contrary that which will ensure its open access: the entire history of modern art shows us that it is not the most common and most general traits which enable us to reach, through art, the most consistent and most profound level of humanity, but rather the maximum originality.[49]

More and more Québécois intellectuals agreed with the French Dominican's designation of the "frenzy of the subconscious"[50] (a concept, it's true, which they still had some difficulty defining)[51] as the richest, most liberated and thus the most living part of a human being. The amazing insights that pierced the subconscious were seen as nothing less than "divine essence,"[52] according to Maurice Gagnon – an author whose style seemed to some to be "too deliberately Surrealist (one finds hints of Breton and Éluard here and there.)"[53] Gagnon argued: "People fear *instinct*, when without instinct, there is no living art – this instinct, which for a Thomist, is the site of spontaneous awareness, and nothing else. It is a driving force in people and goes hand in hand with intelligence; and can bring about excellent results."[54] This "return to instinct" had nothing to do with eroticism or sensualism (or very little), as one can imagine, but rather sought to put the artist in touch with those primitive, inner powers that foster mindful self-awareness. For Hertel, who corresponded with Borduas in January 1942, shortly before the sudden creation of Borduas' first Surrealist gouaches, "to paint, to write with words or with music, is to let the subconscious speak. [...] We are in the age of the expression of the ineffable."[55]

It would be wrong to conclude that Borduas invited his contemporaries to fully abandon themselves to the subconscious in painting. No more for him than for Couturier and Gagnon was it ever a question of cutting himself off from his intellectual faculties. More accurately, his painting attempted to unite his thoughts and sensitivity in an ideal harmony. The unbelievable number of paintings he destroyed clearly shows that Borduas, if able to abandon himself to his intimate impulses while painting, reserved the right, if not the duty, to ruthlessly judge his works afterward. Even if Borduas placed the work of reason after artistic execution (which, because it was done in steps, could give rise to multiple back and forth swings between reason and sensibility), he certainly did not renounce the judgment of intelligence. Initially, free rein was given to intuition, and then intuition was assessed by the artist's knowledge. "Automatism, of the most perfect kind possible, guides the elaboration of the painting. Following this, the sharpest critical sense, again of which I am capable, attempts to intellectually assess the object that has been produced."[56] Borduas' approach demanded ongoing attention while the impulses of the subconscious gushed out in every stroke made by the paintbrush or palette knife on the canvas. Fed by the free play of the subconscious, the act of painting took place "in a particular state of emotion, of inspiration, one could say; in certain cases, as the work of art comes

Jacques Maritain exerted considerable influence over the ideology of the "generation of *La Relève*," men and women who reached the age of majority during the interwar period. "Almost the whole of French Canada," Germain Lesage asserted as late as 1963, "lives by Maritain." (*Le Quartier latin*, October 25, 1934.)

together, self-criticism follows the initially intuitive, unconscious gesture which provides the work's substance, and evaluates this creation as it appears. Self-criticism does not precede the gesture, but rather follows it."[57] The broad dynamic unconscious-conscious movement "strings together all the creative activities in a profound rhythm of transformation, which is that of all living things, namely: that an unconscious need brings about conscious activity, the unconscious result of which, in turn, provides logical signs and relationships for a new conscious manifestation of subconscious needs."[58]

In short, in Borduas' Automatist method, intelligence (defined as "sensitive") was put to good use, even if reason henceforth occupied second rank. Magic was "the ultimate act of intelligence: transforming the unknown into the known, consequently revealing the rational part of all discovery." Love was also an "act of intelligence that demands a total gift for full, and, therefore, selfless possession." As for the necessities, to identify them and comply with them, "a selfless lucidity, which also included reason was needed."[59] Thus, the notion of giving oneself up completely to instinct could not have been more foreign to Borduas' line of thinking.

> When rereading *Refus global*, one is struck by the emphasis placed on highlighting the part of intelligence in the elaboration of a work of art, whereas adversaries of Automatism, incapable of appreciating the paintings themselves, interpreted these explanations in the sense of a total and degrading resignation of intelligence. It is, however, clear, and had been clear from the beginning for many people that automatic writing was only a starting point, a method of working, the only redeeming value of which had to do with to the intensity of the visual experience and the poetic intuition of the artist who practiced it. Borduas started from nothingness, but he was composing a microcosm. He discovered a new meaning for reality.[60]

Nevertheless, this manner of describing Borduas' artistic approach prevents us from grasping to what extent subjecting reason to the need of the unconscious ultimately left little room for reason. Borduas was admittedly not the champion of instinct that certain critics wanted to see in him, but his line of thinking certainly bothered all those who trusted in the Neo-Thomism of the 1940s. There were three reasons: first, personal creation was an incommensurable affair; second, the method for creating was automatic writing; third, creation took the form of a paranoiac screen. Let's attempt to describe these three reasons in greater detail so as to understand why the Automatist method was so vehemently criticized by some art critics, who saw nothing but chaos and disorder in it.

First, if reason were considerably repressed by Borduas, it is because, in his mind, his way of proceeding was destined to lead the painter to create an entirely personal work of art. Diving into the unknown was to enable the artist to express an irreplaceable truth. "What the painter does should express the rhythm of his being and nothing that is foreign to him."[61] Borduas reiterated this idea in a letter dated from February 1947, in which he reproached Jeanne Rhéaume for her "lack of real personality." While she should have been pursuing a moving, prophetic, universal, unique, sensitive and inimitable work of art, Rhéaume seemed "foreign to her object."[62] Borduas was always underlining the necessity for the artist to push himself to the limit and to only express feelings that truly tormented him, letting his artistic imagination run wild. As an immanent work of creation for the artist, art obeyed "the profound necessities of his being," and the century would not be long enough to exhaust the potentialities offered by this inner world.[63] The artist was so perfectly identified with his internal drive that when he saw the finished painting, he could contemplate himself in it. He was his painting, and the painting was him. Having given over his entire soul to his painting, the artist ended up staring at himself on the canvas.

From this demand came the second reason why Borduas stigmatized reason: with the canvas ideally being the perfect mirror of the soul, it was necessary for nothing to come between the painter's creative act and the work of art. As a result, the painter had to somewhat paradoxically forget himself. "That is the artist's job: to forget himself in the work that he's doing and forget himself completely."[64] The painter had to immerse himself completely in his work as it took shape before him. "To always be in agreement with what one is doing," meant never contradicting the natural flow of inspiration and imagination. Had the Surrealist revolution not consisted of delivering art, through dreams and the subconscious, from the former figurative aesthetic, based on the cult of reason and realism? According to Breton, André Masson had enabled Surrealism and painting to come together by letting his hand follow instinctive movements and trace involuntary shapes on paper.[65] Other French artists took their inspiration from automatic writing. Among the influences on Borduas might have been a technique introduced by Matta and named "psychological morphology."[66] Matta suggested spreading colour on a canvas with a rag and then roughing out shapes with a brush according to what the blotches inspired. Borduas had *mutatis mutandis* inverted this approach at the time of his first Automatist experiments, with different result. He proceeded in the following way: forgetting all preliminary ideas, emptying his mind, he let his charcoal move freely according to the whims of his inner impulses. One randomly drawn line provoked another, then another, and again another. Once the drawing was complete, Borduas applied colours using the same technique, without premeditation, once again giving free rein to his impulses in the moment. When a journalist asked him about his method, Borduas answered that he did not have one in the sense that we normally understood the word; he was letting his paintbrush follow a spontaneous, intuitive series of movements. "I do not think," he said, "my paintbrush thinks for me, guided by instinct. My paintbrush determines the composition, dictates what I'm going to do…. No, I don't plan anything at the beginning…I let the forms and colours take shape by themselves on the canvas."[67]

Having freed art from the tyranny of the object and learned methods, Borduas went a step further by liberating painting from the question of the artist's intention. He abandoned all preconceived ideas before starting a painting. He obeyed the purest, most direct, most intimate spontaneity, being guided uniquely by his creative effort. What Borduas called disinterested art was an art that did not yield to any force other than its own intrinsic movement. Only the authenticity of the painter's act counted, each time having to confront his deep-seated emotions and inner demons in a merciless dialogue. By detaching itself from the constraints of intention, "modern" painting redeemed the harsh demands of creativity. The break with morality and ideology (be it bourgeois or proletarian) could not have been more complete. "[French-Canadian painting's] astonishing break with nationalistic academicism (as with all academicism)," wrote Jean Le Moyne, "is a heartwarming scandal. It has finally given us a mission-less art, with no purpose other than its own completion; we finally have works of art that are solely the product of creative urgency."[68] The titles of Borduas' paintings, fruits of inspired happenstance, illustrate the abandonment of a prior message: *Pulsion allègre grave jaune assoiffée* (Warm Grave Impulse Thirst-ridden Yellow), *Aspiration lucide accrochée dans les cerceaux* (Lucid Aspiration Hanging in the Hoops), *Surréelle courbe acrobate* (Surreal Acrobatic Bend), *Souplesse: realité palpable automatique* (Flexibility: Automatic Palpable Reality), *G.37*, *1.45*, *Abstraction no 147* (Abstraction Number 147), *Quand la fleur des vents pique la crête du coq* (When the Flower of Wind Tickles the Rooster's Crest), or *Tapis de l'Île de Pâques* (Rug from Easter Island). These titles were not given to instruct viewers on some external reality that the painting had transposed and that one would have had to decipher through the shimmering of colours and the hodgepodge of lines. On the contrary, these titles taught the art lover to avoid trying to perceive what was visible in a traditional manner. [69] Intention was no longer part of the domain of psychology, but rather of art. The consequence, according to the Automatists, was more important than the goal. (They gave the example of a young girl who, picturing a horse in her mind during a drawing class, produced an elephant.) By deciding to paint in a totally free manner, Borduas also agreed that the painting itself no longer had to carry a specific message. Once again, reason did not count for much.

As for the final motive to exclude reason: Borduas was obviously convinced that, from the viewers' point of view, the value of a work of art came from its sensible qualities and not from its rational properties. "Mr. Borduas wisely stated that the intellectual order (he calls it intellectual discipline), which first affects the production of the work is relegated to the background once the work has been completed, and that it is the work's song that communicates beauty."[70] Borduas insisted on love coming through the canvas, the song vibrating within the paint itself, and joy gushing forth from the painting. For him, this emotion had nothing to do with technical ability or with the painted object. The *Nature morte aux oignons* (Still Life with Onions) by Cézanne was obviously not sublime because of its subject, but because the artist was able to convey a part of his soul on a flat surface. The last thing an art lover needed to appreciate this "convulsive beauty" was reason.

It is worth repeating that Borduas was struck early on by an exercise that Leonardo da Vinci proposed to his students: paint objects that they would see appear while contemplating a decrepit wall. I believe this exercise fascinated Borduas because it solved "the problem of passing from subjectivity to objectivity" by linking together the artist's most intimate sensitivities and the most suggestive physical reality.[71]

The tableau suggested by Da Vinci came from the artist's observations, but what he saw before him was just as much what he sought to express within himself. The decrepit wall served as a "paranoiac screen" (a term invented by Dalí) by enabling the augural reading of the interior motives inhabiting the painter. But Borduas' Automatist paintings also reproduced Da Vinci experiments on a second level: the pictures themselves were paranoiac screens that invited the viewer to probe their own sensibility. They encouraged the formulation of a meaning, an emotional quest, and a poetry that shaped the art a second time. The works took on the same function as Da Vinci's decrepit wall. "A person," said Breton, "will know how to proceed, when, like the painter, he consents to reproduce, without any change, what an appropriate grid tells him in advance of his own acts. This grid exists. Every life contains these homogeneous patterns of facts, whose surface is cracked or cloudy. Each person has only to stare at them fixedly to read his own future."[72] By gazing at the canvas as a graphic transmission of the unsuspected meanings of the world, the viewer could prolong the initial job of deciphering what the painter had achieved and dive even further into the unexpected. "There – if his question is worthwhile – with all the principles of logic scattered, the powers of objective haphazard, which cares little for likelihood, will reach out to him. On this screen, all that he wishes to know is written in phosphorescent letters, in letters of desire."[73] By questioning, viewers could put themselves into a state of total receptiveness, and the meeting between the demands of the subconscious and those of the universe would finally be possible.

Borduas did not want his paintings to convey an allegorical message. He yearned for nothing to remain of former aesthetic judgments, neither image, nor object, nor prior thoughts, nor rational shapes. "A masterpiece," summarized Henri Laugier, "can thus resemble nothing; evoke nothing; it is not necessary for it to speak, to imitate; being beautiful in and of itself is enough, and it is the substantial beauty of the work of art that the true art critic should strive to grasp and explain."[74] Art, freed of the need to represent, to tell a story and to be logical, aimed at being completely autonomous. As art was no longer subject to external interference, it was to be practised in itself and for itself from this point onward. Father Couturier wrote that "art, in this way, is an end in and of itself," that "the artist's creation knows no other necessity for a means or an end" and that art is "useless and unusable."[75] Painting revealed itself as a pure creation, pure poetry, unexploitable, purposeless and generous. Having lost its need for a subject, for technique and all intention, the painting – "an absolute object," – became the subject of its own composition and harmony. It was no longer about expressing something in a particular manner, but rather of letting plasticity express itself in an incandescent and virginal way.

It was not surprising then that very early on music lovers in Quebec paid tribute to abstract painting. One of the first to grasp the meaning of Borduas' gouaches was a musician – Jean Vallerand. He understood that painters were like composers, who had the right to follow their instincts and create works that were sufficient unto themselves and did not represent anything.[76] Jazz, which was being increasingly talked about at the time, was part of this trend toward art that did not describe the outside world as much as it did moods. Contemporary music was appreciated for its melody, aside from its meaning, as much as pictorial art would from then on be appreciated for its musicality. Picasso's *Guernica* needed to be viewed as if listening to one of Beethoven's symphonies or Stravinsky's *Rite of Spring*.[77] Painting was music to the eyes: it enabled one to see the invisible, a bit like music enabled one to hear silence. It was these founding principles that bestowed its lyricism on painting. A painter worthy of this name had to possess "the talent of making the subject sing." This idea had already been formulated by Paul Valéry when he affirmed that the painter was a "soul who sings." Maurice Gagnon observed: "It seems to me that art is [...] according to a discovery made by Valéry: a song turned into matter."[78] To rise to the level of the sublime, a work of art had to bring matter to life, make it vibrate. A preface dedicated to Borduas, which was added to the 1943 edition of *Peinture moderne*, cited in italics an expression used by the master from Saint-Hilaire, noting that "the song – *human sensitivity as expressed in a given medium* – enables profound, essential contact, with the work of art."[79] If emotional intelligence was used while creating a work, it could only be enjoyed through its song. This conviction inspired the final Automatist exhibition in 1954, fittingly entitled *La matière chante* (Matter Sings).

BORDUAS, "PLASTICIEN"

We have seen that the Automatist method can be viewed as an attempt to revoke the divorce between mind and matter, the exterior and the interior. By submitting himself entirely to spontaneity, the artist hopes to go beyond his ephemeral self and fuse with the harmony of the universe. To explore personal, unformulated and secret truths was to dare to descend into the primitive obscurity of the depths of the self. Borduas invited his colleagues to adopt surrational Automatism "so as to abandon all intentions other than going forth into the night, in hopes of passionately grasping the object of our most unattainable and most generous dreams."[80]

In a crossed-out passage from *Projections libérantes* (Liberating Projections), Borduas maintained that society's regeneration could not come from "intentional values – ultimately linked to a self-serving activity (go reread Saint John of the Cross, for God's sake)."[81] This invitation to revisit a Church father to understand spontaneity, and – indirectly – automatic writing, was not frivolous. Compared to all Catholic mystics, Saint John of the Cross may have expressed better than anyone the non-dualist understanding of the universe.[82] "No other mystical writer stressed the sentiment of the transcendence of God as much as he did. [...] For Saint John of the Cross, nothing that our senses are able to grasp, nothing that our intelligence can understand will give us the slightest fragment of God."[83] For the Spanish Catholic saint, reason, intention and memory had to be replaced from the inside by the three theological virtues (faith, hope and charity), which, apart from desire – which always remains – leave nothing but a complete yielding to divine power. It is only by forgetting created things that the believer can move toward an infinite God. Saint John of the Cross did not find revelations, visions or ecstasy in his unconscious. For him, they were nothing but misleading appearances: eternal ideas can only take shape on the mirror of the soul, if the soul succeeds in becoming transparent and pure. Consequently, the mystical approach consisted of purifying oneself, of stripping oneself through an immediate experience and absolute self-possession. The only path to purity, for him, was through blind faith – a total abandonment – which in turn favours receiving divine will. Utter passivity was the way to mystical conscience. By exploring one's inner torments, the individual was united with a constantly changing universe and reached the laws of the cosmos by following his or her own rules and embracing creation in its entirety.

We may presume that it was this integration in the cosmos through the refusal of all explicit intention that struck Borduas about Saint John of the Cross. This idea of combining the expression of personal sensibility with an obedience to "primary needs," to "noble needs," to "profound needs," and to "inner needs" was also present in Borduas' thought. "Make way for necessities!" proclaimed *Refus global*. According to Borduas, to achieve this union, human sensibility had to be able to express itself directly on the material canvas. In this way, Borduas detached himself from the definition of pictorial Surrealism as being a simple representation of last night's dreams. Instead of depicting the memory of nocturnal dreams, the painter had to find the stirrings of his unconscious by working in the medium itself. The painters who Breton frequented (Dalí, Masson) spent their leisure time creating oneiric constructions, at times enchanting but often frivolous, while Borduas worked so that the art of painting became a language in and of itself, so that it could be its own end, so that it would finally lead to nothing but itself. Psychic Automatism or that of imagination, which was the French Surrealist painters' approach, used memory, dreams and hallucinations to produce images that were still very conscious, very rational and very polished.[84] The abstract art that Borduas promoted resulted in raw sentiment by concentrating on the essential. Aesthetic emotion was created by connections between tones and colours, between the lines and curves, which had an emotional effect due to the way they were manipulated. It was the plastic elements of the painting itself that had become the spectacle.

Many times, it has happened to me that perfectly nice people say: "Monsieur Borduas, I really like what you do, I really like the colour. It's just that I don't understand." And I'm obliged to respond very honestly: "I do not understand any more than you do. Whatever you are looking for in the painting, I, too, am looking for it. You are looking for the subject of that painting. I'm as unaware of it as you are." This is always such a revelation for them, for these people. They could not imagine, you know, looking at the painting, that it could be a desire for shape, and a desire for colour and a desire for light, and a desire for harmony, and that this desire could be the sought after object. For them, this desire makes no clear sense. Why? Simply because they have gotten used to seeing other qualities which are secondary, assumed qualities, like the subject, state, science and anything you want, but which is external, expressed by plastic qualities, but outside of the plastic elements themselves.[85]

In a way, Automatism could be defined as an applied art, in the sense that it made the quality of the materials used the actual subject of the painting, and reconciled art with technique in the creative act. It is possible that Borduas was even more sensitive to the material nature of plastic matter because he taught at the École du Meuble, where many courses focused on raw materials. Indeed, training consisted of distinguishing between varieties of wood, calculating density and designing decorative patterns. For future designers, it was important to acquire agility by constantly practicing hand movements in contact with materials. The senses of touch, sight and smell in some cases were indispensable tools for the good upholsterer, cabinetmaker, and ceramicist. In accordance with the philosophy of craftsmanship, Borduas believed that the thoughts automatically executed on a sheet of paper or a canvas were "painters' thoughts: thoughts of movement, of rhythm, of volume and of light and not literary ideas (the latter ideas are of no use unless they are plastically transposed)."[86] The painter thought with paint, just as the writer thought with words. Once the painting had been freed from needing a story and from representation, the formal qualities became an artist's most perfect signature. A certain preference in terms of colour, a certain curvature in the strokes, the manner in which paint was applied to the canvas, the pressure of the hand on the paintbrush – all that most often unconsciously defined his style, revealing the painter's personality.

However, this apologia for an applied art stemmed more from Borduas' monistic attitude than his status as professor at the École du Meuble. As the spirit was already invading physical matter and therefore the artist's paint, splashing colours was the same thing, in a way, as spreading the spirituality of the world on the canvas. The most basic and unsophisticated aspects were invested with the cosmic flow that circulated in an immanent way through all things. Surrational painting, affirmed Borduas, "is matter, it is nothing but matter […]; it is quintessentially concrete," but this concreteness simultaneously seemed to him, as Claude Gauvreau explained, like "materialized human sensibility."[87] The tension toward a more immediate contact with material reality, "the desire to connect with the sensation of materiality," the fascination with a "plastic order" of things came from the conviction that plastic language was itself delirious. "[Whether] I paint a square inside another square, in a circle, or vice-versa, there is always inner life: my own, which creates the painting, and the inner life of the matter, which is also creative. The poet may not depend on ink, but the painter depends on his materials. Because it is in the actual material that we find the real – and a transposed, relived real. Is this not what art is about?"[88] In this way, "non-figurative, essentially materialistic painting" embodied the real presence of the universe for it expressed at once the physical reality and the psychic quality. In light of this equivalency, we can understand Borduas' insistence that lines, shapes and colours in his paintings "express[ed] the psyche" in the sense that they wove "deep connections with the exterior world."[89] The ideal relation between the inner and outer worlds became possible by investing one's subjectivity in the coloured paint itself. "Songs are the vibrations imprinted upon matter by human sensibility. This is what brings matter to life. From this ensues the whole mystery of works of art: whereby inert matter may come to life."[90] This transubstantiation had the stuff of mystifying the profane. A canvas that was nothing more, after all, than colour and lines on a flat surface shone with dazzling life. The artist could breathe life into inert matter and produce an object capable of moving people, charming them, making them laugh and cry.

The Automatist method was the key for this pictorial exploration to the extent that it required "plastic qualities" and qualities "which start purely sensual and become conscious"[91] The subconscious where these qualities come from had next to nothing to do with the Freudian libido or the reservoir of hallucinated and convulsive images that were dear to Breton. This was a human being's primordial turf, its core, made up of all past experiences and emotions that had been assimilated to the point of no longer being dissociated from the person and shaping the uniqueness of one's personality. The "richness acquired" in the past had always come from the exterior world, but this world had been totally integrated by the individual. In that unconscious locus of our innermost thoughts, objects "no longer have shapes that are akin to exterior things." These shapes have become "so [...] individualized, specific to the artist in question" that objects once foreign end up in the unconscious "as transformed as a mouthful of bread."[92] It was there, in the abyss of being, that the alchemy of the inner and outer worlds took place and where harmony was consequently the fullest.

Traditionalist art critics had been taught to believe that a work of art could be approached using two distinct notions: form and meaning. They judged the form by its meaning and its meaning based on the chosen form of the painting. For Borduas, this type of categorization made no sense. "It is the union between matter and sensibility that creates harmony, plastic beauty."[93] Without this union, in the absence of any one part of this equation, a painting could be only chaos or emptiness. Because he placed such emphasis on materials, Borduas used a palette knife with broad strokes of thick paint. And it was because of his insistence on radical subjectivism that the tendency toward non-figuration was so strong. His painting seemed, at least at first, to be the logical result of his aesthetic philosophy. Only surrational Automatism managed to wed on the canvas "the inner life of the matter" and the inner life of the artist. Based on demanding methods, surrational Automatism was the only approach capable of making the flesh, so to speak, become word.

Those who saw it as basically "slinging paint against a wall" (as Pellan put it) understood nothing of the father of Automatism's method. We should take with a grain of salt Jacques Ferron's memory of Marcel Barbeau producing certain works by putting colour on the drum of a wringer dryer and passing reams of paper through it – a technique that would make nice little paintings, once the paper was skilfully cut. According to Ferron, the success of these "automatic" drawings produced by the action of a household washing machine confirmed quite brilliantly the absence of the artist's intent. "Yes, maybe that was true Automatism," exclaimed Ferron. "Since I did not like Barbeau very much, I could not pass up the chance to mock this style of painting and shame his friends, even as they claimed that it took a great deal of talent in order to discern in the products pumped out by the wringer dryer what was worthy of being cut out, framed and exhibited."[94] In fact, Borduas would never have authorized such an interpretation of his teachings. He believed that the artist's subjectivity had to literally inhabit the paint itself. A sunset, a tree reddened by autumn, a stone that was finely sculpted by waves could arouse an extraordinary pleasure for the eye, but they could not be classified alongside works of art, since they had not been shaped by people, but simply by the "mechanical life of the universe."[95] These "quirks of nature," like the chance results of mechanical Automatism (such as *décalcomanie*), were not valued by Borduas because they were unable to bring out the unique personality of an artist.

In a sense, Borduas was more of a *plasticien* than the Québécois Plasticiens of the 1950s, such as Guido Molinari and Claude Tousignant, whom he reproached for having an aesthetic that was too crude, too simplistic and too reductionist. He did not deny that geometrical shapes could express what was human, but he perceived this form of expression as incomplete, since it did not possess enough texture or depth to give an account of humanity's richness. One might as well become a mathematician, Borduas would joke, as practise an art so poor in terms of matter, and thus emotion! The *plasticien* could not inhabit his paintings, other than by performing a contortion, which would sever him from the most genuine part of his being. As for Borduas, he had the impression that he was creating inhabitable worlds, because they were always already informed by the spirit mixed into the matter itself. "Deep down," he concluded, "the element of the world that remains the most permanent for me, the only one perhaps, is the paint, the physical paint itself, the matter, the thick paste. That is my native ground, my land. Without it, I'm uprooted. With it, whether I'm in Paris or elsewhere, regardless – I'm home."[96]

For Borduas, the artist's total gift was much like an escape mechanism. It allowed him to reach a place "beyond things" where subjective conscience threw itself into an eternity of colours and shapes, and strongly resembled a refuge. His attitude allowed him to escape the painful reality of daily life. Opening onto an unknown panorama, a painting offered him an escape from an all too restrictive and destitute French Canada, if not from the whole of doomed Western civilization. "The liberation of man through poetry is taking place," stated Roland Giguère. "Sad reality will soon be replaced by dream, which is becoming a second reality [...] Mankind is now the master of his world, the master of his poetry. Whether we know it or not, this liberation is necessary, and painting offers it."[97] The rejection of external reality not only represented an opportunity to become more at one with the cosmos, but also the condition of a liberating exile. In the eyes of Rémi-Paul Forgues, a young poet who wrote a letter to Breton in 1945 to convey his disgust with French-Canadian obscurantism,[98] Borduas' paintings represented the only way to escape the betrayal of a perverted world. He saw Borduas' paintings as "that inner chamber where we can take refuge when our eyes have been filled with horror, when our ears have been filled with static and our heart with disgust."[99] Material reality, deceptive and defeated, was replaced by the work of art; the latter representing a chance to create a new homeland that would be less treacherous. It offered the possibility of escaping from the world and from oneself into an immaculate universe, which transcended everything because one could project onto it the absolute and love, without fear of ever being contradicted. How distant French Canada, depressing and pitiful, seemed when seen from such an infinite place!

THE CHARGE OF THE
EXPORMIDABLE PAINTER[1]

For me, I would say that Automatism, such as it is defined in Refus
global, *refers to an attitude. It's a more profound way of life and this
particular attitude has been made possible by a pictorial experience,
a very important experience for me: children's drawings.*

—FERNAND LEDUC

The foundation of Montreal's École des Beaux-Arts in 1922 should
not be perceived as consecrating the doctrine of art for art's sake. On
the contrary! Technical knowledge remained very important and the
program for teaching the arts – and architecture in particular – had
been set up to respond to industrial needs. The creation of this school
was first and foremost in response to practical considerations – in
addition to encouraging young French-Canadian students to cultivate
their innate talents in the spirit of a nationalist creed which assigned
the "Latin race" the mission of expressing truth and beauty in the
midst of an uncultured and lowbrow continent. The École des Beaux-
Arts favoured a dual approach, made up of half logic-related subjects
(algebra, descriptive geometry, analytical geometry, shadow theory,
trigonometry) and half aesthetic-related subjects (art history), with a
special emphasis on training for arts that were applicable to the trades
and industry. Professors thus had a penchant for realistic, level-
headed, decorative, moral and practical art.[2] Students learned to
embellish everyday objects (furnishings, wallpaper, linoleum, wood,
wrought iron, glassworks, ceramic). For instance, at the year-end exhibition of student works in 1929, students presented projects such as an

athletic stadium's entrance gate, a design to hide a radiator, plans for religious stained-glass windows, a panel featuring a French-Canadian settler, mosaics depicting Christ's baptism, tapestries featuring French-Canadian lumberjacks or sowers, and interior decoration projects.

It goes without saying that copying at the École des Beaux-Arts was the privileged pathway to learning. The rules of style were taught by forcing students to reproduce oil paintings of grand masters often using black and white photographs, which shaped aesthetic tastes while developing concrete skills. The students were taught "the general and unchanging laws of beauty." Accordingly, in 1928, a Sainte-Croix nun published a practical drawing course, *Cours pratique de dessin d'observation*, which was widely used in the province's schools. Aiming to perfect French-Canadian students' talents for drawing, this manual proposed a series of exercises showing how to reproduce nature. The initial premise was clear: no one is born with a gift for drawing; this gift is acquired through rigorous teaching, emphasizing good judgment and reasoning. By learning to observe attentively, pupils could hope to learn to draw *accurately*, just as was expected by the *Comité catholique du Conseil de l'instruction publique* (Catholic Committee of the Council for Public Instruction). Lessons focused on technical prowess and the identical replication of everyday objects. Probing studies of Manet, Van Gogh, Chagall, Ernst and Kandinsky were viewed with contempt. Teachers said repeatedly that it was better to make a mistake while trying to use the right method than to be right by chance.

The primary preoccupation of such teaching was not an artistic sense: it was intellectual discipline. Declarations made by pedagogues in favour of teaching drawing at the school were based on scientific principals rather than aesthetic ones. The list of objectives published by the *Conseil de l'instruction publique* left little room for ambiguity: "Contribute to the child's basic culture by means of the progressive development of his powers of observation and, consequently, to the affirmation of his personality, to the refinement of his judgment, to the shaping of his tastes, and in the case where he is gifted, to the awakening and development of his aesthetic sense."[3] First, it was a question of developing observational skills, which were the mark of a practical mind-set and prepared children for careers that required this faculty. Secondly, although with less conviction, pedagogues suggested that the refinement of good taste should not be neglected in a Quebec upbringing, and that a basic knowledge of the arts was part of the necessary cultural baggage required of a well-rounded personality. However, reasons for teaching art remained very instrumental. Art helped develop intelligence ("solid, clear and convincing thought"), fed the mind ("abundant and healthy nourishment"), broadened knowledge of history, corrected judgment (it provided "elevated sentiments" and "wide-ranging aspirations"), brought people into touch with the manifest order of things, encouraged moral purity (by means of the link between good taste and good morals), drew people closer to God, enriched the soul ("a beautiful countryside in painting gently recreates and evokes the site and memories of the land"), entertained workers overwhelmed with arduous tasks and distracted them from the trials and tribulations of life by focusing their gaze on beautiful images.[4]

According to Borduas, this "pedagogy of depersonalization" broke and suffocated the innate sensitivity of young French Canadians. "The ruler and the compass, my friend, and make nice circles, nice squares; cut out, paste, copy, trace, but don't invent. Otherwise, you will get a smack."[5] As a young man, Borduas suffered many years under this realist philosophy. He was a conscientious student, capable of copying chromolithographs according to the conventional codes, and this distinguished him from the others in his professors' eyes. He received a first-prize medal in drawing at Sherbrooke's École des Arts et Métiers in 1923, as well as honourable mention in courses given on perspective at Montreal's École des Beaux-Arts in 1925 and 1927.

At the beginning of his career as a teacher, Borduas did not want to question the criteria he had learned from his professors. He continued thinking that geometric devices were "the natural expression of certain aesthetic ideas, which are the essence of all decorative forms." He imagined that "[words] like repetition, alternation, contrast, symmetry, progression, confusion [...] still refer to aesthetic laws [and] these laws are so general that they apply to all construction, all creation that aims to be normal and healthy, whether one is talking about nature or the arts: music, literature, decoration."[6] Yet, evidently, the obsession with identical reproductions bored him. He yearned for more freedom when dealing with shapes and colours and wanted to allow his subjectivity to shine through in his sketches. Describing this

time in his life, he later said: "I looked at paintings as a specialist. I studied technique for technique's sake. The laws of composition governing a picture for composition's sake. Perspective for perspective's sake, execution for execution's sake, appearance for appearance's sake, final touches for final touches' sake. [...] When I was sixteen, I had dreamt of a generous, spontaneous, art, like a never-ending spring that would flow out of my being, of limitless forms of art, an infinite art, and everything kept shrinking, always kept dwindling!"[7]

This stained-glass window project is about as daring as the masters of academicism would allow when Borduas finished at the École des Beaux-Arts. (Paul-Émile Borduas, Project of a stained-glass window: revelation to Mary [with the prophet Isaiah] 1927, gouache and graphite on paper. Musée d'art contemporain de Montréal.)

It is hardly surprising that he sought early on to transform his geo-metrical sketches into liberating projections.[9] In the 1940s, Borduas came into direct conflict with the whole system of conventions in fine arts, the ones supposedly in tune with the laws of nature, allowing the artist to unerringly produce clear, logical and balanced works of art.

THE BÔZARDS

Borduas did not end up becoming a professor in 1937 at Montreal's École des Beaux-Arts, but rather at the École du Meuble where he replaced Jean-Paul Lemieux (who left for Quebec City's School of Fine Arts). The École du Meuble, founded two years earlier in 1935, emphasized technique in the creative process. Director Jean-Marie Gauvreau hoped to spread the precepts of his alma mater, the École Boulle in Paris, on Canadian soil. This school of furniture design's mission was to train cabinetmakers, wood sculptors, tapestry makers, carpenters specialized in making chairs, gem chisellers, steel engravers and bronze fitters. Gauvreau's admitted objective was to purge French-Canadian culture of American bastardized works by producing made-on-site goods for the local market and – eventually – for export. For Gauvreau, knowledge of tradition and folklore represented not only a symbol of attachment to the past, but also an economic development tool. Students in his school were part of the frontline of a national reconquest. This "chisel and wood plane" patriotism was part of a project, to which "buy local" campaigns and support for small industries also contributed.[8] For example, at the end of the 1930s, as part of the government's policy of systematic inventory and economic planning Gérard Morisset recruited Borduas and Maurice Gagnon for his team of researchers, responsible for patrolling the Gaspé Peninsula in search of information on domestic art, tourism, and other forms of artisanal works still being practiced in the region.[10]

Gauvreau was confident he could open three lucrative markets: that of the local bourgeoisie, that of the United States, and that of the Catholic Church. At the time, the clergy were reliable patrons. Gauvreau boasted about obtaining orders for altars, church stalls, kneelers, candleholders, priests' garments, crucifixes and other religious objects. He was eager to replace the false marble, the stucco, the chromolithographs and plasterwork with beautiful objects made from a variety of Canadian woods. As director of the École du Meuble, he was convinced that, with a bit of education and goodwill from beadles and sacristans, Quebec could rid itself of the religious rubbish and mass-produced objects that filled its religious establishments. Hiring Borduas was quite likely part of his project to transform his institution into a prestigious site of church decoration. In Borduas, a disciple of Ozias Leduc, he thought that he had found one of the best representatives of French-Canadian religious painting and a professor who could improve his establishment's reputation in that area.

At the École du Meuble, Borduas found the climate much less stifling than at the École des Beaux-Arts. This is perhaps surprising since this establishment placed great emphasis on national and religious crafts. In appearance, the École des Beaux-Arts and the École du Meuble were similar. However, the École des Beaux-Arts insisted on mimicking the works of grand masters and emulating through imitation, while the École du Meuble, being much more active in trying to integrate industry, was beginning a fight to end mass-produced works of art.

According to Gauvreau, crafts could only rival manufactured goods by exalting their singularity. This led him to seek out those aspects that defined works as exceptional or original. He was conscious of maintaining good relations with the greater public, the government and the business world. Consequently, he respected the professional expectations of parents, civil servants and potential employers. However, at the same time, Gauvreau sought to demonstrate that the craftsman was an artist and that artisanal works could be avant-garde in nature. To those who complained about the old-fashioned nature of crafts, Gauvreau responded with audacious creations. To those who despised outdated folklore, he presented comfortable and modern furniture. Gauvreau was open to incorporating Art Deco or Cubist style into the teaching of architecture, sculpture, cabinet-making, and into so-called minor arts (goldsmithing, glassworks, bookbinding), because students found in such styles "the means of adapting to a highly creative century that is inspired by the distinctive quality that gives great value to useful objects."[11] In this way, the École du Meuble defended modernity more than the École des Beaux-Arts, which had confined itself to pursuing immutable traditions. The roles of the two schools were reversed: at the École des Beaux-Arts, obedience to old formulas and practices; and at the École du Meuble an interest in technical and aesthetic innovations. We must, however, be careful not to transform Gauvreau into an all-out progressive, since he tried to conserve a fragile balance between current aesthetic trends and traditions, to which he wanted to be the heir. Torn between an interest in the contemporary and a refusal to break entirely with the past, Gauvreau lived with this tension that he hoped was creative. Given the context at the time, this was already daring.

What a difference there was between the École du Meuble and Montreal's École des Beaux-Arts, founded in 1922! Divided into two faculties – graphic and visual/plastic arts and architecture – the École des Beaux-Arts offered rigorous artistic and scientific training. In architecture, students took general construction courses, applied sciences, land surveying, reinforced concrete, material science, graphic statistics, mathematics, chemistry and physics. The apprentice architect, combining the qualities of the artist and engineer, could not do without a rudimentary knowledge of plumbing, cabinetmaking, lighting, bricklaying and heating works. Defined as a practical craftsman, a draftsman of well-balanced plans and a good administrator, the architect knew the ins and outs of construction and the details of decoration. He oriented his work in terms of utilitarian layouts and good taste. "The whole of architectural composition can be summarized in a few words: make things logical and beautiful."[12]

In the arts faculty, teaching was no less practical. The sections such as "sculpture," "publicity," "decorative composition" and "painting," were based on observational drawing, drawing from memory and model study. In this context, it was a question of training decorators, commercial artists and painters who could make a living thanks to their artistic talents. Decorative and industrial composition were an integral part of the program. The principal objective of Émmanuel Fougerat, the first director of the school, was to teach youth the challenges involved in technical design and not so much the secrets of pure, detached art. The instruction was based on rational premises and on strict discipline. "Drawing first, painting after,"[13] a female student remembered. A portrait artist himself, Fougerat confirmed that art began with drawing, continued with drawing, and always ended in drawing: "Drawing and still more drawing, always drawing, that's the motto. I explained this to all the students who came to enrol here. Drawing is in everything and everything is in drawing."[14] For Fougerat, drawing was the "unique and indispensable" key for teaching in fine arts. Drawing was practiced ad nauseum and it was necessary to draw not only well, but quickly.

For avant-garde painters, the result of such an education was easy to foresee: "These academic visions prevent a man from finding his essential balance and, in his nature, the demands of the infinite."[15] Progressive critics refused to accept that students should be subject to a set of technical rules or abstract precepts. They emphasized an approach that focused on bringing students to discover within themselves the sources of their art. If the duty of professors was to increase their students' knowledge base, it was also necessary to avoid repressing within them their innate flame of spiritual questioning. The painter's loyalty to the real was not the same as that of the scholar; he was required to go beyond appearances and phenomena; extracting their subterranean and ineffable essence. Unfortunately, professors at the École des Beaux-Arts proceeded in a completely opposite manner. Teaching fine arts was based on the students' ability to copy nature, to demonstrate objectivity, whereas the expression of their subjectivity, of their native poetry, of their ability to enchant, should have been encouraged. In his book on modern painting, Maurice Gagnon advised his students and colleagues at the École du Meuble that academic art was nothing more than "mediocre" and "contemptible." He wrote: "Whereas a work frankly inspired exteriorizes what is most noble and profound within mankind, an academic work, living off past accomplishments, simply repeats, often with illusionary virtuosity. This astounding virtuosity can only dazzle us: these works, empty of sentiment, thought, reflection and love, only show the *pretty* side of things, the wordiness that surrounds them. All things considered, they only speak about what is extraneous to art."[16] At the beginning of the 1940s, many artists like Lyman, Pellan and Borduas backed Gagnon's statements and lashed out in chorus at "outdated teaching principles." Protestors criticized unsparingly bankrupted pedagogical methods and an outdated educational system. They claimed it had taken them years to "disintoxicate" themselves from the formulas they had learned while at the École des Beaux-Arts. For them, art's true path was resolutely elsewhere. It took the form of a fascination with children's drawings.

CHILDREN'S DRAWINGS

In Europe, there was no doubt that progressive Catholic artists were fascinated with the purity of children's art. Maurice Denis, most notably, attached great importance to these works. He boasted of their freshness, their whimsical nature and their truthfulness. For him, children were spontaneously poetic beings, and revealed exceptional gifts for the arts through their drawings. Touched as they were by a detail and charmed by things apparently banal, children were capable of attaining an astounding intensity of expression, without thinking about it. In his mind, children were primitive creators of beauty and harmony – naive innovators – lacking premeditation, who hadn't a care in the world for grownup norms. French poet Charles Péguy went so far as to say that artistic genius and the child were one and the same.

In Canada, the public discovered the purity of sketches made by young children thanks to several exhibitions, notably at the Galerie des Beaux-Arts on Sherbrooke Street, at the École du Meuble, and at the Collège Notre-Dame.[17] Whether it was Arthur Lismer on the Anglophone side or Claudine Vallerand on the French-speaking side, people everywhere in the province were taking an interest in children's talents. After his visit to the exhibition of children's works organized in October 1938 in Ottawa by the Galerie des arts in conjunction with the Musée national des beaux-arts du Québec, Reynald, a respected art critic, rhapsodized over the freshness and spontaneity of children's drawings: "Soon, children will be the only ones in touch with the most lively realities."[18] The fact that pictures created by these young pupils looked like works from the Middle Ages no doubt helped in their appreciation. "You suddenly understand the state of mind of virgin monks who illuminated missals and the book of hours. You can conceive of the abyss separating our rational and practical age from that time when men of genius could […] express with great simplicity […] the images inhabiting their inner world. One feels like proclaiming, while paraphrasing the Gospels: 'Unless you have the spirit of these little children, you will not enter the kingdom of Beauty.'"[19] In a similar way, other art critics also conjured up a nostalgia for the Middle Ages, while denouncing Cartesianism, promoting intuition and praising Christ-like simplicity. This ideological cocktail explains how, in the 1940s, the insistence on childhood innocence slowly became a commonplace theme of avant-garde discourse. In February 1942, Hertel confided, "I am more and more a partisan of instinctivism, which, all things considered, is no more than a great loyalty to that inner dream that has learned, with difficulty and docility, to be innocent. Look at things with young eyes, free from prejudices, and then trust in your dreams."[20]

At his home in the spring of 1948, Paul-Émile Borduas organized an exhibition of children's drawings, of which we have a partial view here. (Photo: Maurice Perron, 1948. Black and white negative, 6 x 6.2 cm. Donated by the Maurice Perron family to the Musée national des beaux-arts du Québec [Neg. 86B].)

Without denying the need for intelligence to sublimate spontaneous sensibility, Maurice Gagnon noted that "the gouaches produced
by children, who are nothing but instinct for a great part of their
youth, are always very beautiful from this point of view."[21] Gagnon
was the first one to concede that the recognition in Quebec given to
this childhood poetry owed much to Borduas. In his opinion, no one
had contributed more than Borduas to legitimizing a pedagogical
method based on students' immediate needs and desires. "This
approach was certainly not invented by me or by François Hertel,"
wrote Gagnon. "It was Borduas who did the most to spread this
approach among us [...]. It respects [the child's personality] and nothing less: moreover, it carries the child's faculties to their fruition."[22]
Borduas had pleaded for some time to have children's drawings fully
and unreservedly recognized. To him, people at a young age were
capable of rediscovering the gestures made by the first artists at the
dawn of humanity, artists who could produce pure and generous beauty because it flowed from their uncompromising intention, rather
than from a desire to follow procedure and imitate models.[23] He
believed that the child, like the caveman, was capable of touching what
is essential. "I repeat, a man who cannot understand the beauty of children's drawings, the beauty of Picasso's *Femme au coq*, will never be
able to understand anything of the true beauty of all plastic arts,
regardless of period or school. He will perhaps like what he sees, but
will not be able to contemplate the mystery of it, a mystery made from
objective beauty."[24] According to Borduas, it was Picasso's genius that
enabled him to revive the poetry of youth and to remain feverish with
joy and self-questioning. Picasso was a great artist because he knew
how to remain a child, splashing his canvases with the same primitive
breath, the same song rising from the depths of his soul. The opposite
was also true: children, who had not yet repressed their natural innocence, could become like many little Picassos.[25]

Ancient art, modern art and naive art were nourished by a single unalterable source: that of the beginnings of the world. While

children may not show much rigour in exercises involving geometry and perspective, they possess a prodigious gift for colour. Without knowing it, they became part of a contemporary art trend that was increasingly liberating itself from the rigidity of lines to benefit from the purity of colours. As such, a direct rapport existed between children's improvised sketches and the latest pictorial innovations. In visual arts classes, there was nothing gratuitous about attentively studying young children's exercises: the professor discovered a naivety that contributed to an understanding of the most revolutionary experiments. While visiting an exhibition of paintings produced by children between seven and twelve years of age at one Montreal school, Marie-Alain Couturier delighted in the freshness of the works. He compared these marvels to the paintings of Matisse, Vuillard and Van Gogh, saying he was happy to find in the works of these artists-in-the-making "natural genius," which develops freely in great painters. Maurice Gagnon also shared his daring opinion that children could paint "as well as modern painters."[26] To appreciate art, art lovers, just like talented painters, needed a new perspective, free from conventions and prejudices. Since education had not yet provided them with goggles to distort their vision, children retained a sensibility that was not yet fossilized and had a soul capable of seeing the world in all its innocence. The child lived in a state of grace, entirely given over to sensibility and spontaneity.

On the other hand, according to the emerging discourse, most adults had given up searching for an ideal. By losing their appetite for play, for love and for joy, they had become blind to true beauty. Their education represented a halt in their natural development and killed the child within them. Traditional ways of teaching art could gloat about producing reasonable adults and rational beings, good and conscientious bourgeois, but this was achieved at the price of losing what made life rich and grandiose: the eruption of the never-before-seen. "Their life is a sterile metamorphosis into a bourgeois life, a disaster."[27] According to Father Louis-Marie Régis, this blindness was displayed by visitors who went through an exhibition of young artists at the University of Montreal in November of 1944. These well-educated people wanted the works to represent something concrete and precise, while they were asked to commune with the artists on a sentimental level and to participate in the harmony that the painters wished to communicate through their canvases. Not finding the realistic scenes that they had hoped to admire, most of the visitors rejected the works on the pretext that they were absurd, ugly or pretentious. "That's the reaction of an aged soul; instead of being like a child and bringing the food to one's mouth to taste it, that is to say, instead of coming into personal contact with the beauty of the object in question, instead of feeling it and perceiving it, they demand a name, a title, so as to be able to compare it with past images, with what they already know; they want our contemplation to be the result of memory and not an experience with the present."[28] In short, adult short-sightedness prevented the visitors from appreciating true beauty.

It is now clearer why Borduas affirmed that the theories he applied to his paintings were acquired during his time as a professor of drawing at the Externat Classique Saint-Sulpice, the Collège André-Grasset, and at the Commission scolaire de Montréal (from 1931 to 1943), or during the drawing classes for children that he initiated on Saturday afternoons at his studio on Mentana Street. In "*Projections libérantes*" (Liberating Projections), Borduas did not hesitate to directly associate with children's art, which he had discovered during his teaching years. "From that time on, I never lost sight of children, because they opened wide the door of Surrealism and automatic writing for me. The most perfect condition for the act of painting was finally revealed to me. I had connected with my earliest feelings about art, which I once expressed something like this: 'Art, the boundless spring which flows freely from Mankind.'"[29] He continued, "Children's drawings [...] are the only confirmation that the path pursued until now will one day lead to victory: even if it be a hundred years after my death."[30] For Borduas, "only children and simple-minded people possess this marvellous gift of having direct contact with forms, without the intermediary of words (similitudes), the power to recreate within themselves the emotive reality of the object right next to them, before their eyes."[31] The influence of children's drawings was subtly there at the time of his first Surrealist exhibition in the foyer of the Ermitage: instead of showing oil paintings, Borduas submitted gouaches, a medium used in primary and secondary schools, which enabled him to reproduce the essence of his pupils' spontaneous gestures.

In his teaching of plastic arts, Borduas had been inspired by the pedagogical method developed by Gaston Quénioux, a method that Ozias Leduc had recommended to him.[32] This "intuitive" method, which was made popular in France at the beginning of the century, emphasized the expression of feelings and not the cold and applied composition of geometrical shapes. Rather than identically duplicating a model or following ready-made formulas, it was a question of starting from the pupil's perceptions. To begin, Quénioux invited teachers to abandon notions of distance, proportion, and perspective, which were much too complicated for young pupils and insisted more on the explicit qualities of colour and shape. Secondly, he suggested that pencil should not be the only medium. They should introduce India ink, modelling clay, watercolours and coloured pencils. Thirdly, rather than only asking young pupils to master certain techniques, the teacher should encourage them to make drawings that opened a better understanding of the world – a knowledge, however, stemming from their own experiences, their personal impressions. By leaving everything open to their interpretation and by putting them in direct contact with nature, the professor allowed his pupils to cultivate their feelings and to produce works that would translate their vision of things. Accurate depiction was less prized than sincerity during the project's execution. With more playful homework assignments (decorative arrangements, illustrations for stories, etc.), pupils awakened their imaginative faculties and, without giving themselves over to pure whimsicality, would discover the pleasures of drawing by exploring their own tastes and spontaneous talents. The fourth and final goal was to see drawing recognized as an entirely autonomous form of art. The study of drawing no longer focused on producing careful and meticulous copyists, but ideally true creators. Logically, it became a preparation for the love and intellectual appreciation of works of art.

The community of the brothers of Sainte-Croix, who supported the rise of *Jeunesse étudiante catholique*, was one of the places where the emerging recognition of children's drawings took shape. "Teaching drawing," Brother Jérôme observed in 1941, "is currently experiencing a beneficial period of evolution in more or less the whole world. The struggle between the old school and the new one is fierce. [...] At Collège Notre Dame, the revival can be felt, without any uproar, as we have gotten used to proceeding prudently and judging the tree from the fruit it bears."[33] Brother Jérôme studied at the École des Beaux-Arts from 1936 to 1938; he came out of it with a disgust for "copying plaster copies." He met Borduas when he had just been hired to give drawing classes on Saturday morning at the Collège Saint-Laurent.[34] This meeting was a "revelation" to Brother Jérôme. "Borduas had retained this freshness, this ingenuity, which makes young people so captivating, and that the majority loses upon becoming adults. Children's drawings delighted him. He spent hours scrutinizing them, one by one."[35] Brother Jérôme, who endorsed Borduas' pedagogical methods without hesitation, abandoned the formal teaching of the tricks of the trade to concentrate on the development of his pupils' individual talents. Generous, lyrical, pure, transparent, inventive, the drawings that his class produced were a delight to their professor's eyes. They represented proof that "children's artistic talents, if they are not diverted, thwarted and spoiled by systematic teaching, can be maintained in terms of their force and initial pureness even into adolescence."[36] Supported by Borduas, and also by Maurice Gagnon, "the best-known art historian of his time, in the province" – not to mention by the philosopher François Hertel, by the architect Marcel Parizeau, by Father Louis-Marie Régis, and by freelance journalists Robert Élie and Éloi de Grandmont – Brother Jérôme based his courses "on instinct, the subconscious, the mystery of spontaneous expression; on gestures and the grace of the present moment."[37] Brother Jérôme's method favoured the development of the child's gift, a gift that could not blossom unless there were no obstacles to the unfurling of his instinct, which made it possible for him to create poetic sketches.

This small revolution was huge in terms of repercussions for the future. It meant that regardless of age and technical skills, children could be considered creators. Teachers needed to recognize within each individual the expression of a profound subjectivity. Freedom was raised to the first rank of artistic requirements, and classic teaching was subsequently judged out of fashion, entrenched in routine, and deadly. In the past, students went from "the mark to the stroke," or in other words, from "doodling to drawing." Exaggerating somewhat, we could almost say that it was now the opposite, in the sense that children progressed by always and increasingly deepening their perceptions rather than by following rules and geometric prescribed techniques. "Children don't have to search for poetry. They have only to let their soul speak and their hands obey."[38] Vivacity became a quality that had to be cultivated.[39]

Maurice Gagnon left a detailed description of his ideal for teaching drawing. He admitted from the outset that his ideas were far from being unanimously accepted and that, on the contrary, his doctrine had caused controversy despite claiming to be more efficient. He was saddened to see the strength of the conservatism reigning within the province's teaching establishments. In his opinion, the vast majority of French-Canadian drawing teachers had not received the training or did not have adequate resources to safeguard the innate gifts of the young people entrusted to them. Lacking support, ignorant and incapable of changing their habits, they were unable to see teaching art in

"There are poets and there are grown-ups," Maurice Gagnon liked to say, quoting Jean Cocteau. Maurice Gagnon in the library of Montreal's École du Meuble. (Collection of the Gail and Stephen A. Jarislowsky Institute for Studies in Canadian Art, Concordia University.)

a new light. Ignoring the progress in teaching over the past twenty-five years, all they could do was make their students conform to the program, killing their creativity at the root. The pupils were constrained by severe discipline, as if they were all destined to become industrial designers or work in advertising. The faithful reproduction of nature and mechanical dexterity had become the ultimate criteria in evaluating their scholarly works. Instead of letting children follow the path of their imagination, helping them when needed by giving them general advice, teachers hastily forced them to go through the textbooks' step-by-step exercises. They were never so content as when students had assimilated their abstract formulas and knew how to patiently copy a dull model or trace a straight line with a ruler. Any inexact perspective was immediately punished, and original use of colour caused general disapproval. Drawing, which should have come from an artist's personality, became a simple respect for rules. After several years of slogging away at sterile exercises, even those who showed the most artistic promise as youngsters had lost the last glimmer of their originality.

Gagnon maintained that children knew how to imagine fabulous worlds in the utmost, joyous and spontaneous way. Protected from over-scholarly lessons, they could create magnificent forms on the whim of new associations, without worrying about respecting criteria set out by official educators. He consequently believed that creativity was to be nourished rather than suppressed, encouraged rather than repressed. "This sensibility expressed through matter confers upon it a new and previously unseen quality. This is what makes a work vibrate, speak to us, and move us. There is no need to be highly intelligent to express oneself through this song (a bird's song is not intelligent and yet still manages to charm us)."[40] Artistic training needed to be purged of its numerous stubborn and unhealthy conventions, which weighed down and blocked the development of free spirits.

What Gagnon called the "personalist method"[41] made such a cleansing possible. It could reveal "poetic essentials" shining within the depths of all beings. It could salvage an individual's most essential quality, which was constantly under threat of being obscured by ideological systems. What was this essential quality, if not the generous gift of oneself, a certain freshness of being, a certain respect of one's integrity? In Gagnon's mind, freedom, poetry, grace, spirituality, movement, life, purity, generosity, sensitivity, creation, youth, risk, all this made up the links of an ideological chain.

> [Much] more than a "temporal" reality, youth must be a spiritual force, a power of the soul. Simply put: in an artist, youth must identify with freedom. What limits and kills freedom in him, puts an end to and kills youth. And he will save nothing of himself, nor of his youth, nor the fruits of his experience if he does not maintain within himself, every day, the demands of absolute liberty: freedom vis-à-vis reality, freedom vis-à-vis others, freedom especially vis-à-vis himself, and his past successes. This is the main lesson past masters teach us: the utmost youthful works of Rembrandt, of Titian, of Greco, of Renoir, of Matisse and Picasso, and of Cézanne, are works produced in old age, because they are the freest. Masters do not give us recipes, but rather teach us to dread and flee them: they teach us courage, audacity, risk and the will to seek out boundless adventures.[42]

According to Maurice Gagnon, the first duty of art teachers was to arouse their students' curiosity.[43] Under these circumstances, a scholarly quality in teaching art was the clearest sign of probable failure; instead of making students reproduce a subject shown in a book, the teacher had to bring them to assimilate the challenges of art. A good sculpture or painting teacher did not so much teach as awaken students to their own desires. For example, showing pupils reproductions of Matisse, Derain, Braque or Picasso was sufficient for them to train their eye as one trains the ear by listening to symphonies. Capable of moving them, these examples had more chance of developing their pictorial sense than lessons *ex cathedra* pulled from some thick, theo-retical work.

As might be expected, Father Couturier was arguing at the same time for a complete reformation of drawing professors' training. In his opinion, this cut right to the heart of Quebec's artistic future. What did the ideal school he dreamed of look like? One in which competi-tive contests, tests and diplomas would be abolished. Teacher training would be reduced to strict limits: perspective, anatomy, the chemistry of colours. All this could be learned in eight days, in his opinion. Besides, this was all an honest teacher could claim to teach. More than codes and tricks of the trade, what would be taught in the future would be audacity and a spirit of adventure, strength and willingness of char-acter; children would be summoned to become their own masters, to train themselves according to their aspirations and penchants. "And for all this, and above all," Couturier wrote, "we would make sure that young people would have a great master present among them and accompanying them or, at least, a great mind capable of cultivating a spiritual climate around them, in which freedom, audacity and an appetite for risk, all of which I have spoken about, could flourish. And when such men could not be found, we would loyally and honestly close the school."[44]

In Borduas' writings, we find a similar ideal for a liberated school.[45] According to Borduas, the distribution of brushes, paint and paper in the classroom always gave rise to an explosion of images full of splendid qualities. In his courses, he therefore refused to make his students take any exams. As much as possible, he left them to freely experiment according to their own devices. "I ask nothing of my stu-dents," he used to say. Instead of imposing precise exercises, he kept quiet most of the time and waited for initial confusion to give birth to personal reflection. At most, he allowed himself to judge the final product, revealing the most precious hidden qualities of the work and entirely neglecting the superficial aspects. When the work was fin-ished, he took it upon himself to make the artist aware of his own power of creation by pointing out awkward, clumsy aspects caused by misguided education. "What we have to do is reveal the hidden qualities of his work, the most precious qualities, the rarest, the most unique, and the most particular ones. We must completely neglect the other side, the abstract qualities exterior to himself which, in fact, the student had been striving for."[46] Plastic materials, Borduas continued, were supposed to reveal life in all its intensity, regardless of the form chosen according to circumstances and temperaments. "The quest for the ideal" began by accepting the sovereignty of untamed impulses. Guy Viau, who was Borduas' pupil, summarized what was new about this method in Quebec:

> The memory that some of us have of Borduas as a professor is mixed with admiration and gratitude. When we set out to take his courses at the École du Meuble, we didn't really know what to expect. But we escaped from the burdensome world of book culture – a hot-house culture – and it was a relief from that point onward to be able use a gouge and chisel, a saw and plane, a T-square and try square, charcoal and a brush, to make or invent something. Men like Borduas, Couturier, Gagnon, Parizeau, introduced us to the heart of concrete reality and their teaching was, above all, about learning freedom and embracing a spirit of adventure.
>
> Borduas especially, right from his first lesson, won us over. We immediately felt that he entrusted each and every one of us with an unlimited confidence. Despite our ignorance and the pressing questions we wanted to ask, it was clear that, for Borduas, the answers were to be found within us. [...] The development of our instinctual gifts, as modest as they were, and the affirmation of our individuality were welcomed by Borduas with fervour and without worrying about references to arbitrary norms, to pre-established concepts, nor with any "inferiority complex" about our past or present works. We worked, however, with great humility,

because Borduas made us familiar with great works through reproductions, be it of Etruscan sculpture, Perpignan's Devout Christ wooden crucifix, Michelangelo, Renoir, Picasso or Paul Klee. And he inspired us to have the courage to measure ourselves against those works. The joy of discovering an appetite for the world and a pride in oneself are what Borduas staked out in our hearts along with anxiety and the will to go beyond ourselves.[47]

This represented a total pedagogical revolution. Teachers no longer demanded that students master anonymous formulas. They encouraged the full expression of their students' subjectivity. "Once one has accepted the path of personal experimentation, once mechanical exercises have been abandoned, as well as imitations and mimicry, the problems of figuration and expression through comparison with proposed models disappear. Now the emphasis is on authenticity of expression itself, on the true, harmonious and objective realities of drawing, as underdeveloped and unskillful as it may be."[48] There was a striking contrast between the Beaux-Arts approach, stuck on classical training in which technical virtuosity came first, and Borduas' method, focused on the particularities of each student. The Beaux-Arts demanded a return to the great masters, whereas Borduas encouraged a communion with oneself, the study of great masters being merely a pretext for self-discovery. For Borduas, the only thing classical painters could teach us was to be free. In 1942, Maurice Gagnon wrote enthusiastically:

Mr. Borduas has been called to play a lead role among us. For him, art is not something that can be taught, it can only be guided. For us, this is a change from the repetition of numerous errors whenever the question of drawing or teaching painting is raised. For him, like for all great artists whose works throughout history are a living testimony to it, the poetic nature of children is an enchanted world that no one other than they can reveal with such purity: lines, colours, unexpected and moving associations. Men can only perpetuate these "virtues" if only they discover how to conserve and preserve childhood instinctual gifts, enriched by the complete possession of oneself, by this sense of being human that fades into an always deeply mysterious poetry. There is absolutely no other justification needed in order to appreciate the instinctual "method."

Instead of being corrupted at first contact with a "deadly teacher," now there will be, at least in some parts of the province, children ready for the great conquest of themselves and of life. These children – let's hope there will be more and more of them, as this is a pressing necessity – will now have more opportunity to attain, for their personal satisfaction and the possible glory of our homeland, the essence of poetry.[49]

From then on, the validity of the young artist's work was guaranteed by its degree of sincerity. Borduas had considerable confidence in the authenticity of spontaneous gestures. He was persuaded that faithfulness to oneself could never betray true art. He did not go so far as to believe, like Claude Gauvreau, that "the only thing that can produce false notes in a painting is a letdown of emotion while the work is being done"[50] and that, without these hesitations and distractions, a work can be nothing less than impeccable. But he did agree with his young disciple that "the integral development of instinctual desires" showed itself, at the very least, to be a promising approach, geared toward the future.

Down with past aesthetic conventions! By following the flow of his desires, the creator's acts had a greater chance of being generous and transcendent. By being faithful to his inner impulses, an artist could hope to give birth to an authentic work of art. Consequently, an artist's first duty was to withdraw from lessons given by fine arts professors. Overall, and by a sudden and radical turn of events, the best education was henceforth a lack of formal training. Wild creation, as professed by Borduas, not only brought out the arbitrary character of official art rules, but ennobled the image of self-taught and marginal painters who were openly in conflict with the norms of the time.

Since a teacher's duty was now to cure his or her pupils of acquired rigidities, Borduas took it upon himself at first to unsettle his own students. He proposed "unhinging" their perception by abruptly criticizing their habits. "They had to experience the fact that authenticity and generosity are synonymous, that the two of them are innately free, unexploitable; they had to rediscover desires strong enough to start them off on a quest to conquer the unknown."[51] Manifestly, such an attitude was a provocation aimed at the traditional milieu of painting. One of his pupils (some historians speculate that he could have been Riopelle) was an exemplary draftsman, capable of reproducing a variety of objects in extremely minute detail. In his youth, he had most probably received praise and encouragement from his teachers. When it came time to evaluate his works, Borduas judged his drawings severely. The student protested, of course. He did not understand why his ability to pastiche classic compositions was being denigrated. He was not the only one at the École du Meuble to complain about his drawing professor's strange criteria. Borduas' pupils came to believe that deconstruction was the most assured path to getting a good grade. They rushed to produce the ugliest works possible, believing that their teacher would appreciate them even more. Bemused by this, Borduas said: "The worse our drawings get, they told me, the better the grade you give them!"[52]

To those who claimed that modern art was easy, something anyone could do, even a child who hardly knew how to hold a brush, the supporters of contemporary art replied that it was entirely the opposite. Academic art was within the grasp of any underachieving fine arts student who could put together a simple version of a Vermeer or a Rembrandt after taking a couple of courses and sufficiently mastering basic techniques. "Repetition," Maurice Gagnon maintained, "is what designates the weak, losers, characterless artists, and academic painters. Their technical skills represent all they are capable of. They worked hard to learn them and they do everything they can to maintain them. They use all kinds of tricks to keep bringing up the same old signs that stand between the true personality of the artist and the canvas."[53] Not only did Gagnon deplore the fact that "skill itself leads to nothing that is living, in any discipline" and "that it replaces spirit and heart," but also that it could be acquired by just about anyone. "A likeness to nature, which is easily discernable, is what makes official art valued, because understanding it requires no effort whatsoever other than following the well-trodden path. This laziness should make us thoroughly disgusted."[54] Couturier argued that a painter could teach his pupils academic rules in a week, while developing singularity in painting could take an entire lifetime of austerity and contemplation. Fernand Léger was not as severe in the lecture he gave in Montreal in May 1945. He allotted a good six months for any student at the École des Beaux-Arts to be able to diligently trace out a portrait of his grandmother.[55]

The advantage for the teacher who focused on developing his students' manual and visual skills, to the detriment of their respective dispositions, was that he could treat his class like a homogeneous whole and not worry about individual personalities. He could forget individuality and concentrate uniquely on a reassuring, albeit artificial, average. Gagnon was saddened by the fact that people in schools were being taught "far too much about how to paint." "It is – naturally – much easier to teach what one knows best, one's own painting style (a method, which annihilates a pupil's entire individuality, imposing the teacher's personality) than to direct the young artists' gifts towards their full development." In Quebec, "disastrous teaching from all points of view, which teaches tricks and methods *to make a good painting* – good, monotonous, and uniformly banal canvases for entire classes left in the hands and clutches of a boring teacher" – such instruction required no tact, no touch, no nuances, and no finesse. It produced good, predictable works for the "year-end exhibition."[56]

Nothing was easier, more comfortable, more reassuring and more trivial than this stubborn approach to teaching.

> If exact reproduction of an object is the goal of drawing and painting, there is no room for "deviation" on the part of the artists, and the role that is imposed upon them is that of a simple and mechanical photographer. They have to erase themselves to follow the model, to annihilate themselves in favour of reality. It seems to me, on the contrary, that the artist's ambition is to fully understand himself in order to achieve noble liberation. Expressed in this way, how enriching it is for a nascent personality to already be able to possess his inner world to the point of expressing it – for the moment, and for who knows how long, with unwavering purity. Isn't the full development of one's personality a form of humanization, better than simply submitting to the model, which is an act that brings about nothing, which adds nothing to personality?
>
> Such logical considerations, at least it seems to me, have hardly dawned on our educators for the moment. This is inconceivable. The teaching of drawing, such as it exists in our province, is done using such facile methods that all teachers (here, I mean academic teachers who abound in our dear Canada) have persevered on this erroneous path. The easy corrections that they apply demand no special quality of judgment or greater talent than that of the most common of mortals (don't be upset with me, I beg you, for being demanding with respect to these teachers). In such a system, facility becomes the *raison d'être* or the philosophy: I don't dare say, laziness. Judging the proportions of a vase drawn on paper in comparison to a vase in reality is one of the easiest things to do. Attributing grades according to whether the proportions of a drawn object correspond more or less correctly to its model is much less challenging than giving pupils directives that will allow them to grow, to develop in the real direction of their talents and faculties.[57]

A pedagogical method, using complex Socratic methods that placed students in a perpetual state of readiness, was just so much more demanding! Avant-garde painters argued that it was much more difficult for a teacher to get students to engage in a febrile quest than to bombard them with abstract theories. "Teachers must exercise great vigilance and one must admit that this method requires greater self-restraint and more thought than a course on the principles of art and the techniques of perspective."[58]

Tearing down the veil of fear and inhibition, teachers had to help their pupils determine the unexplored qualities that made them unique beings. They were to help students find themselves. Producing a non-figurative canvas required no sparing of effort and discipline. Maintaining, as much as possible, full emotional tension during the painting of a canvas was an "exhausting and severe endeavour."[59] When Marcel Barbeau presented his most recent compositions to Borduas in the fall of 1946, the latter disdainfully rejected them and criticized their lack of depth and a certain confusion between form and content. For Borduas, there were rules that "one could not recklessly overstep."[60] Nonetheless, these rules had nothing to do with the authoritarianism of traditional teaching. Barbeau was the first to recognize this. After stomaching Borduas' criticism, he reworked his canvases in accordance. The hastily made changes ended in pitiful results. Depressed, barely making ends meet, Barbeau did not create anything for several months.[61] Achieving the purity of contemporary art was by no means easy!

The bourgeois who visited Borduas' studio or his exhibitions were not convinced by the arguments made by modernist painters. In vain, Borduas replied that the results of his advice were there for anyone to see. His disciples' talent was sometimes acknowledged early on (Claude Vermette, Jean-Paul Mousseau). Many of his students had been admitted to the Contemporary Arts Society, clearly proving the effectiveness of his methods. His own wife, Gabrielle, took a long time to accept his approach to painting, and she was not alone. The most conservative minds refused to endorse an approach that seemed to belittle any kind of skill. If a work of art was the unforeseeable fruit of a singular imagination, it seemed impossible to judge it using *a priori* conventions, which could only be external to the free expression of personal impulses. In the case of academic art, one understood what to appreciate: one only had to trust the exterior qualities of the work in question – the mastery of a certain technique, its ability to conform to the imposed discipline, to obey the styles and codes of a school or the photographic reproduction of reality. By starting from what was already known and using proven techniques, a painter could achieve expected results. As for the artist who favoured living art, he proceeded in an entirely different manner, throwing himself into the unknown to discover a part of the mystery of the world. This caused deep frustration among those who believed in academic principles because they realized how such an aesthetic theory could cause grave disruptions. Once the link between the work and reality was broken, it became difficult to judge its inherent value. Since the only exterior requirement was to create what was previously unseen rather than reproduce the known, critics were alarmed at the thought that the most hideous of objects could be considered a masterpiece, as long as it demonstrated some novelty. Certain quick-witted collaborators of *Le Quartier latin* made fun of this radical relativism in an ironic interview with Guy Beaugrand-Champagne, the pseudo-founder of *slice-ist Automatism*. After an ochre period, during which he painted, due to a natural need, on his diapers, Beaugrand-Champagne "thickened his material" and varied his colour palette. While quoting Toulouse-Lautrec, he agreed with the French artist that: "Painting is like sh.. you don't explain it, you only smell it!"[62] This parody shows, by means of its absurdity, people's resistance to a vision of art that was counter to the presupposed aesthetic principles of conservative French Canadians. It is hardly insignificant that the article on *slice-ist Automatism* was signed: "A sportsman."

Copie de la Vierge d'Écouen, XVIe siècle (Drawing of the Virgin of Écouen, sixteenth century), 1926. Black chalk, white chalk and Conté pencil on paper. 62.8 x 48.2 cm. Collection of the Musée d'art contemporain de Montréal. Donated by Ms. Gisèle Verreault-Lapointe and Mr. Paul-Marie Lapointe. Photo: *MACM (D76 1 D 1).*

Autoportrait, v. 1928 (Self-portrait, v. 1928) oil on canvas, 21.7 x 16.1 cm. Collection of the National Gallery of Canada (no. 15780), Donated by Mrs. Paul-Émile Borduas.

La Jeune fille au bouquet ou Le Départ (Young Woman with Bouquet or The Departure), 1931. Oil on canvas, 35.9 x 17 cm. Musée des beaux-arts de Montréal. Donated by the J.-A. DeSève Foundation. Photo: MBAM, Brian Merrett.

Maurice Gagnon, 1937. Oil on canvas, 50.2 x 44.8 cm. Collection of the National Gallery of Canada (No. 15794).

Femme à la mandoline (Woman with Mandolin), 1941. Oil on canvas, 81.3 x 65 cm. Collection of the Musée d'art contemporain de Montréal. Photo: Richard-Max Tremblay (A 66 38 P 1).

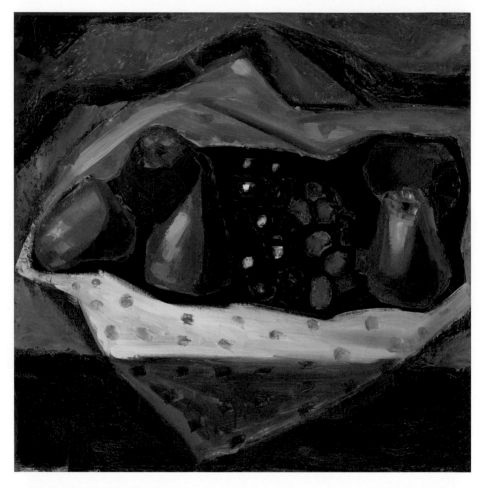

Les Raisins verts (Green Grapes), 1941. Oil on canvas, 60 x 61 cm. Collection of the Séminaire de Joliette, dépôt des Clercs de Saint-Viateur de Joliette.

Abstraction verte (Green Abstraction), 1941. Oil on canvas, 24 x 36 cm. Musée des beaux-arts de Montréal. Purchase subsidized by the Canadian Government under the terms of the Cultural Property Export and Import Act, and the Bequest of Harry W. Thorpe. Photo: MBAM, Brian Merrett.

Sans titre (*Les trois formes hérissées*), (Untitled, The Three Bristling Forms), 1942. Gouache over charcoal, 25.9 x 37.3 cm. Musée des beaux-arts de Montréal. Donated by Mr. Denis Noiseux and Mrs. Magdeleine Desroches-Noiseux. Photo: MBAM, Christine Guest.

Sans titre (*Un oiseau*), (Untitled, A Bird), 1942. Gouache over charcoal, 27.2 x 25.2 cm. Musée des beaux-arts de Montréal. Donated by Mr. Denis Noiseux and Mrs. Magdeleine Desroches-Noiseux. Photo: MBAM, Christine Guest.

Arelquin (Harlequin), 1942. Gouache on paper, 55.9 x 43.2 cm. Collection of the Gallery Leonard and Bina Ellen, Concordia University. Donated by Dr. and Mrs. Max Stern, 2000. Photo: Richard-Max Tremblay.

Abstraction, 1942. Gouache over charcoal, 59.2 x 43.5 cm. Art Gallery of Ontario. Donated by the Junior Committee Fund, 1977.

Léda, le cygne et le serpent (Léda, Swan and Snake), 1943. Oil on canvas, 47 x 56 cm. Collection of the Musée d'art de Joliette. Donated by Dr. and Mrs. Max Stern.

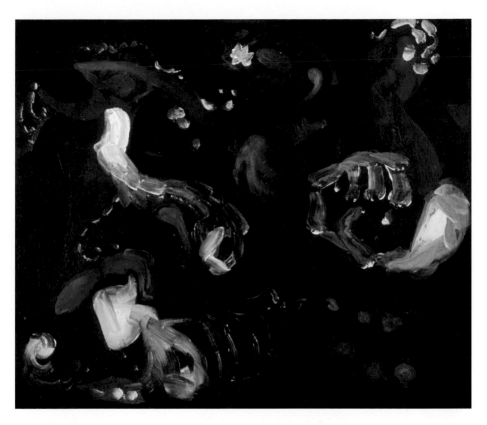

Viol aux confins de la matière (Rape at the Limits of Matter), 1943. Oil on canvas, 40 x 45.8 cm. Collection of the Musée d'art contemporain de Montréal.

3.45 or *Palette d'artiste surrealiste* (3.45 or The Surrealist Artist's Palette), 1945. Oil on canvas, 57.5 x 76.2 cm. Collection of the Musée d'art contemporain de Montréal. Photo: Richard-Max Tremblay (A 71 57 P 1).

8.47 or *Les Carquois fleuris* (8.47 or The Flowering Quivers), 1947. Oil on canvas, 81.2 x 108.7 cm. Musée des beaux-arts de Montréal. Donated by Mr. and Mrs. Maurice Chartré. Photo: MBAM.

14.48 or *Cimetière glorieux* (14.48 or Glorious Cemetery), 1948. Oil on canvas, 65 x 80.9 cm. Musée des beaux-arts de Montréal. Donated by Mr. Denis Noiseux and Mrs. Magdeleine Noiseux. Photo: MBAM, Christine Guest.

Opposite Page:

Above. *La Pâque nouvelle* (New Easter), 1948. Oil on canvas, 30.5 x 38.1 cm. Collection of the Gallery of Leonard and Bina Ellen, Concordia University, Purchased, 1983 (983.11). Photo: Denis Farley.

Below. *Les Coquilles* (The Shells), 1950. Ink and wash on paper, 37.5 x 44 cm. Collection of the Musée d'art de Joliette. Donated by Pierre Laberge, C. A., syndic.

Translucidité (Translucidity), 1955. Oil on canvas, 51 x 61.1 cm. Collection of the Musée d'art contemporain de Montréal.

For teachers graduating from the École des Beaux-Arts, who were trained in accordance with the classical canons of beauty and truth, the goal of painting exercises was to fortify young children's personalities by teaching them to demonstrate style, logic, harmony and discernment. To produce a work or make art involved combining individual expression and submission to learned rules. It seemed unthinkable for an error to be beautiful, for a vice to be pleasant to look at, or for an immoral act to show any aesthetic qualities. Beauty came from moral perfection. How in such a context could a drawing teacher be indifferent to his students' "bad taste?" How could he allow drawing errors to get to the point of becoming "horrors?" Neglecting order, proportions, elegance, unity, harmony and the power of the brushstroke were equivalent to abdicating one's pedagogical responsibilities. "Therefore, I have no trouble saying to deformists," wrote René Bergeron, "that giving priority to instinct over intelligence, dreams over reality, the subconscious over intelligence, is pure degradation."[63] Bergeron compared the urge to abolish all hierarchies in art with musical experiments organized in Russia after the Revolution, when orchestras were left to perform without a conductor. Musicians' freedom had certainly been respected, but the revolutionary ideal concerning the inalienable equality of the performers was maintained at

SCIENCE INFUSE . . .

Abstract painters had to bear the public's mockery and jeers. One of the most common criticisms was that any child could produce such scribbles. (Jacques Gagnier, *Le Quartier latin*, November 10, 1944.)

the cost of the symphony. For Bergeron, professors who renounced their guiding role had no reason for being. It was better to kick them out rather than pay them to cause disorder! A teacher could certainly let his students choose the path best suited to their own temperament, but only if he guided them toward a single goal: the attainment of truth and beauty. Bergeron much preferred "pompier painters" to arsonists and pyromaniacs. Many others also showed themselves to be just as severe.[64]

In his drawing classes, Borduas had to confront standards established in a previous century. Gagnon presumably spoke for his friend when deploring the fact that many venerable institutions were suspicious of young people and sought to break "very admirable and legitimate ambitions."[65] Borduas and some others were accused of sinking into subjectivism. "They shouted that the personalist method was Rousseauism,"[66] Gagnon wrote with regret. The public, who had initially applauded Borduas' first experiments, increasingly gave him the cold shoulder. For members of the educated Montreal bourgeoisie, one or two Automatists were fine, but an entire school of them was too much. Some people, disdainfully amused by the works of Borduas' disciples, openly laughed at the Automatist method.

Take, for example, not an art exhibition, but one of Claude Gauvreau's plays, called *Bien-être* (The Good Life), created in May 1947. The play is important, because Borduas claimed it was on that specific evening that he became fully aware of his marginality within the milieu he had frequented up until then. In the room, people with whom he thought he was on good terms suddenly became strangers to him.[67] *Bien-être* was not the smash success that Gauvreau had expected it to be. Jean-Paul Mousseau remembered that Marcel Barbeau, who was acting in Jean Mercier's *Pièce sans titre* (Play Without a Title) that was presented alongside Gauvreau's in a double feature, had such stage fright that he could not move. And as for Mousseau himself, he forgot to say his only line. Such disorder put the audience in a good mood. *Bien-être* followed immediately after. From the first words spoken: "Hands in the abyss making leaves. This is a wedding," the audience could not contain their "exorbitant generalized and uncontrollably hysterical laughter."[68] Then the "décor fell apart," just before the intermission. "When the play began, there was a general kerfuffle in the room. I think there weren't many people, maybe between 125 and 150 – supposedly people who knew a thing or two about theatre. People were yelling, shouting, and booing, and Claude and Muriel carried on until the end, without stopping, and it was a beautiful thing to see."[69] When the evening ended, there were hardly more than ten spectators left in the room.

THE ONE BY WHOM SCANDAL COMES

Instruction at the École du Meuble included courses on life drawing, sketching, observational drawing and industrial drawing. In fact, a quarter of the time spent at the school was devoted to learning drawing in all its forms. Jean-Marie Gauvreau stated: "Drawing is a universal language. It is a fierce weapon and brings definitive honour to the artist who knows how to wield a pencil."[70] Borduas had been recruited by the École du Meuble to teach drawing as applied to cabinetry and ornamentation. Given his ideas and his teachings, it is easy to see how his very presence at the École du Meuble was itself the subject of scandal. At the time, obviously, no one contested a professor's right to refine his students' culture and broaden their horizons. In 1948, a professor of decorative composition noted: "We pride ourselves on the fact that many of our students before leaving our school no longer think or express themselves in the same way."[71] But, for old-school professors, this transformation assumed a marriage between tradition and progress, without affronts to good taste or threats to Christian morality. Learning about art was part of a well-rounded man's education and served as his entry into a culture of distinction and good manners. It was as indispensable to see clearly, as it was to speak French properly or dress decently. In opposition to this philosophy, Borduas said that he was not overly worried about the aesthetic value of artistic works and violently objected to the criterion of usefulness. It was not enough for him to simply contest traditions, to shake up received ideas, and to call into question a certain way of painting: he actually advised his students to break radically with all forms of heritage, to the point of being able to approach a canvas without any preconceived ideas. He rejected more than just a certain tradition; he seemed to be sweeping away the past as a whole. He was condemning not only an antiquated education, but also calling into question the notion of lecture-style teaching and presentation.

More and more students visited Borduas in his office, asked him for advice, and harassed him with questions. The most daring began doubting canonical ideas which, until then, had been massively instilled in them. Facing scorn and incomprehension, they became even more uncompromising and found, within their conflicts with established order, an opportunity to radicalize their will to rebel. Discussions that had begun in class continued in the corridors, in salons and cafes. Having dealt with problems related to art, they digressed and covered social issues such as war, education, religion, literature and love. The self-righteous elite criticized Borduas for turning his teaching into a school of libertarianism. He was accused of mixing his drawing lessons with advice that was only good for sowing the seeds of doubt in students' minds. Poor families, who sacrificed much for their children's education at the École du Meuble, counted on the earnings that their children would receive to make ends meets and did not look favourably when they came back home with creative experiments (tempera works, transfers, projections, splatterings, drippings, spatula paintings). In his apologia *Projections libérantes* (Liberating Projections), published in 1949, Borduas highlighted the rampant conflicts that developed little by little between his more audacious students and his less open-minded teaching colleagues.

Early on, a common front was established with the students against prejudice, ignorance and the unknown. They helped me as much as I could help them myself and they knew it. We made an unspoken pact and it held magnificently. It is possible that this agreement was enough in itself to justify the choices they made, which threatened to disrupt the school. Their dedication to studying drawing made them find the other subjects on the program of study boring and sterile; this, despite the administration's eager attempts to reduce work done in class, despite the systematic opposition of the applied arts professors and of the entire section of students who did not take my classes, despite my efforts to make the usefulness of these subjects understood. Besides, it was self-evident that their disgust only applied to the prevalent way of teaching and not to the course topics themselves; and this was because the students could now compare two states of being: the passive one and the active one, and could assess them clearly.[72]

Borduas claimed that his vision of art never tainted the way he taught his classes and that he took great care to scrupulously respect the program of study at the École du Meuble. This defence does not ring true, because we know that Borduas believed that the full development of a student's gift would not lead him to carpentry. He spoke with disdain about a young man who gave into the pressures of his stubborn environment and gave up a brilliant career in painting ahead of him. One sign of Borduas' influence was the fact that some of his students at the École du Meuble joined the Contemporary Arts Society whereas their training should have lead them to a more conventional career. Jean-Paul Riopelle, who burned bridges that could have led him to a more respectable profession in his parents' eyes, went so far as to deliberately fail his drawing classes. The École du Meuble was becoming a school of fine arts, or better yet, a school of modern art, which was a considerable digression from its initial vocation.

At the outset, the director of the École du Meuble dismissed the works inspired by Borduas as insignificant, inoffensive pieces done at the artist's leisure, which were undertaken during spare time as an aside to real scholarly exercises. However, it was not long before Gauvreau reprimanded the drawing professor – who never liked lecturing – for not keeping his lessons in line with the principles of art, as applied to the furniture industry. He would have liked Borduas to work on his talents as a designer and not as a painter. "[Jean-Marie Gauvreau] told me that Paul-Émile Borduas had initially been hired to teach drawing to students taking carpentry and industrial design. Instead of doing what they asked him to do, Borduas turned his courses into painting courses. They warned him that this did not correspond to the director's expectations, but he ignored them."[73]

The person who was the most shocked by the methods touted by Borduas was obviously Charles Maillard, who had been the director of the École des Beaux-Arts since 1925. A specialist in industrial and anatomic design, he refused to abandon the discipline associated with well-organized composition in favour of what he called "the closed field of abstract painting." What Maillard deplored above all else in so-called modern works, which he considered shoddy and unskilful, was the poor drawing[74] and the lack of rigour in traced lines. He could not accept colour replacing well-drawn lines, as in the works of impressionist imitators who thought they could make up for their technical deficiencies by splattering colour. "Disorder in thought, which corresponds to disorder in form, is the common and accessible ground of all mediocrities."[75]

On one hand, as I explained earlier, imagination and creativity were valid, according to Maillard, provided they did not make people lose sight of art's ultimate goal, which was to praise the virtues of nature, religion, and folklore. "He would never dare deprive [students] of the discipline of their art, by claiming that they must remain purely instinctual, and say that instinct alone is enough to lead an artist back to the source of inspiration."[76] Painting's mission was to idealize natural, Catholic and French-Canadian realities. Furthermore, Maillard, who criticized Borduas and his followers in passing, found it inconceivable for a professor to leave his students without clear indications regarding the necessary successive steps to follow to succeed at drawing. The masters had not reached the peak of their art form by yielding to the disorder of their impulses. In painting, Maillard maintained that ignoring the elementary rules of proportion and colour inevitably condemned one to fail.

In his battle against all that went beyond the audacity of *Impressionism by numbers*, the director of the École des Beaux-Arts had several allies. Among these were former pupils in positions of power at the *Commission des Écoles catholiques de Montréal* (CCM – Montreal Catholic School Board). A former director of drawing at this Commission thundered, "We must fight against some of the ultra-modern aesthetic influences coming in from the outside and trying to infiltrate our teaching. Certain enthusiasts of modernism (who are not part of our staff) advocate questionable theories from the standpoint of our own program, in addition to the fact that they are only aimed at a purely artistic culture. They invoke the 'subconscious, originality, personality, pure ingenuity' and even propose getting rid of all technical methods, which would lead us straight to anarchy and absolute graphic liberty."[77] In an interview granted to *Actualités canadiennes* (Canadian Current Events) at CBC Radio-Canada in 1944, Francesco Iacurto lashed out more specifically at lovers of childish doodles, saying: "Modern artists are con artists, dishonest people. Modern art is the negation of art. People no longer know how to draw; drawing is set aside, junked. Even in Montreal, there is an evil school where they are deforming children's minds by making them believe that their shapeless scribbles have some artistic value. This is a regrettable turn of events."[78]

Despite Maillard's efforts, the supporters of non-figurative art continued to gain ground. Maurice Gagnon was publishing books, participating in exhibitions, giving talks, writing articles, teaching courses and trying to make the avant-garde's position known. Father Couturier, who was very active during the last year of his stay in Quebec, began a series of five weekly programs on modern art on the radio in July 1945. He also sat on the jury of the provincial government's painting award with, among others, Fernand Léger, in addition to publishing a monograph on Marcel Parizeau and supervising a revised edition of *Art et Catholicisme*, which contained an important supplement: "Note on abstraction." Montreal's Contemporary Arts Society had been encouraging discussion on current art trends since 1939 and supporting personal initiatives. Under the enlightened leadership of John Lyman as president, Borduas as vice-president and

Robert Élie as secretary, the Contemporary Arts Society worked hard to assure free art's legitimacy throughout the country. To convince the greater public of the soundness of his stances, Borduas increased his participation in debates organized in schools and other institutions, and also campaigned for the Contemporary Arts Society to divide its jury for the annual exhibition to include abstract painters. Members of Borduas' group shone, individually and collectively, at various exhibitions (in the Hall of Honour at the University of Montreal in November of 1946; in Franziska Boas' studio in New York in January 1946; in Montreal on Amherst Street in April of 1946 and on Sherbrooke Street in February-March 1947; in the Maeght Gallery in Paris in 1947, etc.). New recruits joined the first group of faithful. In July of 1949, Father Couturier, who was invited to summarize trends in art throughout the country for a radio audience, remembered that art had made a prodigious leap during the Second World War. "The barriers of conformism, the authority of schools and official academies, were crumbling. In the double wake of Cubism and Surrealism, extremely audacious initiatives kept popping up. There was a hint of insurrection and total independence in the air, although this did not prevent certain talented individuals from orienting themselves toward less radical paths."[79]

By 1945, observers had the impression that "modern" painters, from this moment onward, constituted a large and unified group of artists. Jean Le Moyne believed that painting was ahead of other forms of cultural expression in Canada.[80] Claude Gauvreau exclaimed in 1946: "Finally! Canadian painting exists. We have few poets, and even fewer composers, but now we have painters."[81] René Bergeron went so far as to say that supporters of living art had won in Quebec, that they controlled artistic institutions and occupied key positions on official award committees. Consequently, it was reasonable to speak of their works in terms of a new academicism. Bergeron even claimed that the *Salon des Indépendants* would have made more sense if it had attracted more realist artists. Such talk was clearly an exaggeration.

However, at the end of the war the winds of change seemed to have begun blowing and the battle against traditionalism's worst excesses appeared on the verge of being won.

The first to suffer from this evolution would be Charles Maillard, Borduas' sworn enemy following his brief stint at Montreal's École des Beaux-Arts twenty years earlier. For some time, enlightened people had been calling for Maillard's head. The director's sly manoeuvres, which he used in order to maintain his ascendancy, his nepotistic links with Charles-Joseph Simard, undersecretary of the Secretariat of the Province of Quebec, and his arrogance, which made him believe that he surpassed the Impressionists (to his students who pointed out the likeness between his canvases and those of Van Gogh, he responded by saying: "Yes, it may look like Van Gogh, but it is much better!")[82] ended up making his establishment a nest for conniving and the object of ridicule. Not only did the students learn to paint badly there, but the atmosphere in the offices, the studios, and the classes had become intolerable.

In 1940, Jacques de Tonnancour, who had been disgusted by the topic of a still-life imposed at a year-end examination, slammed the door of the École des Beaux-Arts and left. A month later, in reaction to the stupidity of his professors, he wrote a text whose title speaks for itself: "L'École des Beaux-Arts or the Massacre of the Innocents." In May of 1941, during the *Salon des Indépendants*, which Father Couturier had organized, Maillard felt obliged to send the newspapers a letter in which he praised the training offered at his establishment and took a dig at Father Couturier and his disciples. The Dominican did not take long to respond. He answered that Maillard's teaching could be judged by the "mediocrity of the painting normally coming out of this school" and "the inferior quality of the works annually presented at the 'Exhibitions' he organizes." Couturier spoke with full knowledge of the facts. The year before, he had been invited to teach at Montreal's École des Beaux-Arts and observed students deserting the classes in droves (twenty-five out of thirty dropped out before the end). The students found it troubling and incomprehensible to see a professor, for whom it was not enough to reject usefulness, drawing, morality and figurative art, telling painters and sculptors to mock Paris' École des Beaux-Arts. Couturier, upset by having been so cavalierly treated by Maillard, and understanding the extent to which the latter was part of an old guard whose influence was damaging art and religion, led a campaign from that moment on to undermine Maillard's credibility. Louise Gadbois, John Lyman, Borduas and Pellan shared Couturier's opinions and added to them: the teaching approach at the École des Beaux-Arts was so harmful to students' ability to create that the first duty of any graduate was to purge him or herself of formulas that "had failed everywhere else."[83] At the same time, without citing Maillard's name even once, Marcel Parizeau wrote a letter to newspapers that clearly expressed his sentiments: the works shown at the last salon of student work from the École des Beaux-Arts showed no "sense of enrichment" and were not worth even speaking about. Highlighting the mediocrity of the works would have only hurt certain people.[84] Simone Aubry, who incidentally was Paul Beaulieu's wife, one of the directors of *La Relève*, did not mince her words either when she enumerated her grievances with her alma mater, qualifying the atmosphere at the École des Beaux-Arts as "empty" and "debilitating."[85]

The rise of Montreal's avant-garde convinced Maillard to hire Pellan as a professor in August 1943. He wanted to promote his school in comparison to Gauvreau's and show his magnanimity. It is also important to mention that he was ill and had considered giving up his main painting course for some time. However, Stanley Cosgrove, whom he preferred over Pellan, was studying at the time in Mexico and not yet available to replace him.[86] While he could not be criticized for not making room for living art in his establishment, Maillard had miscalculated the consequences of his decision. Far from calming things down, it caused tempers to flare. "More and more, over the course of the year 1944-1945, tensions mounted, rumours circulated to the effect that the École des Beaux-Arts had become a place for scheming and bullying."[87] In May 1944, Pierre Gélinas, an admirer of André Breton,[88] published a satirical tale set in a mythical Philistinia featuring a character named Moronos Blockheadionn, a Carthaginian dimwit who was a professional tramway conductor, but also a painter in his spare time. Moronos is named director of the School of Fine Arts thanks to trickery, flattery and scheming. He makes the school unlivable for people working there, to the joy of the Philistinians, who delight in being able to count on such an illustrious nobody. "If Philistinia's School of Fine Arts has remained the symbol of artistic abjection for thirty years, we owe it all to Moronos Block-headionn."[89] Upon reading such a tale, one realizes the extent to which Maillard had been entirely discredited in the minds of zealous supporters of living art.

In a lecture given in May 1945, Fernand Léger declared that he had wasted his time on the benches of Paris's École des Beaux-Arts. To those few people who protested his recollections (among them René Chicoine, a follower of classicism), Léger responded tit-for-tat, draw-ing applause from the audience. Certain people even shouted: "Down with Maillard! Down with Maillard!" In summary, "It is fair to say that no one stood up to defend Maillard, who was identified by sharp tongues as the director of the École des Beaux-Arts. […] The audience was very large and the unanimity and satisfaction of the people who were present was clear. In fact, it was one of the first manifestations of its kind and everyone seemed to be happy to give his or her opinion on the state of what had been going on for a long time."[90]

A month later, on the eve of the annual student exhibition, Mail-lard ordered two works to be taken down, fearing they might offend the morals of the Quebec public, including several teachers, both male and female from religious groups, accompanied by their young pupils. Having first agreed to the director's request, Pellan did an about-face and asked the two incriminated students to touch-up the offending works. The first one – a nude by Mimi Parent – was decked out in a red and blue polka-dot bathing suit. The second – a Last Supper, which had been judged too realist in style – was transformed into a drinking scene and a beret, with a red pompon on it, was placed on Christ's head, while the chalice was rendered as a glass of beer. This ridiculous solution only fed the controversy. On the evening of the opening, students demonstrated, using the war cry "Down with Maillard and academicism," and plastered the walls with stickers featuring the same message. "[This] demonstration is the end result of a thoughtful and steady movement initiated by young people and all serious art connoisseurs against narrow-mindedness, scheming plots and authoritarianism in art."[91] The director, who was only too happy to find an occasion to fall out with Pellan, took it upon himself to denounce this uncouth insolence in front of the greater public. Against all expectations, the press – the liberals of the newspapers *Le Canada* and *Le Jour* as much as the nationalists of *Le Bloc* – did not take Maillard's side. On the contrary, they ganged up with Pellan to demand his dismissal. "It is important to note that this is no longer a question of isolated manifestations against Mr. Maillard, but rather a popular trend and a spontaneous movement."[92] In the fall, during a dinner-talk held by the university student club, forty or so people loudly applauded Éloi de Grandmont's speech, which was a general attack on the crippling nature of Maillard's teaching.[93] The situation at the school seemed to have become suffocating to the point where the only possible outcome was the director's departure. In December 1945, Maillard finally left. The fact that he was appointed by a Liberal government when the Union Nationale party was returning to power most certainly did not help his cause.

Maillard's eviction did not mean that the battle for wildness, the primitive, childhood, life, originality, truth, nature and abstraction had been won. Maillard had not been cavalierly kicked out, but had simply, and somewhat honourably, retired. The conservative forces at the École des Beaux-Arts and the École du Meuble continued to make their presence felt. Borduas' allies had to deal with a growing popular reaction. As Automatism defined its vision more and more clearly, the rebellion against these pictorial innovations also became increasingly intense. In 1948, Brother Jérôme fell into a deep depression. "[I] can no longer tolerate children's drawings, which are marvellous in their sensitivity and freshness, being called sacrilegious scribbles…. I feel rejected by everyone, they take me for a mental case. […] I am isolated, as if I were in a concentration camp."[94] Hurt by the jeers of his fellow brothers, including Gérard Petit, the author of an incendiary book opposing modernist art,[95] Brother Jérôme wrote to his superior to ask for a short leave to rest. "I have dealt with so many attempts at bullying me and have seen so many grimaces in front of things that I absolutely know to be correct from an artistic point of view! The moral spring in my heart is broken, despite the clarity of my vision when I am faced with a child's drawing."[96]

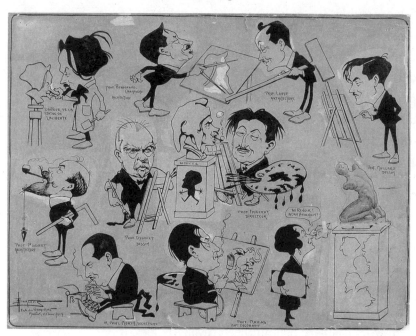

Albéric Bourgeois, École des Beaux-Arts, 1924. Feather, brush and ink, lead pencil and water-based paint on cardboard, 50.6 x 64.8. (Musée des beaux-arts de Montréal. Donated by Mrs. A. Bourgeois. Photo MBAM, Jean-François Brière.)

Borduas himself was faced with an increasingly "untenable"[97] situation at the École du Meuble. In the winter of 1946, a strike by graduating students, led by Barbeau, Roger Fauteux, Bernard Morisset, Maurice Perron and Riopelle, among others, protested against the old-fashioned teaching style of their cabinetmaking teacher. The situation looked strangely like the struggles that had taken place one year earlier at Montreal's École des Beaux-Arts, as if Borduas, from behind the scenes, wanted to accomplish with Gauvreau what Pellan had managed to do with Maillard. It was the wrong thing to do. Gauvreau reacted strongly to his turbulent professor's supposed scheme by withdrawing his courses on documentation and decoration, and by only letting him teach a drawing course. He avoided a scene by permitting Borduas to keep his full salary. Who could have complained about such an arrangement?

For Borduas, the problem was that his stances, which had become increasingly radical, had alienated him from an important group within Quebec's artistic community. For instance, the Contemporary Arts Society founded in 1939 by John Lyman and for which Borduas served as vice-president. Academic painters in the C.A.S. felt more and more frustrated by the growing importance given to young painters who, after being named "junior members," continually badmouthed the "old fogies." The fact that the youngest members (however internationalist) were French-speakers, whereas the eldest (however Francophile) were mostly English-speakers, did not help them get along. "According to a former associate member, the most elderly, who were mostly English-speaking, were afraid of giving too much power at the time to the young French-speaking artists for fear of changing the balance of the organization."[98] Over and above these language issues, the Francophone and Anglophone painters had denounced the "ridiculous" tendencies of modernist art for years. They lashed out at the growing influence of the Automatists and their desire to remove dilettantes and traditionalists from seats of power. A public letter signed by twenty-five people, among them Adrien

Hébert and Marc-Aurèle Fortin, Francesco Iacurto and several Anglophones, showed their exasperation. "It isn't enough to simply patiently wait for this regrettable movement to stop on its own. Meanwhile, advocates for this art are slipping into influential positions in art galleries, in schools, in newspapers, trying to destroy what has made art great over the centuries."[99] In December 1947, Julien Hébert wrote from Paris to Jacques de Tonnancour that Borduas and his *"fils de l'esprit"* (spiritual offspring) could not go on dictating Montreal's artistic agenda. "I say to hell with them,"[100] he concluded.

Adding to this first division among the members of the Contemporary Arts Society, there was soon another, which was much more dangerous to Borduas: one pitting Borduas followers against Pellan supporters. Strengthened by their initial breakthrough in exhibitions and galleries, Borduas' disciples were not content with denigrating Barbizon school-type sketches made by William Goodridge Roberts. They also made fun of Pellan, accusing him of being too timorous and abandoning the anguish of pictorial research for the soft comforts of an outdated Cubism. "Unfortunately, the sectarian mind-set reigns among young people. We can appreciate their enthusiasm, but not their blind judgments. Whoever chooses Pellan cannot be Borduas' friend. Who is the greater of the two: is it Pellan or is it Borduas? And they're off, banner in hand, and to hell with the rest of the universe!"[101] The Contemporary Arts Society, the sounding board for these conflicts, was in danger of being crushed under the weight of the mutual hatred between the two great Montreal painters. "During the war," John Lyman confided, "Pellan returned to Montreal, and he, too, with his followers joined the C.A.S. Thus, it became divided into two factions, each of which sought to prevail. [...] I could not admit seeing that the Society, oblivious of the purpose for which it was founded, namely, aesthetic liberty for its members without distinction, should become an instrument of sectarian contention."[102] The hostilities were such that, when Borduas was ultimately elected president of the C.A.S. in the winter of 1948, the group rallying around Pellan (which included Jacques de Tonnancour) preferred to withdraw, rather than accept such a leader.

The loss of Pellan's support had direct repercussions on the general appreciation of Borduas' work. Art critics and amateurs felt free to despise his creations, considering him to be a clumsy draftsman at a time when being able to draw was seen as the first requirement for artistic legitimacy. Wicked tongues, fed by professional jealousy, spread rumours that Borduas did not know how to finish his figurative paintings and that Maurice Denis, during Borduas' time at the Ateliers d'art sacré in Paris, had found what he considered imperfections in the drawings submitted by the master from Saint-Hilaire.[103] Whereas the most famous signatory of the manifesto *Prisme d'yeux* (Prism of Eyes) was described as a natural-born draftsman, deeply concerned with the technical perfection of the finished work, Borduas' strokes by comparison seemed inexact and weak and his lines artificial and faulty. Pellan did not hesitate to insinuate that the difference between Borduas and himself was that he knew how to draw! "In painting, I deplore Surrealism having favoured Automatism and accepted works that I find too simplistic [...]. It has produced sloppy painters."[104] On the same subject, Jacques de Tonnancour told an interviewer: "As an artist, I would say [that Borduas] had unequalled vision. But, as a painter, he was not very gifted."[105] Even François Hertel, Borduas' former companion, was increasingly disgusted by the work of Borduas and his disciples. Whereas Pellan was in "perfect control," "produced many sketches and drafts" and "conscientiously destroyed them before producing a finished work," the Automatists accumulated "puddles of colour dripping in all directions, without form – informal, as they wanted it to be – without real harmony." "Giving oneself to creative happenstance is nothing but a giant sham. [...] Those who do not thoroughly control their works are paltry creators. Automatism, in writing as in painting, is the alibi of the impotent."[106]

These malicious remarks remind us that artists of Borduas' generation, even many years later, had difficulty giving him his due. What must they have thought of him while he was alive! At the École du Meuble, at the Contemporary Arts Society, and in French-Canadian society in general, tensions had reached a boiling point. The confrontation to come had been foreshadowed and the end could only be terrible. It was.

WHEN MY DREAMS
HEAD OFF TO WAR![1]

*Within a foreseeable future, men will cast off their useless chains. They
will realize their full, individual potential according to the unpredictable, necessary order of spontaneity – in splendid anarchy.*

—PAUL-ÉMILE BORDUAS

Four years after his manifesto appeared, Borduas attempted to mini-
mize its critical dimension. "The meaning of this total refusal was
distorted," Borduas tells us. "It was just a refusal of facility and conformity. Besides, there is never any total refusal – the title isn't mine –
what should have been used was global acceptance, of life and its
riches... Even the term "liberated art," which we were so severely
criticized for using, does not imply anything other than a new perspective on the world, free from constraints and academicism, open to
everything, basically!"[2] A revolution, however, had occurred. The progression of Borduas' line of thought can be measured in terms of the
company he kept, going from spending time with Ozias Leduc, to the
Ateliers d'art sacré of Maurice Denis and George Desvallières, to the
small circle that formed around Maurice Gagnon and Marie-Alain
Couturier, before briefly making himself the leader of the Automatist
group and returning to solitude. Borduas had built his relations with
the progressive Catholics of his time around a knot of ambiguities.
How had it suddenly come undone? How are we to understand the
break, which occurred in such a decisive and brutal fashion, between
him and the clergy and deeply pious laypeople?

One of Borduas' difficulties had to do with his hot-tempered character. He did not take lightly to compromise or to red herrings. Just

reading the first two lines of a text brought to him by Pierre Gauvreau and Jean-Paul Riopelle was enough to make him throw the pages "violently into a corner of the studio."[3] When Thérèse Renaud and Fernand Leduc visited him at his house in Saint-Hilaire in the winter of 1952, he appeared bitter and surly to them. The discussion had barely begun when he reared up and angrily said, as he had written in 1948: "Only Breton is incorruptible," and then he showed his guests to the door. The two former disciples protested, proclaiming their friendship, and worried about the bus, knowing that it departed for Montreal only several hours later. Ultimately, they stayed, but something seemed broken.[4] "Borduas simply did not tolerate people doubting him. You had to get out of his way."[5] Those who dared contest his radical vision of things were stricken from his list of friends.[6]

Borduas' intransigence did not just stem from his temperament, but also from the status of the artist in the twentieth century who heroically embodied the refusal of materialistic values. The disinterested nature of his creative acts was in opposition to the profiteering character of commercial transactions. His anxious and domineering passion made him look like a mystic, constantly driven toward transcendence: "Just as the mystical revelations of saints come from their ardent life, the works of modern painters are vindicated by their life. Borduas' works proceed from asceticism itself, where sacrifice is an implacable rule. This is because art is the fruit of rigour: eliminating all that is accessory in order to present what is essentially painting and drawing; like pure poetry, modern painting has sought out and found anew the basic elements."[7] By refusing to compromise with an impure world, the artist embodied an ideal image of sainthood. His isolation from the rest of society drew him closer to visionaries, who in troubled times had sought to safeguard the uncompromising sense of the absolute. The persecution that Borduas faced was in this sense the proof of his integrity. The archetype of the artist was that of someone who single-handedly fought battles against mass misunderstanding and who carried out his revolution at great cost. Outcast by society, he lived in misery and his death occurred amid a sea of indifference. Only a handful of followers, hunched over his tomb, swore to carry on his teachings.

The first Impressionists, rejected by art salons, expelled from fine arts schools and snubbed by collectors, also had to face the scorn of their contemporaries. By revolting against widely accepted aesthetic norms, they brought upon themselves the disdain of "official" art critics. In Europe, the bourgeois public made fun of the Impressionists, but later bought their oil paintings for a small fortune. And, in Canada, it took even longer for this art form to be recognized for what it was worth.[8] This was more proof that, always behind the times when it came to creative evolution, so-called cultivated art lovers inevitably held yesterday's creators in high esteem and dragged their contemporaries' names through the mud. The artist could not count on public opinion to reassure him as to the quality of his paintings. Rather, it was by rejecting the opinions of uncultured and unsophisticated masses that the artist had the best chance of formulating honest and correct judgments.

In Borduas' case, by accepting the romantic vision of the poet having been rejected by "counterfeiters," "touch-up artists," the "incalculable crowd of exploiters," "innately sad souls," "the forces of fear," and other "hypocrites," he depicted true artists as uncompromising heroes ready to brave "general disapproval" in order not to betray "their quest for beauty, rigour, and purity."[9] There was something elitist in Borduas' conception of the artist, which may not be surprising coming from a man who "loved monastic cells"[10] and who had the strict self-discipline of a former student at the Ateliers d'art sacré in Paris. By his own admission, having little faith in others, he sought to distinguish "ardent souls, among the crowd, who could deeply transform the human adventure." "The principal signatory of *Refus global*, who forged over the course of several years the utmost elevated conception of the artist, generously conveyed extraordinary personal talent and moral strength to the small group of men and women he united around him. These qualities could be found in the notions of purity, integrity and generosity, rooted, as is well known, in the soil of Judeo-Christian doctrine."[11] The true artist was the one who fled the frenzied crowds, who turned aside honours and, on the contrary, made it his duty to listen only to his inner demons.

The time during which Borduas grew up was waiting for and expecting the arrival of luminaries capable of giving direction to a French-Canadian youth's need for action. Intellectual periodicals ardently called for the coming of a leader and tried to formulate a doctrine. In the 1940s, a master was first and foremost someone who was on the path to sainthood, a person overflowing with faith and willing to give himself over entirely and wholeheartedly to making truth triumph. Among a generation of young people, this desire for such a luminous authority was widely felt. In Borduas' case, he was someone who sparked such a burning enthusiasm in many young people.[12] "We have found in Mr. Borduas," Fernand Leduc emphasized, "a vigilant source of enlightenment that shows travellers the way, and we intend, by drawing on the strength of his example, to always stay on this path and not back down, regardless of the sacrifices."[13] For Leduc, who had just left his religious community, artistic fervour verged on asceticism. He believed that the broadening of human horizons could be accomplished by the concerted action of a phalanx of incorruptible volunteers, who would refuse any compromise with a condemned world and who would march firmly towards purity. Leduc's wife, Thérèse Renaud, confirmed that her husband had integrated an ideal of contemplation and prophetism[14] from the time he spent with the Marist Brothers and confessed that she had also been "looking for a master [a guru, we would say today]."[15] Jean-Paul Mousseau remembered the seriousness that characterized group discussions during the first years, saying: "Anarchists? Not really. We wanted to be rigorous. We were very intolerant. Perhaps there was a bit of Christian education at the base of it all."[16]

Fervour and asceticism were encouraged by the fact that, more than literature, music or architecture, painting lent itself to the formation of small groups. Pictorial creation was, to a large extent, a collective endeavour, due to relations created during school years, exhibitions, or salons, which at times brought together artists with little in common. Rejected by hostile juries, the *Indépendants* and especially the *Refusés* (Rejects) ended up creating a group identity themselves, which highlighted their opposition to stagnant traditions. Such solidarity gave cohesion to their efforts, which would have otherwise been difficult to reunite under a single label. The broken communion between avant-garde artists and the broader public resulted in manifestos, and these documents described obscure practices that were difficult to grasp for the untrained eye.

Young artists frequented Fernand Leduc's studio on Lorne Crescent. Among them were several who gravitated around Borduas. From left to right: Marcel Barbeau, Pierre Leroux, Claude Gauvreau, Madeleine Arbour and Fernand Leduc (Photo: Maurice Perron, 1946. Gelatin silver print, 19.5 x 34 cm. Donated by the Maurice Perron family to the Musée national des beaux-arts du Québec [1999.207].)

As if these reasons were not enough to create a clannish atmosphere, there was another, even more decisive cause. It was that the dynamics characterizing modern art were subject to the pull of academicism on one side, which was considered sterile, and the pull of the avant-garde on the other, which was discursively defined as the only legitimate art form.[17] Contemporary art was forced to update its forms constantly and the artist, by necessity, was brought to adopt the latest trends. The push forward was a key concept to this way of defining creative acts. The famous cry of *Refus global*: "The past must no longer be used as an anvil for beating out the present and the future!"[18] could be directly applied to revolutionary art. As a result, budding artists who chose to imitate their elders or canvases that were mere pastiches, condemned themselves. It was no longer enough for an artist to simply trace out his path. He had to produce works that participated in a general artistic regeneration, that disrupted established codes, that got other young disciples to follow along and try to establish a particular style. The multiplication of artistic schools (Primitivism, Romanticism, Naturalism, Impressionism, Nabism, Fauvism, Cubism, Abstractionism, Dadaism, Surrealism, Futurism, Expressionism, Symbolism, Purism, Orphism, Unanimism) inevitably caused excommunications and ostracisms. André Breton, who lived to provoke sensational schisms, was symptomatic in this respect. Perhaps more than any other aesthetic trend, Surrealism built itself upon the dynamics of rupture, creating in this way a necessary game of exclusions, which exacerbated its subversive power.[19]

THE LATEST TREND

At the beginning of the 1940s, it was no longer possible to pretend that the history of painting had stopped with the Fauvists or Nabis. It was clear that another upheaval of considerable scale had made its mark on the arts in Europe during the first half of the century. "For weeks, months and years, a deep disquiet has come over us. It is because more and more works are presented to us as masterpieces, although they mystify us, displease us, and make our skin crawl. We feel that a new, powerful, and irresistible world is being built in our absence. How are we to remain indifferent to it?"[20] *La Voix des Amériques* (the French office of the radio station, Voice of America, run by Denis de Rougemont in New York) diffused a trailblazing vision of art by broadcasting the thoughts on the matter of refugee intellectuals such as André Breton, Fernand Léger, Georges Duthuit, Amédée Ozenfant, Jacques Maritain, and Marie-Alain Couturier. Among art lovers, avant-garde catalogues and magazines, such as *Minotaure* (1933-1939) and *Verve* (1937-1960) circulated at the time.[21] To a large extent, illustrated books succeeded in popularizing and making readily accessible disconcerting contemporary works of art. In addition to being able to soak up this culture via these daring publications, Montrealers also had the pleasure of admiring collections that rich European art aficionados brought with them. The Second World War, "despite causing atrocious tragedies across the world, was good for young intellectuals here as it allowed us to see an abundance of world masterpieces from all periods and all disciplines, ousted by the Nazi invasion of Europe"[22] For example, Henri Laugier's personal collection included drawings by Picasso, which Borduas enjoyed analyzing for the benefit of his students. There were also itinerant exhibitions, including those of the Dutch masters, which Borduas and his disciples appreciated enormously. Important collectors, such as Max Stern, who was the owner of the Dominion Gallery, founded in 1942, also became arbiters of the pictorial revolution. Thanks to such events and these connoisseurs, the artistic elite in Quebec gradually opened to "experiments and successes, ranging from Impressionism to Surrealism."[23]

Louise Renaud, who had initially gone to New York to enroll in painting courses, accepted a job as an *au pair* for Henri Matisse's son, as she needed money.[24] Pierre Matisse's gallery (which Couturier knew well[25]) regularly gathered Surrealists in exile, including Yves Tanguy, André Breton, Man Ray and Marcel Duchamp. Louise shared with her friends the marvels she saw and the talks she heard throughout her stay in America. Among the things she brought back to Montreal was a copy of Gisèle Prassinos' book, *La Sauterelle arthritique* (The Arthritic Grasshopper). Prassinos was a fifteen-year-old author who inspired a sister-author in Quebec, Thérèse Renaud, to write *Les Sables du Rêve* (The Sands of Dream), a collection of poems written when she was also fifteen years old, using similar writing techniques. Borduas, Fernand Leduc, Mimi Lalonde, Françoise Sullivan, Claude Gauvreau, Jean-Paul Riopelle, and Jeanne Renaud also visited New York for brief periods during which they explored museums and the plethora of galleries on 57th Street. "When I arrived at the New York's Museum of Modern Art," Claude Gauvreau remembered, "I felt like I was entering paradise on earth."[26] Irène Legendre (named to the École des Beaux-Arts upon her return) studied with Alexandre Archipenko and Amédée Ozenfant between 1939 and 1944 and took philosophy courses with Jacques Maritain. Madeleine Laliberté also frequented Ozenfant's studio. Charles Daudelin had visited Fernand Léger's studio, as well as that of Henri Laurens. From that point on, people talked about "returning from New York," in the same way others had spoken about "returning from Europe"[27] before the outbreak of the war.

Several exiled French intellectuals took advantage of the war to establish contacts with the French-Canadian milieu. Among the speakers who were invited to Montreal and Quebec, Fernand Léger retains special status. One of his talks, given at the Ermitage in May 1943, consisted of an impressive overview of the history of art, using slides to support his presentation. During this talk, Léger formulated a thesis according to which "visual realism," by attempting to replicate the exterior world so as to better espouse the times and the environment, could not prolong the development of the arts, as art strove on the contrary for "pictorial realism" or "conceptual realism," which deals with the objectivity of the work itself.[28] By wanting to imitate nature, the Renaissance had pursued a paltry illusion. In contrast, primitive art, popular art, Egyptian art and Byzantine art had fostered invention and freed up form, making colour, volumes and shapes the subjects of their paintings. The day after this conference, there was the opening of an exhibition of Léger's most recent works (the series entitled, *Plongeurs* (Divers) was included among them). In May 1945, Léger gave another talk, but this time on colour and architecture, in which he summarized his theory of the disassociation of colour and form. In his opinion, pure colour existed. He confessed to being fascinated by formal methods of painting. The subject of a painting was not hidden within the canvas but behind it, in an infinite space, which obliged the viewer to immerse himself or herself in the baroque universe of the painter. Léger preferred contrast over perspective. Technique was replaced by powerful emotions. Coincident to Léger's second talk, a collective critical work, called *Fernand Léger, la forme humaine dans l'espace* (Fernand Léger, The Human Form in Space),[29] was published by Éditions de l'Arbre.

Henri Laugier, another intellectual refugee in America, sensitized Quebeckers to the incommensurable potential of abstract art by his participation in diverse cultural events in Montreal, through his friendship with Father Couturier, by the encouraging remarks he made to Maurice Gagnon, by frequenting Pellan's studio, and through the discussions he had with Borduas.[30] Following Couturier's momentary departure for New York in 1943, Laugier wrote to him: "Do you know that I have been summoned to be your successor – or even to replace you – as propagandist for modern art in Montreal? I am beset by the numerous Clubs that poison Montrealers and make real workers turn away from their work, using them as entertainment for idle capitalists. And despite all this, I have promised myself to give a few talks, one of which will be "Introduction to toxic art!"[31]

It would be difficult to ignore another refugee of the war, even though he is not French, namely Alfred Pellan. Having been awarded several prizes and distinctions, Pellan, who was also the first-ever recipient of a grant given to an artist by the provincial government, left the École des Beaux-Arts in Quebec City when he was twenty years old to settle in Paris. Between 1930 and 1940, with no set plan, he discovered the works and writings of people like Pierre Bonnard, Max Ernst, Pablo Picasso, Paul Klee, Antonin Artaud and André Breton. And, this was when he was not meeting these painters and writers in cafés. As a recognized figure in multiple art galleries, salons and museums, Pellan had shown his works in Paris, London, Prague and New York. Within ten years, a hundred or so articles and notes on his works had appeared in both Europe and America. When Pellan came back to Canada, having fled Europe due to the war, he brought with him, like a treasure chest, a half-century of pictorial experiences. Guy Sylvestre, the editor of the literary page of the daily newspaper, *Le Droit*, spoke of Pellan as having played a decisive role in the acceptance of contemporary art in French Canada. "Alfred Pellan's return to Montreal in 1940 has to take on the proportions of a great event in our embryonic artistic life. His forceful personality allowed certain aesthetic tendencies found within the souls of young artists to manifest themselves openly. Without Pellan, such manifestations would have simply been ridiculed."[32] Irène Legendre, in her *Petite Histoire de l'art moderne* (Brief History of Modern Art), confirmed that Pellan was "the incontestable pioneer of modern art in the province" and that he exercised "a considerable influence over the young generation."[33] In 1943, Maurice Gagnon published an extremely praiseworthy booklet on the painter.

Jean-Charles Harvey admitted to changing his mind about abstract art after visiting Pellan's grand exhibition (161 works) in Quebec

City, which was shown in June 1940 at the Musée de la province du Québec, later known as the Musée national des beaux-arts du Qubec. "I didn't like the first abstract works I saw, especially in various magazine reproductions. In art, every innovation shocks our expectations. We form ideas that are too cut-and-dried. In the past, I had firmly thought that painting should be the exact replication of a given subject or a historical or symbolic scene, derived from known facts. Since then, I've had many discussions about this issue with artists and art lovers. They provided such good answers to my objections that today it is impossible for me to see as unreasonable what I though was absurd before."[34] For Harvey, as for a whole flock of other art lovers, Pellan created a formidable crack in the aesthetic canons that the French-Canadian elite had accepted until then. "We know that Alfred Pellan left his mark on Canada. He is the one who sparked modernity in our eyes. [...] With Pellan, modern art, in its most adventurous creations, established itself in the very heart of the young generation."[35]

It seems that Borduas' assimilation of so-called modern trends, and especially Surrealist ones, was also in part due to Pellan. "Paul-Émile Borduas was teaching at the time at the École du Meuble and seemed happy to become friends with Pellan, who preached to all those willing to listen about Apollinaire, Éluard, Picasso, and Breton's *Surrealist manifesto*. Borduas took advantage of this to bring himself up to speed, since his stay in France in 1929 had been filled with decorating churches in the Department of Meuse, while Pellan had been involved in the Parisian effervescence."[36] Confronted by Pellan's exuberant canvases, Borduas could not hide his admiration and compared his friend to Raphael, who was then generally considered the greatest painter of all. His influence over Borduas was at first so strong, Marcel Parizeau insinuated that the gouaches exhibited in the foyer of the Ermitage had been inspired by the paintings that Pellan had made in France and brought back to Canada.[37] In 1945, Claude Gauvreau wrote: "A few years ago, at a time when there were two memorable exhibitions in Montreal, Pellan's and then the exhibition put on by the

Galerie des arts featuring works by Braque and drawings by Picasso, enthusiasm gleamed in the sun and a group of young people's hearts were filled with faith and hope."[38] In this last quote, the mention of Braque and Picasso is not insignificant. At the time, Borduas was still struggling with a style inspired by these two masters.[39] Years after making the prodigious leap from sacred art to Surrealism, he continued to create semi-figurative works, which borrowed from Cubism and Fauvism (for example, *La Fustigée*, that dates from 1946). Pellan's influence could be felt in these experiments.

Pellan presented a challenge to French-Canadian creators. Since the avant-garde was defined by an ability to remain on the cutting edge of creation, it was fatal for artists to suddenly feel like they were being outclassed by the "master of [French] Canadian painting." As never before, Pellan's return stimulated pictorial exploration and research. Artists in Quebec were suddenly projected into the midst of the Parisian School's most advanced trends. At the same time, he forced them to imagine a path that could equal his own approach to art, if they wanted to continue to belong to the avant-garde. Now that Pellan was ahead, everyone else was logically behind and following. They needed to conceive a way of not being entirely left behind. They were confronted with an alternative: either condemn modernism in the name of healthy Western traditions (which went no further than Impressionism, or perhaps Fauvism) as Clarence Gagnon did in his posthumously published pamphlet, *"L'immense blague de l'art moderniste"* (The Giant Joke of Modernist Art),[40] or define a branch of visual arts that would situate itself beyond Pellan, "the most advanced and perhaps the first and only of our modern artists."[41] What could this artistic branch be? What would this visionary and prophetic tendency be? Finding an answer to these questions did not take long: for French Canadians, stalled twenty years behind Europe, it was Surrealism.

In 1938, Jean-Paul Lemieux hastily attempted to discredit Surrealist art, which in his opinion represented a "degeneration of Cubism" and a "combination of colour for colour's sake and form for form's sake, without any concern for the subject being treated."[42] But, there was a sense that pictorial evolution was moving in this direction. A year before, the media coverage surrounding Edwin H. Holgate's exhibition had presented Surrealism as "the most advanced art in Canada."[43] In 1940, in his history of modern art, Maurice Gagnon affirmed that classical art had gone through a cycle of conflicts, from Impressionism to Cubism by way of Fauvism, and that Surrealism had closed the cycle. Impervious to the great revolution embodied by creators like Marcel Duchamp, almost all art histories written between the time separating Jean-Paul Lemieux and Pierre Gauvreau called Surrealism, as fostered by Breton, the last stage in the pictorial quest. This virtually unanimous interpretation delighted some and exasperated others. As for the Quebec Automatists, they were not embarrassed to call Surrealism the only valid aesthetic movement of the time. In their eyes, it formed an unsurpassable horizon. It constituted the last word on cultural creation. When Breton announced to Fernand Leduc in a letter that he wanted to include Leduc and his Montreal friends as members of the international Surrealist group, Leduc answered: "Surrealism is at present the only living movement with a reserve of enough collective power to rally all the generous energies and guide them in the direction of developing life's full potential."[44] Still in February of 1950, and even long after, Claude Gauvreau, who turned a blind eye to certain decisive aesthetic innovations in the post-war period, considered that: "Surrealism most certainly had not been surpassed by any other European movement."[45]

Pellan agreed with almost everyone in supporting the idea that Surrealism, as least for the time, was the pinnacle of the evolution of painting in the Western world. Nevertheless, he drew conclusions that were opposed to those of the Automatists. For him, it was not enough to rush blindly into the latest trend in painting, excluding all others. Rather, it was better to explore all the old and new traditions, assimilating multiple historical veins of thought, and developing an encyclopaedic knowledge of approaches to painting. His career was dedicated to producing a personal synthesis of the École de Paris' different interpretations. His ideas coincided with those of intellectuals who thought that Surrealism had reached its peak around 1935, that the trend had gone out of fashion, and that one should not be restricted by it. He feared sharing an infatuation for something that was already worn out in Europe. It was better used as a creative resource, just like all other movements. In Pellan's courses, students most certainly learned to trust their instincts to reveal the "poetic world," the "surreal world"[46] that slumbered within them. However, making the collaborative works called "exquisite corpses," for example, was only seen as an experiment among many others, a technique that one had to become familiar with. Breton, who knew about the existence of a small group of disciples in Montreal, did not bother to meet Borduas when he visited Quebec in 1944, whereas he took time to see Pellan again, having known him in Paris. It was over the course of their meeting in the Gaspé that Pellan reiterated to the Pope of Surrealism his desire to integrate in his painting all historical aesthetic knowledge, a wish that Breton found perfectly absurd.[47]

As for Borduas, he presumed that "everything had been said about the visible world."[48] Figuration had exhausted itself by means of rigid imitations of nature and had given all it had to give. To regenerate style, it was necessary to look elsewhere. In Borduas' opinion: "The cycle of exterior nature came to an end with Renoir, Degas, Manet. The cycle of true expression, of the medium being used, as intermediary between the artist and the visual world, was closed by Cubism. Only one path remains open: toward the invisible world, specific to each artist, Surrealism."[49] Consequently, any painter who was satisfied with putting a little bit of Surrealism into the realist mix understood nothing of the revolution that was taking place. A period in art had definitively ended, was finished and emptied. It was time to embrace the new pictorial age, by accepting "the total risk in global refusal." Here, we can better understand the misunderstanding between Pellan and Borduas: the former saw things in terms of addition, whereas the latter saw things in terms of going beyond, and wanted to take all of Canadian painting in unexplored directions. Pellan later accused Borduas of making Surrealism, which he knew as well as Borduas, an exclusive obsession, a rigid recipe, whereas Borduas would accuse Pellan of not acknowledging the real potential of Surrealism and of not going beyond a static interpretation of Cubism.[50] This dialogue of the deaf could not have been more complete. Gabrielle Borduas, the painter's wife, explained what led to the falling out between the two painters by saying:

> Borduas had had unlimited trust in Ozias Leduc and became – as much as Leduc was classical in his ideas – abstract in his later years. Unlike Pellan, Borduas was not an interpreter. He was not inspired by what was being done in Europe, but rather discovered his own personal way of painting, which became the Borduas style or manner. Pellan did not at all approve of Borduas' explorations and even warned him against them. He assured him that he was making a mistake by working in such a way and that it would lead him nowhere. Borduas, angered by this and beside himself, taunted Pellan by saying that he was ready to fight him at the Forum. As each of them held strongly to their own ideas and individuality, Borduas and Pellan went their separate ways and never again spoke to one another.[51]

Adding to this first split was the conflict over the interpretation of Surrealism itself. From an exclusively pictorial point of view, Pellan's paintings are much closer to the vision of Breton who long remained hostile to non-figurative art. Like the dream-like works that Breton's early companions admired, Pellan's oil paintings would have been less out of place than Borduas' in an exhibition of works by René Magritte or Yves Tanguy. It was more the literary figures gathered around Borduas – Thérèse Renaud of *Les Sables du Rêve* (The Sands of

The second Automatist exhibition in February 1947 at the Gauvreau's house, 75 Sherbrooke Street West. Paul-Émile Borduas seated in front of his painting *Sous le vent de l'île* (Leeward of the Island) (Photo: Maurice Perron. Gelatin silver print, 26.0 x 33.5 cm. Donated by the Maurice Perron family to the Musée national des beaux-arts du Québec [1999.212].)

Dream), Paul-Marie Lapointe of *Le Vierge incendié* (The Virgin Burned), Suzanne Meloche of *Aurores fulminantes* (Livid Dawns), and Claude Gauvreau – who can be associated with the Surrealist tradition. However, from a philosophical point of view, Pellan was much less Surrealist than Borduas. Having no theoretical or political ambition, Pellan's revolution was confined to remain within "the plastic arts' ivory tower." The manifesto *Prisme d'yeux* is indicative of this ecumenical and eclectic stance. "While writing up the manifesto," declared Jacques de Tonnancour, "I could think of nothing but general ideas with respect to living art – so general in fact that one could ask if *Prisme d'yeux* was actually going in any particular direction."[52] Signed by Pellan, the manifesto, which appeared a few months before *Refus global* and which was a response to Borduas' growing authority in Montreal art circles (it was circulated in the media during the same week in which Borduas was elected as president of the Contemporary Arts Society), set its sights on nothing other than reforms to pictorial forms of expression. With respect to this, an anecdote, showing the bourgeois side of Pellan, is amusing. One day when he was in Montreal, he apparently invited Breton to spend an evening with him at some judge's home. Breton reacted to this invitation by saying: "At a judge's house? Why not at the executioner's!"[53]

As for Borduas, he was attracted to Surrealism because of its social ideology. He felt that there was an engaged quality to Breton's writings that corresponded well with his own.[54] "If our movement is like Surrealism," Riopelle stated, "it's because we think the same way."[55] Impressionism, Fauvism, even Cubism had not directly sought to overthrow the framework of Western society. These aesthetic trends had been content to claim the right to practice art outside of the academic canons dominant at the time. Breton, who had come from literary circles, adopted a different approach, and was always tempted by the need to clearly define his positions, to publish manifestos, to strike up associations with communist political parties, and wage a merciless war on the bourgeois world. He supported a philosophy and a spirituality, as much as he did a creative method. For Breton, it was not enough to put the established aesthetic approach on trial: he hoped to go further and formulate an all-encompassing critique of Western institutions and values. He gave his aesthetic actions a political flavour. Borduas seized upon this ideology and used it as a formidable weapon for contesting the dominant social order, which Pellan had never really considered. "Borduas brought the same energy to both non-figuration and his anti-bourgeois feelings, and he kept it right to the end. If you dissociate these two sides of the problem, separating the painter from the revolutionary, preferring his painting to his rebellion or his rebellion to his painting, you'll never understand either."[56] By making art, metaphysics, morality and politics come together, Surrealism contributed to the grand battle materializing between Borduas and French-Canadian society.

THE END OF A WORLD

The time has come, my dear Guy, for us to get together and adopt an unequivocal stance, to state clear-cut positions. At all costs, we must form a group that is small, uncompromising, respectful of what is essential in a work of art, doing group shows. [...] Borduas believes this is the only possible attitude at the moment. —FERNAND LEDUC

In the 1940s, Quebec Automatists shared the conviction that a planetary upheaval was imminent. In their eyes, the total and irremediable failure of religion, of the economy, of politics and of culture was forthcoming. "From here, we feel like we are watching the end of the European world [...], the end of Christian civilization."[57] They were not the only ones who believed that Western Christian civilization was going to be wiped out by an ultimate spasm, after five centuries of agony. Several artists, including the Catholic Albert Gleizes, prophesized the death of the Western world, which would happen after a period of devastating catastrophes.[58] For Gleizes, the cycle of civilizations followed a trajectory like that of living organisms: after a period of gestation, civilizations developed, attained maturity, entered an inevitable period of decay, and ended up disappearing. Just when societies seem most stable and flourishing, sclerosis can be felt in the appendages, religion becomes ritualistic and dogmatic, justice serves the privileged class and art gets locked into inviolable canons. Such was the uncontestable *fatum* of human history: between moments when civilization is alive and dynamic, celebrating visionaries and messengers of life, moments of incredible collective enthusiasm and audacity; between these gestational moments of a new civilization, there is always a difficult and painful period of transition during which apathetic generations feebly cling to the *status quo*. According to many observers, the 1940s corresponded to such a historical period of in-betweenness, when the languishing flame of the previous civilization was slowly fading and the light of a new one had not begun to shine overtly.

Far from depressing them, the conviction that the world as they knew it was coming to an end gave the Automatists great hope. They shared the conviction that a more human society would rise from the former's ashes. "It is not about the end of a world, but rather the beginning of a new one."[59] The modern world was dead, and another was waiting to be born, a thousand times more poetic and marvellous. "The day has come. We must renew our understanding of the world."[60] The Automatists felt like stakeholders in a "time of wild revelation," in an "unforgettable and frenetic time."[61] Fernand Leduc savoured this historic moment during which "the declining civilization's rubbish was still present and tried to stop the germination of new elements," this moment of "total decomposition," which was essential to give "rise to a fermenting life." It's a heroic time, an age of martyrs, of saints and cursed artists."[62] Jean-Claude Dussault, who met the little Automatist group shortly after the publication of *Refus global*, trembled with messianic emotion, saying: "Along with the others I, too, shared in the prophetic excitement as we waited for the 'grand evening,' assured, as we were, that we would be carried by the changing winds of history."[63] In June of 1950, when North Korea invaded South Korea, an event that led to the involvement of the United States and its allies, Claude Gauvreau's friends rejoiced at the thought of perhaps witnessing the "triggering of the third world war."[64]

This (non-Christian) eschatology was no doubt related to the craze for divorces, destruction and sacrifices, festering among the Automatists. They felt it necessary to cause apocalyptic disorder, so to speak, the fire of which would destroy all worn-out traditions once and for all. They would not avoid confrontation with oppressive powers, as a new civilization could only come about following a cruel and violent battle. "Obviously," Fernand Leduc wrote to Borduas in April 1948, "we have gotten to the point where we are savagely calling for the same destruction that made us shudder in the past. Massive and systematic destruction that erases all signs, including the memory of the present civilization. Mankind can no longer do anything for the salvation of mankind!"[65] Leduc concluded his letter with these prophetic words: "It is, however, no longer possible for me to see the manifesto written for our planned exhibition, in terms of anything but destruction, as this exhibition must be the flagrant sign of it."[66] Such cataclysms foretold a grandiose ending, which was finally going to unveil, in a supreme battle, the relics of the ancient world and the germination of a new one. "What's best on the way down," Borduas argued approvingly, "can only come about after what's worst. We should cynically foster this with all our violence."[67]

Everyone was preparing for the final assault against the province's obscurantist forces. So that "destiny inexorably is accomplished," heroic souls had to agree to deal the final blow to this dying civilization. The young Claude Gauvreau – who, when he was fourteen or fifteen, saw himself as a "steel robot, with heavy and unpardoning movements, steeped in determination and infallibility" or "a superman who was invincible to all blows, strolling along under a white sun"[68] – sought to be part of history's prophetic current. "Exalted by their new faith and totally disinterested, the new prophets do not back down when faced with threats and massacres. Their heroic behaviour, which is of course the most eloquent of models, causes their disciples to increase."[69]

One did not have to adhere to a political party to bring about the anticipated revolution. The tumult of human existence could only be tamed once another silence was forced upon the world, so people were asked to look into their hearts, to resist mundane invitations, and to make sure that a deceitful universe had no hold over them. The revolution that the Automatists were proposing was, in essence, spiritual. They wanted to change human sensibilities: "We did not have a real political engagement apart from our experimentations and the range of our ideas."[70] The expected transformation of the world involved a new way of seeing and of feeling first and foremost. "I never thought about liberating Quebec," Bruno Cormier maintained. "It was about freeing myself. Being a man, the most human possible."[71] Mousseau shared Cormier's view: "*Refus global* is more than anything else an ethic."[72] The word *anarchy* itself had to be understood in the broad sense (or, as Claude Gauvreau would have said, "generic"[73] sense): it primarily designated a fertile ground for creative activity. The revolution that Borduas foresaw was personal and moral.[74] This perspective did not encourage dropping out and even less defeatism, as the support for the asbestos strikers or the struggles in favour of freedom of speech (see the condemnation of the Padlock Law) show. On the contrary, this perspective made people aware of the need to become involved (what Borduas called "a passionate getting in touch"), although that contact first came about by bearing witness (hence the central use of letters to newspapers,[75] exhibitions, and discussion forums), and not through political action in the strict sense of the term.

The most patent example of this revolutionary attitude was the manifestation of the *Rebelles* at Montreal's Musée des beaux-arts in 1950. During the spring salon, seventeen individuals, including Jean-Paul Mousseau, Claude Gauvreau, Marcelle Ferron, Madeleine Arbour, Robert Roussil and Marcel Barbeau, marched into the exhibition hall wearing sandwich boards. Their panels bore anti-bôzard slogans – *Make way for living art! Cosgrove "mort pion"* (a pun meaning – dead pawn and *"morpion"* – crab lice), *On strike against the shitty jury, Poor Goodridge tired, Soon, an exhibition for the rejects*. Borduas had applauded this declaration of "collective poetry," as he considered it from the sole point of view of the conversion of the protestors themselves. "Whether the crowds secretly booed you or admired you changes nothing! Whether this battle brought followers or not, this does not change anything either: all of that pertains to external consequences, which will never change anything of a liberating act's positive value because it liberates the very person who commits it: in this affair, the question of the bystander is irrelevant."[76] Borduas did not care about the immediate repercussions of these actions on ignorant masses or the stubborn elite. By liberating themselves from conventions and proprieties, the *Rebelles* made a statement that involved them all; they could not back down. Who cared, under these conditions, what the impact of hostile and scatological slogans was on the posh and preppy audience at the spring salon? The value of an action had to be judged in terms of the author's moral fortitude.

The small group of Automatists where enthralled by an unshakable confidence in the resources of what Pierre Mabille called a new "egregore," an aggregate of individuals who could eventually expand to the point of invading all spheres of society.[77] There was hardly any doubt in their minds that the big bang to come was going to sweep away the old world and that an ideal society would rise from the ashes. Their role in this revolution had already been set out. Mabille had written it in golden letters: "I have insisted too much on it to reiterate the inevitable death of the whole Christian system. It is not enough to just watch its decomposition as bystanders. Our efforts are needed. The irrational survival of empty, useless, structures calls for removing the rubble, a clean sweep, as the revolutionary songs say. I affirm that nothing will remain tomorrow of what lies hidden under the sign of the cross or that prospers under its recommendations. The centuries to come will only retain the words of those who, having experienced difficulty and sacrifice, demonstrated the necessary unwillingness to compromise."[78] The "accumulated vivid forces" will then act like a spark that will set the whole of society ablaze. For Mabille, poets and artists together had the mission of spreading this gospel. They possessed the skills to "reveal to mankind the world they contain within themselves and which they shape, without knowing it." In this way, they will mark "the beginning of a new human cycle."[79] Through their message, they accomplished their individual destiny and expressed the emancipating language of the future. Because they embodied the emergence of an irreversible ethic that was going to swallow up the old traditions of the Christian world, it was incumbent upon them to produce works as powerful as atomic bombs, works which as Fernand Leduc wrote, "would bring about cataclysms, cause mass panic, command rebellion, all kinds of rebellion."[80] The young Automatists' need for provocation had nothing gratuitous about it: the grand awakening of the masses would only come about after an exemplary poetic explosion.

The exaltation felt by the Quebec Automatists was palpable. The future seemed radiant for the prophetic egregore gathered around Borduas. "No backtracking is allowed," wrote Borduas in February 1947. "The bridges have been burned, salvation is before us in complete generosity."[81] Under the impression that he could count on a growing number of solid allies, Borduas looked to the future with confidence. "Yesterday," *Refus global* proclaimed, "we were alone and irresolute. Today a group exists, with deep and courageous ramifications, some of them already spreading beyond our borders. [...] Let those moved by the spirit of this adventure join us."[82] The "escalating breakups," in Bernard Teyssèdre's words,[83] would reach their peak in 1948. Among a variety of events that year, we can cite Borduas' withdrawal from participating in the sixty-fifth spring salon; aborting the plan to publish texts and works by Automatists in the second issue of *Ateliers d'arts graphiques* when Borduas' group abandoned the project; scuttling the Contemporary Arts Society in February, even if the actual dissolution was only voted in November. Tensions had reached a boiling point.

In this effervescent context, Borduas believed it important to publish a text to disseminate his circle's ideas. "Within the group, there is a powerful desire to act, a great anxiety; we need to clarify things. We must eradicate misunderstandings, give contradictory elements some sort of order and unity."[84] In 1946, they pondered founding a journal that would make the Automatists' opinions better known, clarify their points of view and circulate works that were still improperly recognized, as well as publishing a catalogue to coincide with an art exhibition. They finally decided on the publication of a manifesto, in the purest Surrealist tradition (in June 1947, the French group, *Cause*, published its *Rupture inaugurale* (Inaugural Rupture), co-signed by Riopelle). The highly artisanal *Refus global* was typed up by Claude Gauvreau and Maurice Perron, and printed on a Gestetner copying machine. The pages were folded and put together by hand, without any binding, using a paper cover folded to hold loose pages. An initial printing of 400 copies came out in bookstores on August 9, 1948. In addition to the manifesto itself, the volume also included, by Borduas, *"En regard du surréalisme actuel"* (About Today's Surrealism) and *"Commentaire sur des mots courants"* (Comments on Some Current Words); by Claude Gauvreau, *Au Coeur des quenouilles* (In the Heart of the Bulrushes), *Bien-être* (The Good Life) and *L'Ombre sur le cerceau* (The Shadow on the Hoop); as well as Françoise Sullivan's paper *"La danse et l'espoir"* (Dance and Hope), Bruno Cormier's *"L'oeuvre picturale est une expérience"* (The Pictorial Work is an Experiment and an Experience) and Fernand Leduc's *"Qu'on le veuille ou non"* (Like It or Not). All of this was accompanied by a few illustrations.[85] Some people have suggested that the manifesto was published in the summer to avoid any confusion between Borduas' teaching duties and his pamphleteering activities, but according to Bruno Cormier, there were unexpected delays that prevented the manifesto from appearing in the spring.[86]

Hopes were high that this war cry would wake the province from its slumber. "We wanted to give birth to a gigantically influential egregore,"[87] recalled Claude Gauvreau. "We believed that a small group with a few clear-cut and precise ideas along with the qualities of their work, their freedom, and the freedom they discovered within themselves could overturn a society."[88] But, these illusions came to an abrupt end. The manifesto did create some waves, but it was quickly forgotten. French-Canadian society was not about to topple over from one day to the next due to the powerful shock wave elicited by Surrealist prose. In three months, 270 copies of the manifesto were sold. This number can be compared with the 6,000 copies sold of *Art et Bolchevisme* (Art and Bolshevism), published in 1946, in which the author vehemently criticized "modernist" scribblers and accused them of being agents of dehumanization.

```
                    S O M M A I R E


  1.  Paul-Emile BORDUAS.........  REFUS GLOBAL

  2.  ................. COMMENTAIRES SUR DES MOTS COURANTS

  3.  Claude GAUVREAU...........  AU COEUR DES QUENOUILLES

  4.  Claude GAUVREAU...........  BIEN-ÊTRE

  5.  Claude GAUVREAU...........  L'OMBRE SUR LE CERCEAU

  6.  Bruno CORMIER.............  L'OEUVRE PICTURALE
                                  EST UNE EXPERIENCE

  7.  Françoise SULLIVAN........  LA DANSE ET L'ESPOIR

  8.  Fernand LEDUC.............  QU'ON LE VEUILLE OU NON



                    _____


  Couverture de Jean-Paul RIOPELLE, texte de Claude GAUVREAU.

                    _____
```

Table of Contents of *Refus global*. The amateurish appearance of the publication did not prevent the religious and political powers at the time from reading it as a serious threat to their hegemony. (Paul-Émile Borduas et al., *Refus global*, Montréal, Mithra-mythe, 1948.)

The context in which *Refus global* was published could not have been any less favourable. Maurice Duplessis had just been re-elected Premier, having obtained eighty-two of the ninety-two seats. The provincial government did not hesitate to crack down on those it considered enemies of established order, which was apparent when they raided the offices of the newspaper *Combat* (the French-Canadian communist party's newspaper) by invoking the Padlock Law. The fact that alarmed souls complained loud and clear about André Gide receiving the Nobel Prize in Literature in 1947 was one sign among many others of the conservative climate reigning within the province. In October 1948, a few months after the publication of *Refus global*, *Quartier latin* was censured, and in the winter of 1949 its editorial team was forced by university administrators to step down for unclear reasons, but high among them were rumours circulating that certain articles had been considered too scandalous.

Within the Church, the brief, religious bright spell that occurred during the war, was followed by a darker time. After a few years of experimentation and openness, the Vatican put a stop to the aesthetic initiatives that Father Couturier proposed in his magazine *L'Art sacré*, as well as to innovations, be they pastoral (liturgical renewal), theological (personalism) or social (worker-priest movement), that had begun to shake up Catholic institutions. The Dominican Order was particularly affected by Rome's reaction, which would ultimately culminate in what Thomas O'Meara called the "1954 repression," when the Holy Office momentarily put a halt to the showing of the most daring works of modern art in Catholic churches.[89] Even though the Dominicans continued to keep the fire of reform burning, they had to publicly retract their most audacious opinions.

In the context of such censorship and general repression, who could Borduas count on to lead his crusade against entrenched authority? Most certainly not his colleagues at the École du Meuble! Father Marie-Alain Couturier had gone back to France, and his status as a priest made him, in any case, increasingly suspect in the eyes of the Quebec Surrealist brotherhood, which adhered to Breton's vehement anti-clericalism.[90] Henri Laugier had been called to Algiers at the end of 1943. Marcel Parizeau died in August 1945 at forty-seven. Maurice Gagnon handed in his resignation as a professor in October of 1947.

As for Jean-Marie Gauvreau, he was tired of quarrels among opposing members of the teaching body. "I am no longer willing to compromise the school's future," he wrote in April 1947, "with theories or with movements that do not concern it."[91] He did not want his establishment, which employed forty professors at the time, to fall prey to discussions that were not appropriate for a school of applied arts. He did like to think that his institution was praiseworthy, not only for its technical prowess, but because it could also hold its own vis-à-vis the snobbish pretentions of the Beaux-Arts. But, he first and foremost wanted his students to concentrate on manual work, such as making furniture for dining rooms out of tiger maple or bedroom sets out of white oak.

Borduas' popularity with the most active elements of the École du Meuble caused the creation of clans, with students bitterly taking sides for one kind of teaching against others and reviving the quarrel of the Ancients and the Moderns. Some accused the father of Automatism of playing on his popularity at the expense of his colleagues by fuelling students' infatuation for the gaudiest and most outlandish fads. Elzéar Soucy, the oldest professor in the school, turned purple at certain painting styles that were presented as ideal, when they had none of the good old Canadian spirit. "For the love of God! Let's not follow the Cubists, the Surrealists, the Futurists, and all those who thought they were ahead of the pack and are already out of fashion."[92] Such talk exasperated the young people gathered around Borduas. They could no longer tolerate the outdated principles of aging men like Soucy and were anxious to launch full-throttle attacks on the teaching establishments in Quebec, the "inheritors of papal authority, infallible, unjustified, grand masters of obscurantist methods" who were responsible for "the reign of exploitative memory, of stagnant reason, of harmful intentions." We can easily imagine Jean-Marie Gauvreau's reactions to such words.

The few students who had converted to the avant-garde during those years could not have harboured any illusions with respect to most people's sentiments. In the end, Borduas could count on only a handful of disciples among the 500 students enrolled at the École du Meuble. Partly out of obedience and partly out of fearing the consequences of open dissent, the majority of students continued to support the director. The situation was hardly more promising at the École des Beaux-Arts. In 1941, Armand Filion, president of the Beaux-Arts Alumni, expressed his lack of respect for those, who – avoiding the mould of realism – docilely accepted to make their works fit the forms of modernism.[93] Still in 1945, when a small group of Beaux-Arts students was hammering out the war cry: "Down with Maillard!" the student association condemned the rebels' lack of discipline and reiterated its confidence in Maillard. Whether at the École du Meuble or the École des Beaux-Arts, Borduas' influence was never enough to seriously diminish the young French Canadians' fearful respect of academic authority.

On examination, the signatories of *Refus global* were a minuscule group, united by unique personal relationships. Pierre and Claude Gauvreau were brothers. Thérèse Renaud (sister of Louise and Jeanne) had known Françoise Lespérance and Jean-Paul Riopelle for a long time, and Riopelle himself was an old friend of Maurice Perron. Françoise Sullivan had been friends with Pierre Gauvreau and Bruno Cormier since childhood. Pierre Gauvreau wed Madeleine Arbour, Marcel Barbeau married Suzanne Meloche, Jean-Paul Mousseau was married to Denise (Dyne) Guibault (Muriel's sister), Fernand Leduc was Thérèse Renaud's husband and Jean-Paul Riopelle wed Françoise Lespérance. There was perhaps only Marcelle Ferron, a friend of Gilles Henault's, who gravitated outside this limited circle.

Borduas was extremely disappointed when several people he respected declined his invitation to sign his surrational text, considering it too contentious. Among the youngsters, Guy Viau and Mimi Lalonde were frightened by the anticlerical content of the document. Yves Lasnier feared that his reputation would be tarnished and that this would cause financial difficulties for this family's company, which made and distributed church candles. Rémi-Paul Forgues, Madeleine

Desroches-Noiseau, Madeleine Lalonde, Suzanne Meloche, Serge Phoenix, Pierre Mercure and Adrien Vilandré also preferred not to compromise themselves by signing the provocative document. Among the elders, neither Maurice Gagnon nor Robert Élie, nor John Lyman signed *Refus global*. One after the other, two letters of *adieu* sent by Borduas in February 1948 forever compromised his friendship with Lyman and Gagnon. "Given the action that I am obliged to pursue on the cutting edge of 'events,' all sentimental baggage must be eliminated."[94] François Hertel, who was back in Montreal in October 1947 before moving to Paris for good in May 1948, cast only a distracted glance at *Refus global*. A hasty reading of the document was enough to convince him of its banality. He was not interested in defending a "little man [...], haughty, aggressive, and pretentious."[95] As for Pellan, we know that Borduas had not spoken to him since Pellan accepted the position of painting professor at the École des Beaux-Arts in 1944.[96] As a result, from the entire progressive milieu in Quebec, only sixteen signatures, Borduas' and those of his disciples, were attached to the bottom of the manifesto. A very small gathering.

What was most shocking in *Refus global* was obviously not the aesthetic opinions of the signatories, as those are largely absent from the principal text. Neither was its erotic or socialist character, stigmata of French surrealism. *Refus global* made no overt mention of sexuality and it broke with communism. Gérard Petit, who denounced Surrealism in his critical work *L'art vivant et nous* (Living Art and Us) under the pretence that this trend was encouraging licentiousness and vice, would have searched in vain in *Refus global* for anything comparable to Georges Bataille's erotic rants or quotes from Lenin. From this point of view, there was no danger to the morality of those who feared the infamy of "erotic obsessions" or "paranoid emotional states."[97] In his writing, Borduas continued to use the categories of good and evil, aligning himself with a sense of justice, of generosity, of duty, of knowledge and of the community spirit. There was nothing there to cause a public outcry.

No, what primarily scandalized people in the manifesto were the social and cultural considerations, which adopted views contrary to the dominant ideology. Neither praise given to "resplendent anarchy" nor a wish to get rid of "the holy water and the French-Canadian tuque" were pleasing in a province still dominated by clerico-nationalism. The parts dealing with religion turned off religious readers. The prose in the manifesto no longer fit with the vague notions of spirit and contemplation that had rallied Catholic personalists around Borduas after his 1942 talk, *"Des mille manières de goûter une oeuvre d'art"*. His later philosophical doctrine excluded divine transcendence. Even worse, the apostate, pillorying Catholicism, was pointing his finger at a form of Christianity walled up in its dogma and inward-looking, distancing itself from universal aspirations toward a "burning human fraternity." Borduas could not forgive the Church for seeking refuge "inside its liturgical fortress." He argued: "A marvellous world is being built, which is going to make this execrable Christian isolation explode: this solitude of the soul within the refusal of the universe."[98] Much like Hertel who was scandalized by clerical hypocrisy and turned against theology, the Church and God in a grand gesture of disdain, Borduas chose to condemn a moribund religion. Some said of Hertel that "[he] refused the destiny that had made him a member of French Canada's ruling elite. You cannot go further than that in terms of negation."[99] In fact, one could go further. Hertel had left the Church quietly, in silence, whereas Borduas outwardly profaned the religious idols of his youth. The former sacred art painter was boisterously turning himself into a sacrilegious intellectual and iconoclast.

The fact that some religious people, including Brother Jérôme, had been able to morally endorse the manifesto and that signatories of *Refus global* could claim the text did not deny the existence of God but only denounced the undue power of the clergy on temporal affairs;[100] both confirm the thesis of this study. But, this does not change reality. *Refus global* was undoubtedly an attack on belief in any divinity.

Robert Élie explained in the clearest manner possible what was problematic in the manifesto for a Christian personalist. He agreed with the idea that the artist was like a sorcerer and that individual visionary ideas allowed him to penetrate the mystery of life's secrets. He agreed with Borduas that in children's games, chance, the shimmer of the light, a detail in one of Cézanne's paintings – "everything has meaning, everything is light, everything is flowing with life." He also agreed with the virulent critique of a technological society. For him, as for Borduas, rationalism was opposed to pure and gratuitous art. He lashed out at the separation between the bourgeois elite and the avant-garde. He endorsed criticizing academicism. He understood that the artist could feel the need for isolation when he or she was not condemning a society that was nothing but "a vast enterprise of debasement." Moreover, he followed Borduas in his critique of French-Canadian society's routines and fears. But that is where his support ended. Élie could not accept a call to embrace a passion that was not somewhat temporized and controlled by reason. If passion could embody love, as Borduas suggested, it was often the face of hate, too. Élie also did not understand why *Refus global* identified Western civilization with Christianity, and made the irreversible downfall of the latter a consequence of the decadence of the former. Finally, and especially, he acknowledged that divine transcendence was the fulfilment of a human being's infinite aspiration, whereas Borduas, in his opinion, confused irrationality with surrationality; animal instinct with the call of the absolute.[101] Gérard Pelletier's analysis in *Le Devoir* adopted a similar argument to Élie's. He accepted all the arguments in *Refus global* except for the most central one: the negation of God's existence.

What Pelletier and Élie formulated in nuanced and polite terms was in the end not so different from what the province's right-minded elite thought, but in a less sophisticated manner. A note in the newspaper, *Montréal-Matin*, probably by Roger Duhamel, summarized what observers, who did not know much about modern art, did not like in the Automatists' manifesto: a pamphleteering prose, shaky grammar and spelling, simplistic anticlericalism.[102] People were surprised that a middle-aged man could write so poorly and lash out with such little regard for the majority's religion. The fact that the main signatory taught at a respectable institution added insult to injury. "If some nobody wants to take pleasure in door-to-door salesman anticlericalism, in poorly written French, that's up to him. But when it's a matter, as in Borduas' case, of a man called to shape youth, to make his mark in teaching, there's a difference."[103] For nationalists and clerics, the *Ministère du Bien-être social et de la Jeunesse* (Minister of Social Well-Being and Youth), official overseer of the École du Meuble, could not *not* react to this serious attack against the most sacred principles of the Union Nationale political party. Indeed, the deputy minister did not take long to inform Gauvreau that Borduas was being suspended.[104]

The École du Meuble – like the École des Beaux-Arts and the *École d'arts graphiques* (School of Graphic Arts) – not only had a mandate to provide solid professional training and teach the fundamentals of the trade, but it was also obliged to serve the well-being of French-Canadian youth by providing them with moral guidance. It was understood that the teaching staff's duty was to enforce good morals in scholarly establishments. This was even more true for the first two schools, because they were reputed to house careless and bohemian youth that needed method and discipline more than students in law or medicine. High moral standards for the teaching staff were also important. Claude Gauvreau had written: "The freedom of teaching does not give thoughtless morons the right to abuse the confidence of young minds and impose on them all kinds of conformist prejudices."[105] Those who were partial to conserving the fine arts tradition thought he was right, but now they reproached Borduas for using his position of authority to instil controversial ideas in his students. The rules at the École du Meuble stipulated that "professors who utter atheistic, immoral or amoral statements in front of students" would be susceptible to sanctions. This was clear enough, and it would have been a waste of time for Borduas, who certainly understood what was at stake, to claim he was indulging in "extracurricular activity." The manifesto was perhaps published outside the school year, but not outside a full-time professor's duties. Incidentally, with respect to the publication of "*Projections libérantes*" (Liberating Projections) the following year, there is no need to bring up a conspiracy theory to explain why it received such poor coverage in the press: the author was no longer a professor, and his writings were of no consequence from the point of view of institutional morality. In August, Jean-Marie Gauvreau could write to Borduas in this way:

> I discovered an article that appeared in the *Petit Journal* on the 15th of August 1948, entitled "Our Automatists declare the downfall of Christianity and prophesize the coming of the reign of instinct." You will not be surprised, I think, at my utter surprise to discover that a professor at the École du Meuble was the main protagonist of this kind of movement, because it is very difficult to disassociate your name from the position that you occupy. When acting in this way, I cannot believe, given your experience, that you did not realize the severe sanctions you were exposing yourself to. I wanted to know more about your attitude and your line of thought and so I read your manifesto. Do I need to add how much it pains me under the circumstances to need to ask an old collaborator for his resignation as a professor of the École du Meuble, so as to save him from, most probably, further and worse problems?[106]

There were four reasons invoked by Jean-Marie Gauvreau to justify Borduas' dismissal. The first was that a professor could not profess anticlerical views and anarchism without consequence. Second, that the publication of the manifesto was an act of insubordination, not having been approved prior its publication by the director of the establishment employing Borduas. The third recognized that the personal relationship between Gauvreau and Borduas had already reached a point of no return.[107] And fourth, Gauvreau could not accept that third-year students under Borduas' supervision did not yet know how to draw correctly.[108]

The last reason is not to be taken lightly. Borduas' moral teaching was not the only thing that raised questions. His teaching of techniques made him the object of growing suspicion, as we saw in the previous chapter. Claude Gauvreau was probably right when he affirmed that the master from Saint-Hilaire proved himself to be a generous, intelligent, attentive and open-minded professor; however, when Gauvreau declared that Borduas was always objective in his teaching, he had a curious way of defining this impartiality: "Mr. Borduas' teaching is recognized for its impeccable objectivity; he makes his pupils conscious of the *reality* of their own paintings, he unlocks their sensibilities in such a way that they manage to understand objective plastic form, he makes them sensitive to the subtleties of materials, he teaches them to judge not using abstract and conventional concepts, but by using their own personal knowledge."[109] This summarization is faithful to what we know of Borduas' pedagogical approach, but we must admit that for a drawing professor at the École du Meuble such praise had much to unsettle those who were hearing it. "Whereas Borduas aimed at forming painters, [Jean-Marie] Gauvreau, for his part, stuck to forming competent artisan-decorators. At the time, these were held as contradictory, and thus irreconcilable, objectives."[110] Hence, Borduas was dismissed from the École du Meuble in the fall of 1948 on grounds that he had committed a triple insubordination: professional, religious, and pedagogical.

Borduas argued during a press conference that the least they could have done was to ask him to resign instead of so cavalierly showing him the door. Yet, Gauvreau had already written to Borduas to suggest that it would be preferable for him to withdraw quietly. "If I may give you some advice, it would be to immediately hand in your resignation in writing, as this will involve less material disadvantages."[111] In this way, Borduas could have recovered his pension and avoided the dishonour of being fired. It seems, however, that he believed until the end that he would win the fight he was engaged in. When he learned of his dismissal, he thought of involving the media, just as Pellan had done three years before to his advantage. He even wrote to the Dominican Father Louis-Marie Régis to ask him to publish a review of the manifesto. He did not seem fully conscious of the irreversible nature of what he had done. He was wrong to accuse Gauvreau of evildoing (in the same way Pellan had targeted Maillard), because this time the firing had been decided at the Minister's office.[112] Some historians have interpreted the manifesto's publication as a well-thought-out act, the consequences of which Borduas had foreseen. In their opinion, Borduas had long thought over the implications of his bravado. Ten months before *Refus global* came out, Borduas had written to his former comrade, John Lyman, that his text involved his "whole life with no possible chance of escape." In my opinion, these words must not be taken for anything other than what they are: a refusal to soften the tone of his prose and to compromise. Today's reader will search in vain in this passage for any hint of Borduas' prescience. And Claude Gauvreau's testimony does not prove Borduas' foresight, either. Gauvreau met Borduas when the painter had just received the letter confirming his dismissal issued by Minister Sauvé. "Knowing what to expect is useless," Borduas had told Gauvreau. "It's nonetheless a shock!" But Borduas had received the news at the end of the month of October, when his definitive suspension could no longer surprise anyone.

Upon consulting archival documents, it seems more probable that the signatories of *Refus global* showed themselves to be a little naive. Their age, no doubt, excuses the naivety of their fight against men hardened by behind-the-scenes scheming and wheeling and dealing. For example, Jean-Paul Mousseau and Thérèse Renaud were twenty-one years old, while Jean-Paul Riopelle and Claude Gauvreau were twenty-five and twenty-three years old respectively. They lived in the hope of smashing down the walls of incomprehension and disdain that victimized them, of pulling Quebec out of its guilty stagnation, and of throwing themselves into the current of universal history. Such energy made them blind to the repercussions their actions were likely to cause. They lashed out without restraint at the powers that be; first and foremost at the Church, when this institution was still very powerful in sectors such as education, where they were trying to carve out a place for themselves. It is true that the Church's monopoly was being contested by other cultural organizations such as Radio-Canada (CBC Radio) and the National Film Board, but that did not help. "We never thought," Fernand Leduc confided, "that Borduas could lose his job, that we would be blacklisted and that they would prevent us from demonstrating. We just never thought about it."[113] Maurice Perron, Mousseau, Barbeau (but not Marcelle Ferron) shared the same somewhat naive confidence.[114] Bookstore salesman Henri Tranquille, no stranger to controversy, did not anticipate any trouble and was as stunned as the others by the outcry that *Refus global* provoked.[115] Borduas himself seemed to show his surprise at the widespread frantic reactions, when he said in a slightly disabused manner: "People may have thought I wanted to shake the foundations of society [with the publication of *Refus global*]. That was not at all the case. Others before me had said everything that I wrote. And, all the ideas were in the air. They could be spoken, but not written down. But, I don't regret a thing."[116]

Borduas himself became the victim of a total refusal: he who had denounced formulaic teaching, the Catholic Church, and French-Canadian society, found himself repudiated by pretty much everyone. What they were targeting were his anarchistic views and his militant atheism. In the province of Quebec, the quarrel focused less on the quality of the paintings than on the validity of Surrealist texts. At the time of Borduas' dismissal, few called into question his contributions to art. Many art critics recognized a definite quality in his paintings even if they preferred more restrained creations, like those of Alfred

Pellan. They distinguished Borduas the painter from Borduas the philosopher, finding merit in the one, and little value in the other. In fact, they frequently mocked his prose, going so far as to condescendingly claim, as Robert Élie did, that the master from Saint-Hilaire did not understand what he painted. This was their way of forgiving his strong language. Jacques Dubuc, for example, had no problem recognizing the value of criticizing intention in art, the goal of art being to free up "objective mysteries." He only condemned the Automatists for applying an attitude appropriate for artistic creation to the political domain. Increasing intention seemed to him a better philosophy for human societies than a utopia of "resplendent anarchy." "In the end, if we analyze the Surrealist experiments, we see that they put on the wrong eyeglasses: they delved into the area of philosophical thought with a kind of approach that was not of the same nature. Their basic intuitions are artistic, moral." While Dubuc accepted "the profound desire to change the sources of modern life directed by personal interest," he did not believe it was possible to transpose "the search for authentic life," as it applied to art, into other areas of human activity.[117] But these fine distinctions could not erase the fact that Borduas had talent, a talent which had been recognized by art lovers in Toronto, New York and Paris. One clear sign of resistance by certain official circles was the cancellation of a Borduas retrospective being organized by the team of *Le Quartier latin* at the University of Montreal. But Borduas did win first prize at the sixty-sixth Spring Salon in 1949 at Montreal's Musée des beaux-arts. And, Minister Omer Côté, of the Union Nationale agreed to sponsor the exhibition of the *Quatre Peintres du Québec* (Four Painters from Quebec), which Borduas was part of, at the Musée national des beaux-arts du Québec in 1949; a decision that indicates how the government's sanctions did not primarily concern Borduas' painting but rather his teaching, in the broad sense of the term.

Eventually it was not only Borduas' painting that was celebrated, but the whole movement that he had set in motion and that had become a force to reckon with in the 1950s. Brother Jérôme wrote to Borduas in 1958: "All your students, Robert Élie, Guy Viau, Claude Vermette, J.-P. Mousseau, Gérard Notebaert, etc., are now in key positions or on the edge of being publicly recognized. All your ideas are making headway and appear to be crushing everything that opposes them."[118] It was not, however, a complete triumph, far from it. There was still resistance, which blocked full recognition of an art freed from the weight of tradition, to the point where certain members of the academy were pretending to fear the imposition of a new ensemble of pictorial rules if ever Automatism were recognized. Pierre Gélinas criticized Claude Gauvreau in 1954 for having taken on the role of the grand inquisitor of styles and of replacing reasoned argumentation with categorical condemnation. "We are witnessing the establishment of a new academicism (that is to say, the pretention of being the only one who holds the whole and immutable truth, while, like all religions, calling for the extermination of infidels.) [...] History has curious turnabouts; Mr. Gauvreau is showing the same attitude to people who do not share his views, as Mr. Maillard was correctly condemned for by Gauvreau's predecessors: of being intransigent, self-important and having the kind of boundless assurance that only faith tolerates."[119] Obviously, the fundamental difference was that Gauvreau's intransigence turned toward social justice and human emancipation, and not toward religious preaching and the securing of privileges. What did it matter? Those who felt that their position was threatened tried to associate the movement that Borduas initiated with facile formulas for painters looking for a fight. It was to no avail. The old established aesthetic was falling apart in its entirety due to a development in the teaching of the arts that transformed artist-bohemians into salaried professors, by the rise of public cultural institutions, and by an expanding art market.[120] In 1962, Borduas was granted a first retrospective at Montreal's Musée des beaux-arts. His ideas had finally triumphed, twenty-five years after obtaining his position as a drawing professor at the École du Meuble. Unfortunately for him, he was unable to attend this moment of historical revenge. He died in Paris shortly before, in February of 1960.

The condemnation of *Refus global* by the self-righteous elite did not ring the death knell for the art revival movement in Quebec, as this gallery opening at the Librairie Tranquille in July 1949 shows. From left to right: Pierre St-Germain, Rolland Boulanger, Charles Doyon, Jacques Delisle, G.G Mac-Donald, Roger Guil, Henri Tranquille, and an unidentified art critic. (Photo: Maurice Perron. Gelatin silver print, 25.5 x 25.5 cm. Donated by the Maurice Perron family to the Musée national des beaux-arts du Québec [1999.289].)

CÉZANNE'S ONIONS

Art's redefinition at the end of the 1930s meant that painting was no longer considered a pastime or a technique useful for architecture or cabinetmaking. It was no longer an idle bourgeois pleasure, nor was it the useful skill of an artisan and a professional. Rather, it became a dynamic principle of society and morality, and simultaneously a formidable means of expressing one's soul. It was capable of civilizing matter, of even touching the spiritual aspect of life, and manifesting the "power of the spirit." However, throughout this period, people remained true to the Thomist definition of art being a mix of reason and passion, and did not accept French-Canadian artists abandoning themselves to their impulses and their personal instincts. That was the real background of Father Hyacinthe-Marie Robillard's and Henri Girard's violent rejection of Automatism.[1] They believed that Surrealism in painting was entirely a materialist endeavour with no interest in transcendence. Yet, people felt that this was the only direction for the evolution of painting and that the "boundaries of poetry," which Maritain spoke about, were being more and more contested from the inside. The "boundaries of our dreams" would never be the same again.

We should not forget that this revolution was made possible by the energetic action of many people, including those who ended up breaking away from the Automatist phalanx. In October 1943, Jean-Gilles Flynn dated the rebirth of painting in French-speaking Canada from the outbreak of the Second World War, even if it had been in the works over the course of the previous ten years or so. "Lyman, a very erudite intellectual, organized a circle over which he exercised a healthy influence: he founded a society. Father Couturier gathered a group of people. And, as the elements came together, Pellan came back to Canada at that precise moment and was very influential. I will add that Maurice Gagnon contributed a lot to the movement by forming taste and bringing sympathizers to the movement with his courses and the papers he gave in *collèges.*"[2] Another witness corroborated the fact that the "airing out started by the Contemporary Arts Society," "the renewal undertaken by Maurice Gagnon, P.E. Borduas and Marcel Parizeau," "the brilliant splash created by Pellan's return" and "Father Couturier's talks" pushed young people to call academicism into question for good.[3]

Furthermore, internationally, the functioning of Western society radicalized the process of art for art's sake and progressively emancipated painting from considerations that had nothing to do with aesthetics themselves. The doctrine of art for art's sake, indeed, responded to a process of autonomisation taking place in all spheres of human activity. Just as the liberal economy folded back on itself more and more and science became its own law, art sought to free itself from all principles that were exterior to the creative process. It is hardly surprising that, for many artists, this philosophy ended in anarchy. Even Irène Legendre's *Petite histoire de l'art moderne* (Brief History of Modern Art) which she dedicated to Alexandre Archipenko and Amédée Ozenfant and which was anything but provocative, could do nothing other than disassociate art from morality, from codes, from techniques, from cultures, academic lessons, colours and lines, and concrete reality. Here, her line of thinking coincided with that of Father Couturier who wrote: "The more the artist elevates himself, the more he frees himself; rids himself of materials and methods. [...] Great artists are independent: they do what they please, they do what they want with what they want."[4] Art had become an end in and for itself and its magic was lodged within its irreducible gratuitousness.

Little by little, Catholic art critics had opened up to abstract art and finally grasped the importance of the three breaks Father Couturier had spoken about: The break with the official milieu of painting, with plastic mimesis, and with rationalism. Such awareness allowed for a fertile dialogue to develop between Christians and Surrealists. Hence, in the 1940s, André Rousseaux was able to acknowledge that Surrealism was "one of the remarkable forms in which the Surreal could reenter a world that had been deprived of it."[5] Having reconciled himself with Breton's writing, Rousseaux showed how the Pope of Surrealism's works used a vocabulary filled with Christian words like faith, grace, gospel, communion, revelation, mystery and incarnation. He invited Christians to draw on the Christian sap flowing implicitly within Surrealist texts. Many followed his advice. René Bergeron is a particularly interesting case of such a conversion. In 1945, he lashed out at avant-garde artists and cursed the critics who took advantage of their positions of authority to call into question the École des Beaux-Arts and lecture style of teaching. "I heard you say: 'Down with school! Down with academicism! Down with Maillard! Down with titles!' I heard you say to a young female artist 'no schooling or formal training' – which is nonetheless the 'most authentic example of painting' – that she should not see what others are doing and that she should consequently not visit museums, for fear of losing in these establishments her 'pure naivety.'"[6] It was this same man, who fifteen years later, in *L'Art et sa spiritualité* (Art and its Spirituality) had an epiphany. In his mind, modern art no longer deserved to be universally condemned. Admitting he had erred in certain past judgments, he went so far in his *mea culpa* to purposely include reproductions of Borduas and Riopelle's works in his book.[7]

What contributed to this rehabilitation was the conviction that abstraction was better at pointing out the correspondences between the visible and the invisible, by means of shape, colour and volume, than realistic art using a story or objects. Painters who gave themselves over to such an art would have discovered, by speaking the language of the heart, how to reveal the secret poetry of the universe and make their canvases a place of personal meditation. In the eyes of personalist

Catholics, people like Dali, Masson and Matta practiced an art of enchantment superior to the sloppy works of Italianist painters cluttering church walls. They transcended the false classicism of a sectarian and limiting Davidism. "We now suddenly realize that those we believed were anarchists have prolonged tradition in such a perfect way that, without them, the chain would have been broken. They were the living tradition, they embodied a moment of evolution in art, but adopted a form that it took us a while to recognize."[8] Progressive Catholics believed that in Borduas they found a witness to the long tradition of nostalgic yearning for the absolute. In Quebec, he was the one who had best known how to transcend matter and see through it to the secret dimension organizing the universe. He was able, or so people said, to express the sublime essence of beauty, free and personal, which shone beyond the natural world. This art, totally free from physical reality, was said to point in the direction of the ineffable. That such poetic creation confounded the naive art lover and left him feeling lost was entirely normal, because the true artist comes into his own by continually searching for novelty. His conflict with the elite petite bourgeoisie bore witness to the authenticity of the painter's quest and the irrepressible need to be at one with that part of himself seeking to come into contact with the impalpable truth of the world.

In his autobiographical essay *Nègres blancs d'Amérique* (White Niggers of America), Pierre Vallières drew a portrait of a Montreal artist, called Maurice. He had met him in 1957 during an exhibition of his works at the Musée des beaux-arts. As a diligent reader of Mounier, Ramuz, Bernanos, Berdiaeff, Unamuno and Teilhard de Chardin, and a personal friend of Albert Béguin, Maurice felt a personal responsibility for the world crisis. He believed that true revolution began in people's minds and continued in their hearts. It did not occur by means of a disruption of social structures or economic relations. He fled the noisy crowds and political turmoil to better find peace within himself and rediscover the metaphysical meaning of reality. "It was necessary to live in being for being's sake, as one lives in art for art's sake, to discipline one's mind according to the individual search for what is essential: the basis of human existence."[9] Maurice could spend hours contemplating Cézanne's canvases, as if they were a door behind which lay the obscure pathways of the soul. He stood before Cézanne's *Nature morte aux oignons* (Still Life with Onions) "as *believers* do when adoring the host, seeing God within it." Vallières wrote: "Maurice believed that true engagement, for each and every man, meant accessing his original purity through art and prayer and drawing from this exercise, for mankind's benefit, not only a sort of grace that would wash humanity of its stain, but a light that would show the heart of the world to mankind."[10] Night, darkness, misery itself became trials greeted with joy, as the artist always became one with the absolute through a certain catharsis, in a more or less painful and angst-ridden crossing.

There is no doubt that this Maurice would have contemplated Borduas' creations "as believers adore the host." For that reason, many misunderstandings were inevitable between the master from Saint-Hilaire and progressive Catholic art critics. When Borduas was drafting *Refus global*, he was no longer Christian. He had followed a trajectory that placed him in deep contradiction with his former allies from *La Relève*, a journal that (in perhaps a significant coincidence) folded in September 1948. His painting had nothing Catholic about it anymore. During his exile in France, he would even end up distancing himself from Surrealism, which he considered too close to "the purest of Christian poetry." But that, precisely, no longer mattered for personalists, who agreed that the richness and depth of Borduas' works back when he was trying to impose himself as a church painter had nothing to do with their subjects or their religious intention. Why would it have been otherwise after he turned toward abstract art? "I don't believe I'm twisting the meaning of the words," wrote Guy Viau, in the Christian magazine *Maintenant* "by affirming that even as an unbeliever, Borduas was a deeply religious thinker. To a large extent, his works bear witness to this and are situated, as he himself said, 'beyond the visible.'"[11] Thus, there was a certain connection with people like Robert Élie, Gérard Pelletier, Roger Rolland, Guy Viau, Charles Lussier, Irène Legendre and Gérard Lortie. Trusting in a hidden God,[12] these Christian intellectuals agreed to initiate a dialogue with atheism, socialism, anarchism and Surrealism. They assimilated the subversive strength of doubt and wanted to make life a journey off the beaten path. Consequently, discovering God could only take place if one attempted to reveal the signs of His presence, signs that were no longer available in a single block through the dogmas of an institution, but rather appeared in the obscure depths of the self. For them, Borduas' highly disturbing works from his last cycle, *Translucidité* (Translucidity) or *L'Étoile noire* (Black Star), could not have been more beautifully painted.

This attempt to strike a balance between Christian mysticism and Borduas' paintings was clearly foreign to the painter's way of working. They made him a mystic searching for a reality situated beyond things, and not always already in things. Nothing could have irritated Borduas more. "It is unpleasant for me to hear myself being characterized as a mystic. I would not say that a tree is mystical because it bathes in the universe. I would not say that, either, about a man who has a pressing need to live all his potential."[13] What Borduas wanted was to live fully, without constraints, to savour the joys of existence, to establish, as he would say, "the most elementary of contacts, the most immediate, the most humble, the most of 'vulgar' of contacts with everything"[14] and give priority to an "amorous union with the whole of everything that is."[15] According to this anarchist, he had experienced enough new emotions and made enough discoveries in this world to live a thousand lives in wonder and joy. Offended by a morality full of contrition, taboos, inhibitions and limitations, he confessed, incidentally, that the title of his celebrated manifesto had been poorly chosen: his utopia did not envision a refusal, but rather a global or all-encompassing acceptance of life and its richness. Borduas was a man of love, of passion, of delight, and of terrestrial pleasures. He cared little for promises of eternal life because he felt an urgency to simply live his life here on earth.

Marxist theory had contributed to Borduas' abandonment of a supernatural interpretation of history. The notion of the soul could not survive this materialistic vision, which defined passions in terms of "behaviours of the material world, which were linked to the biological development of matter itself."[16] For the father of Automatism, the soul was nothing but a "difference of intensity" in matter, a certain "finesse in matter" or a "thinking quality of matter."[17] Nevertheless, Borduas did not recognize that this monistic view retained something of personalism, in that it still invited people to commune with the universe. After he moved to the United States, Borduas insisted even more on the impersonal character of the reconciliation he dreamed of: chance gave way to accidents, light to space, society to the cosmos, France to America. Nostalgia for the Middle Ages and his romantic perspective had disappeared. The hope of complete union with the cosmos had also vanished. After so many disappointments, failures and denials from friends, Borduas cared little about being "nothing more than a solitary man."[18] More than ever before, he accepted the personal contemplative nature of the creative act. "Painting 'in light,' however abstract, is still, personalist morbidity – even more moving after WOLS [pseudonym of Alfred Otto Wolfgang Schulze] – all of that, is *fi-nished!*"[19] He came to realize that the universe is "impersonal, totally impartial personalist morbidity – entirely cold and indifferent to who we are."

Had Borduas changed fundamentally? Even if in a letter sent to Claude Gauvreau, he wrote that his painting "was heading off in the direction of another world [compared to his latest abstractions], a more impersonal and more general one," focusing less on "nice little silly elements" so that he could "find divine impersonality – which we would call today – cosmic,"[20] Borduas continued to wish for an intimate union with some cosmic reality. For instance, what he liked about Jackson Pollock's paintings was that they managed to conjugate "the reality and the unforeseeableness of a grain of sand" and "the emotional quality of the painter."[21] He wrote: "Pollock…exasperated by not being able to express the intensity of an indeterminate feeling, […] takes the magnificent risk of turning his nose up at what he can like in painting and gives free rein to his ardent and energetic passion without really worrying about results. In this way, accidents, which he multiplies infinitely, show themselves capable of expressing at the same time physical reality and mental qualities without the aid of images or Euclidian geometry."[22] These words seem to indicate how Borduas' thought had not radically changed while in exile. The master from Saint-Hilaire still sought to cause "accidents of a human nature," which would allow for spiritual exploration through the manipulation of matter. In this way, and in this way only, progressive Catholics were correct to say about Borduas' painting, what André Malraux said about art in general, that it aspired toward an absolute that had deserted the world. "[Art] is not a religion, but a faith. It is not something sacred, but rather the negation of an impure world."[23] Filling the void left by the decline of religions, art promised to mend the torn fabric of human existence by opening onto an unnamed other-worldliness even though that transcendence was now revealed through the immanence of artistic and plastic endeavours. It was this belief, as this essay has shown, that created space for dialogue in the 1940s between Borduas, the impertinent atheist, and the most enlightened Catholics of his time.

NOTES

THE THRESHOLD

[1] Maurice Gagnon, *Sur un état actuel de la peinture canadienne*, (Montreal: Société des Éditions Pascal), 1945, p. 85. Bernard Morisset, "Nous sommes avec vous, Borduas!" *Le Canada* (October 2, 1948): 4. André Jasmin, "Le climat du milieu artistique dans les années 40." In *Peinture canadienne*, (Montreal: Presses de l'Université de Montréal), 1970, p. 22.

[2] Robert Élie, "La peinture: Borduas," [1946], in *Oeuvres*, (Montreal: Hurtubise HMH), 1979, p. 585.

[3] Read, among others, Jean-Philippe Warren, *Un supplément d'âme. Les intentions primordiales de Fernand Dumont*, (Sainte-Foy: Presses de l'Université Laval), 1998.

[4] Jean Éthier-Blais, *Autour de Borduas. Essai d'histoire intellectuelle*, (Montreal: Presses de l'Université de Montréal), 1979, p. 183.

[5] François-Marc Gagnon, *Paul-Émile Borduas: A Critical Biography*, (Montreal and Kingston: McGill-Queen's University Press), 2013.

[6] Jean-Éthier Blais, *Autour de Borduas*, p. 88.

[7] Robert Élie, "Borduas à la recherche du présent." *Oeuvres*, (1968), p. 605.

[8] As inspiring as it may be, Anne Davis' book *The Logic of Ecstasy: Canadian Mystical Painting 1920-1940*, (Toronto: University of Toronto Press), 1992) cannot serve us directly. Davis wished to show how the painters Emily Carr, Fred Varley, Bertram Brooker, Jock MacDonald and Lawren Harris portrayed a certain mystique in their landscapes, whereas I am trying to understand how religious progressives wished to dialog or rather recuperate an art that was increasingly fleeing their grasp.

[9] Charles Doyon, "S.A.C. 46." *Le Jour* (February 23, 1946): 5.

[10] Jacques Ferron, Claude Gauvereau. From "Du fond mon arrire-cusine" translated by Ray Ellenwood in *Exile, A Literary Quarterly* 3. 2. 1976: 20-57.

[11] Patricia Smart, *Les Femmes du Refus global*, (Montreal: Boréal), 1998. Also see Rose-Marie Arbour, "Identification de l'avant-garde et identité de l'artiste: les femmes et le groupe automatiste au Québec (1941-1948)." *RACAR – Revue d'art canadienne* 21. 1-2 (1994): 7-21; "Le cercle des automatistes et la différence des femmes." *Études françaises* 34. 2-3 (1998): 157-173. Patricia Smart, "Seven Women Who Dared to be Different: The Women Artists of Quebec's Automatist Movement." Florence Bird Lecture, Carleton University, Ottawa, 1997.

[12] Marie-Alain Couturier, *Dieu et l'art dans une vie. Le père Marie-Alain Couturier de 1897 à 1945*, (Paris: Éditions du Cerf), 1965, p. 342.

OUR ANXIETY

[1] Esther Trépanier, *Peinture et modernité au Québec (1919-1939)*, (Quebec: Nota bene), 1998, p. 10. Also see Yvan Lamonde and Esther Trépanier (Dir.), *L'Avènement de la modernité culturelle au Québec*, (Quebec: Institut Québécois de recherche sur la culture), 1986. For more information dealing with artistic education during the first half of the twentieth century, see Olga Hazan's *La Culture artistique au Québec au seuil de la modernité. Jean-Baptiste Lagacé, fondateur de l'histoire de l'art au Canada*, (Quebec: Septentrion), 2010.

[2] François-Marc Gagnon and Louise Dupont-Tanguay's bibliography established in 2006, comprises eleven pages. I invite the reader to consult the following site: www.borduas.concordia.ca/about. See Louise Fournel (directly linked to the topic of Borduas), "Création picturale et expérience du sacré chez Paul-Émile Borduas," Doctoral thesis, University of Quebec in Montreal, 1987; as well as Pierrette Jutras, "Mises en scène de la peinture non-figurative autour de Refus global (1935-1960)," Doctoral thesis, University of Quebec in Montreal, 2002. In addition, Louise Vigneault's very insightful book, *Identité et modernité dans l'art au Québec. Borduas, Sullivan, Riopelle*, (Montreal: Hurtubise HMH), 2002.

[3] Letter from Paul-Émile Borduas to Jean-Paul Riopelle, Saint-Hilaire, February 21, 1947 in Paul-Émile Borduas, *Écrits II*, Vol. 1, *Journal, correspondance (1923-1953)*, (Montreal: Presses de l'Université de Montréal), 1997, p. 193. Gilles Lapointe, "Un soleil noir dans le sablier automatiste: la constellation Breton," in Claude Beausoleil's (Dir.), *Héritages du surréalisme*, (Montreal: Éditions du Noroît), 2010, pp. 51-63.

[4] Esther Trépanier, *Jewish Painters of Montreal: Witnesses of Their Time, 1930-1948*, (Montreal: Les Éditions de L'Homme), 2008.

[5] Christopher Varley, *The Contemporary Arts Society, Montreal, 1939-1948: La Société d'art contemporain, 1939-1948*, (Edmonton: The Edmonton Art Gallery), 1980. Louise Déry, "L'influence de la critique d'art de John Lyman dans le milieu artistique québécois de 1936 à 1942," Master's thesis, Laval University, 1982. Louise Dompierre, *John Lyman (1886-1967)*, (Kingston: Agnes Etherington Art Centre), 1986. Molly Pulver Ungar, "The Last Ulysseans: Culture and Modernism in Montreal, 1930-1939," Doctoral thesis, (Toronto: York University), 2003.

6 Marcel Fournier and Robert Laplante, "Borduas et l'automatisme: les paradoxes de l'art vivant," in Paul-Émile Borduas' *Refus global, projections libérantes*, (Montreal: Parti pris), 1977, pp. 103-145.

7 Marcel Olscamp, "Un air de famille. Entre *La Relève* et *Refus global*: la génération cachée." *Tangence* 62 (2000): 7-33.

8 Pierre Popovic, "Les prémices d'un refus (global)." *Études françaises* 234. 3 (1987): 19-30.

9 Pierre Gélinas, "Pellan, par Maurice Gagnon." *Le Jour* (December 18, 1943): 5.

10 For more information on Jacques Maritian's influence in Quebec, see Yvan Lamonde and Cécile Facal, "Jacques et Raïssa Maritain au Québec et au Canada français: une bibliographie." *Mens* 8. 1 (2007): 157-274. Florian Michel, *La Pensée catholique en Amérique du Nord. Réseaux intellectuels et échanges culturels entre l'Europe, le Canada et les États-Unis (années 1920-1960)*, (Paris: Desclée de Brouwer), 2010.

11 Robert Charbonneau and Claude Hurtubise, "Ce que nous devons à Jacques Maritain." *La Nouvelle Relève* 2. 2 (1942): 70. Marie-Thérèse Lefebvre, "L'influence de *Art et Scolastique* de Jacques Maritain au Québec dans les années vingt," in Sylvain Caron and Michel Duchesneau (Dir.), *Musique, art et religion dans l'entre-deux-guerres*, (Lyon: Éditions Symétrie), 2009.

12 Jacques G. de Tonnancour, "Art et logique." *Le Quartier latin* (March 3, 1940): 5. He uses the same words in "Des beaux-arts..." *Le Quartier latin* (March 15, 1940): 5.

13 Thérèse Renaud, *Un passé recomposé. Deux automatistes à Paris. Témoignages, 1946-1953*, (Quebec: Nota bene), 2004, p. 20. François Gagnon, "Contribution à l'étude de la genèse de l'automatisme pictural chez Borduas." *La Barre du jour* 17-20 (1969): 228.

14 Jean Le Moyne, "Signes de maturité dans les lettres canadiennes." *Le Canada* (October 12, 1943): 11. "In the last few years, Montreal has become an interesting place. Many of the European refugees who came here to live have raised the cultural level of the city considerably." Paul-Émile Borduas, "Local Art Exhibitions." *The Standard* (October 20, 1943): 16.

15 Marie-Dominique Chenu, "Paroisse et oeuvres. Les exigences de *l'Action catholique*." *Revue dominicaine* 40 (1934): 343-358.

16 Jacques Petit (Dir.), Maritain-Mounier, *Correspondance 1929-1939*, (Paris: Seuil), 1973, p. 116.

17 According to notes taken by André Laurendeau, Centre de recherche Lionel-Groulx, P40/C6, 12, quoted by Yvan Lamonde, "*La Relève* (1934-1939), Maritain et la crise spirituelle des années 1930." *Les Cahiers des Dix* 62 (2009): 172.

[18] E.-Martin-Meunier and Jean-Philippe Warren, *Sortir de la Grande Noirceur. L'horizon "personnaliste" de la Révolution tranquille*, (Sillery: Septentrion), 2002. Michael Gauvreau, *The Catholic Origins of Quebec's Quiet Revolution, 1931-1970*, (Montreal and Kingston: McGill-Queen's University Press), 2005.

[19] Charles Péguy, *Lettre à Lotte*, quoted by Henri Daniel-Rops, *Notre Inquiétude*, (Paris: Perrin), 1963, p. 282.

[20] A.G., "Daniel-Rops." *Le Quartier latin* (November 29, 1934): 10. "Along with Péguy's, only Daniel-Rops' work, inspired by the doctrine of the New Order, can bring us the true revolutionary formula which is French, that is to say personalist." Jean-Marie Parent, "L'oeuvre de Daniel-Rops." *Le Quartier latin* (April 16, 1937): 4.

[21] Henri Daniel-Rops, *Notre Inquiétude*.

[22] Pierre Dournes, *Daniel-Rops ou le Réalisme de l'Esprit*, (Paris: Fayard), 1949, pp. 73-74.

[23] Gilles Hénault, "Un homme nous parle," [early 1940s], in *Interventions critiques* (Montreal: Les Éditions Sémaphores), 2008, p. 147.

[24] "Without knowing it and without even knowing the word, we were practising a Christian existentialism. Emphasis was put less on practising the rites than on loving thy neighbour; less on sexual morality than the requirements of charity and justice. At the time, it was a new language." Guy Cormier in "Les 50 ans d'un mouvement mal aimé." *La Presse* (January 14, 1978): 4.

[25] Paul-Émile Borduas, "[La transformation continuelle]." [1946-1947], *Écrits I*, (Montreal: Les Presses de l'Université de Montréal), 1987, pp. 282-283.

[26] Paul-Émile Borduas, "Refus global." [1948], *Écrits I*, pp. 327-328.

[27] Claude Gauvreau and Jean-Claude Dussault, *Correspondance, 1949-1950*, (Montreal: L'Hexagone), 1993, p. 130.

[28] Letter from Paul-Émile Borduas to Harry Bernard, Saint-Hilaire. (September 26, 1948), *Écrits II*, Vol. 1, p. 260.

[29] Gilles Pierne, "Le néo-thomisme et ses assomptions possibles." *Le Quartier latin* (March 3, 1944): 4.

[30] Ibid.

[31] François Hertel, *Pour un ordre personnaliste*, (Montreal: Les Éditions de l'Arbre), 1942, p. 294.

[32] Ibid., p. 292.

[33] Maurice Blain, "Sur la liberté de l'esprit." *Esprit* 193-194 (August-September 1952): 203-204.

34 Esther Trépanier, "Art moderne et catholicisme au Québec, 1930-1945: de quelques débats contradictoires." *Thèmes canadiens/Canadian Issues* 7 (1985): 330-342. Carmel Brouillard, "Les témoins d'une renaissance catholique." *En avant!* (August 12, 1938): 3.

35 Gérard Pelletier, Gérard Pelletier Archives, Library and Archives Canada, Fonds 11939-0-3-F, document 14-5, p. 69. [Anonymous], "Henri Charlier." *JEC* (September 1937): 11.

36 Letter from Paul-Émile Borduas to Olivier Maurault, Paris, July 17, 1929, *Écrits II*, Vol. 1, p. 118.

37 Françoise Caussé, *La Revue L'Art sacré. Le débat en France sur l'art et la religion (1945-1954)*, (Paris: Les Éditions du Cerf), 2010.

38 "[The] single most important vitalizer in modern French Church Art." [Anonymous], "Father Couturier." *The Voice of Prouille* 1. 2 (June 1945): 4. Joanna Weber, "The Sacred in Art: Introducing Father Marie-Alain Couturier's Aesthetic." *Worship* 69. 3 (1995): 243-262.

39 Marie-Alain Couturier, "Les artistes." *Le Quartier latin* (March 24, 1944): 10.

40 Simone Aubry, "À propos d'Art et catholicisme." *La Nouvelle Relève* 1 (September 1941): 117.

41 Claude Gauvreau, "Aragonie et surrationnel," [1954] in Claude Gauvreau, *Écrits sur l'art*, (Montreal: L'Hexagone), 1996, p. 280.

42 Jacques G. de Tonnancour, "L'avènement des indépendants." *Relations*, 2e année, 18 (June 1942): 161.

43 Robert Élie, "Art et catholicisme." *Architecture, Bâtiment, Construction* 3. 23, (March 1948): 46. "Father Couturier, whose dynamism and clear, frank ideas astound many people, was, just as Fernand Léger is, the support that we needed at that precise moment in our evolution. These two men – driven by no personal interest – reassured us on the value of what we had produced. A good thing to learn from others and which clarified our positions." Maurice Gagnon, *Sur un état actuel de la peinture canadienne*, p. 122. Monique Brunet-Weinmann, "Le père Couturier au Québec (1940-1941): un vent de liberté." *RACAR* 14. 1-2 (1987): 151-158. "Présence du père Couturier au Québec (1940-1945). De la modernité à l'abstraction," in Antoine Lion's (Dir.) *Marie-Alain Couturier (1897-1954). Un combat pour la liberté*, (Paris: Serre), 2005, pp. 67-85. Robert Schwartzwald, "The 'Civic Presence' of Father Marie-Alain Couturier, O.P. in Québec." *Quebec Studies* 10 (Spring-Summer 1990): 133-152. Robert Schwartzwald, "Un apport singulier à l'avènement de la modernité au Québec. Hommage au père Marie-Alain Couturier, O.P., à l'occasion du cinquantième anniversaire de sa mort," in Ginette Michaud and Élizabeth Nardout-Lafarge's (Dir.), *Constructions de la modernité au Québec*, (Montreal: Lanctôt Éditeur), 2004, pp. 65-86. Claude Bergeron, "Aux origines de

l'architecture religieuse moderne: la phase suisse et savoyarde," in Monique Moser-Verrey's (Dir.), *Les Cultures du monde au miroir de l'Amérique française*, (Sainte-Foy: Presses de l'Université Laval), 2002, pp. 157-180.

⁴⁴ Letter from Marie-Alain Couturier to Paul-Émile Borduas, Ottawa, Couturier Collection, Yale University, Ms 251, D – 6Aj 9.

⁴⁵ Paul-Émile Borduas, "Projections libérantes." [1949], *Écrits I*, p. 424.

⁴⁶ Jacques Dubuc, "[Si j'étais Jésus-Christ...]." *Le Quartier latin* (December 17, 1943): 4.

⁴⁷ Robert Élie, *Borduas*, (Montreal: Les Éditions de l'Arbre), 1943, p. 18.

⁴⁸ Paul-Émile Borduas, "[Je vous dois des explications (3)]." [1942], *Écrits I*, p. 601.

⁴⁹ Paul-Émile Borduas, "Projections libérantes." pp. 450-451.

⁵⁰ "Of the books that I had Borduas read, two authors moved him deeply, Pauline Réage's *Story of O*, Kierkegaard's *Sickness Unto Death* and *The Concept of Dread*." Letter from Michel Camus to André-G. Bourassa, April 10, 1983, quoted by Gilles Lapointe, *L'Envol des signes. Borduas et ses lettres*, (Montreal: Fides), 1996, p. 71. However, these readings occurred late in his life.

⁵¹ "To have no preconceived ideas helps one work better in mystery, in the unknown..." Paul-Émile Borduas, "[Je n'ai aucune idée préconçue]." [1942], *Écrits I*, p. 637.

⁵² Robert Élie, "L'art dans la cité," [1935] in *Oeuvres*, p.18.

⁵³ Lucien Hébert, "L'art pour l'art." *Le Quartier latin* (April 2, 1936): 11. For art in the 1930s, see François-Marc Gagnon, "La peinture dans les années trente au Québec." *Annales d'histoire de l'art canadien* 3. 1-2 (Autumn 1976): 2-20. Trépanier, "La peinture des années trente au Québec." *Protée* 17. 3 (Autumn 1989): 91-100; "Modernité et conscience sociale: la critique d'art progressiste des années trente." *Annales d'histoire de l'art canadien* 8. 1 (1984): 80-108. This history, like all history, is complex, and the exotic trend was never marginalized to the point where it disappeared from Quebec in the interwar years. Dominique Garand, *La Griffe du polémique. Le conflit entre les exotiques et les régionalistes*, (Montreal: Hexagone), 1989.

⁵⁴ Arthur Laurendeau, "L'artiste." *L'Action française* 4. 4 (April 1920): 150.

⁵⁵ Ibid., pp. 150-151.

⁵⁶ Jacques Maritain, *Art and Scholasticism and the Frontiers of Poetry*, translated by Joseph W. Evans, (New York, Charles Scribner's Sons), 1943, p. 101.

⁵⁷ Quoted by Lai-Kent Chew Orenduff, *The Transformation of Catholic Religious Art in the Twentieth Century: Father Marie-Alain Couturier and the Church at Assy, France*, (Lewiston: The Edwin Mellen Press), 2008, p. 30.

[58] Marie-Alain Couturier, *Art et Catholicisme*, (Montreal: Éditions de l'Arbre), 1941, p. 91; "Problèmes d'un art religieux canadien." *Revue dominicaine* (June 1940): 281-285. Henri Ghéon, revivalist of Christian theatre, explained, in an interview given to French Radio Canada in the summer of 1938, how Naturalism only attained the truth of appearances, whereas true art should aim to explore the underlying truth. "God," he exclaimed, "wants the maximum. [...] He cares nothing for bland, neutral, mediocre, emasculated art which has sunken to the same level as exceedingly pious prayers and candy-coated statues of saints."

[59] Maurice Gagnon, *Peinture moderne*, (Montreal: Éditions Bernard Valiquette), 1940, p. 195.

[60] "Borduas was a religious painter and had to go door-to-door to the priests to get work. Some of them ordered sketches into which the painter put a lot of conscientiousness and time. After seeing them, the 'customers' rejected the sketches without compensating their author whose name and style were, in their eyes, not Italian enough." Guy Viau, "Les chrétiens et Borduas." *Maintenant* 2 (February 1962).

[61] Jean Éthier-Blais, *Autour de Borduas, essai d'histoire intellectuelle*, (Montreal: Presses de l'Université de Montréal), 1979.

[62] [Anonymous], "L'art canadien et l'école d'art canadien, intéressants aperçus exposés par monsieur Charles Maillard dans sa causerie de samedi soir." *Le Devoir* (January 26, 1931): 2.

[63] Robert Rumilly, "Entrevue avec M. Charles Maillard, directeur de l'École des beaux-arts." *La Petite Revue moderne* (November 1934): 222-223.

[64] Alfred Ayotte, "Le R. P. Couturier à Montréal." *Le Devoir* (March 30, 1940): 2. Robert Rumilly, "Entrevue avec M. Charles Maillard" pp. 223-223.

[65] Jean Chauvin, "M. Charles Maillard." *La Revue populaire* 20. 7 (July 1927): 8.

[66] École des beaux-arts de Montréal, Rapport du secrétaire, 1926-1927, p. 5.

[67] [Anonymous], "L'art canadien et l'école d'art canadien, intéressants aperçus exposés par monsieur Charles Maillard dans sa causerie de samedi soir." *Le Devoir* (January 26, 1931): 2. "The director of the École des Beaux-Arts added that today's art has become destitute. A deplorable artistic movement exists, which has a harmful influence on the production of artwork, and this movement was triggered by the Jews who have never produced truly artistic works and who are on a mission to have the last say in art."

[68] Esther Trépanier noted how, already in the 1920s, there was a shift toward exoticism and a praising of the universal human dimension in art. "Un *Nigog* lancé dans la mare des arts plastiques." *Le Nigog*, Archives des lettres canadiennes 7 (Montreal: Fides), 1987, pp. 239-267. Armand Guilmette, "*Le Nigog* et la modernité." *Protée* 15. 1 (Winter 1987): 63-153.

[69] Quoted in Éloi de Grandmont, "Jacques de Tonnancour est-il le fruit mûr de nos Beaux-Arts?" *Le Canada* (June 12, 1945): 7.

[70] Paul-Émile Borduas, "Manières de goûter une oeuvre d'art." [1943], *Écrits I*, p. 229.

[71] Julien Hébert, "Pellan." *Le Quartier latin* (December 19, 1941): 7.

[72] Henri Girard, "L'École de Paris." *Le Canada* (October 22, 1936): 2.

[73] François Hertel, "Retour d'Europe. François Hertel nous dit…" *Le Quartier latin* (October 3, 1947): 3.

[74] Camille Laurin, "Éloi de Grandmont." *Le Quartier latin* (October 24, 1947): 5.

[75] One day Borduas confided in Pierre Gauvreau that he hated the Nationalists. Quoted by Marie-Andrée Chouinard, "Un cri de révolte." *Le Devoir* (May 9, 1998): E11.

[76] With respect to Simone-Mary Bouchard's paintings, Françoise Sullivan was able to write, in an article in 1943, on feminine painting: "This naive young girl paints with a charming and peasant delicateness" the scenery of her native region. "Here is at least," she concluded, "a good painter for lovers of Canadian paintings." As we can see, Sullivan's encouragement with respect to practicing a primitive art contained a certain condescending attitude toward the works of these "charming" and "peasant" artists. Françoise Sullivan, "La peinture féminine." *Le Quartier latin* (December 17, 1943): 8. According to Éthier-Blais, Borduas was opposed, in 1948, to the presentation of Bouchard's works at the Canadian Art Exhibition planned at the Musée d'art moderne in Paris. On the popular primitive art market triangle formed by Charlevoix, New York and Montreal in the late 1930s, see Laurier Lacroix's article "Les barbares, nos premiers modernes ou "comment New York a volé…" au secours de l'art moderne dans la province de Québec," in Yvan Lamonde and Denis Saint-Jacques' (Dir.) *1937: un tournant culturel*, (Quebec: Presses de l'Université Laval), 2009, pp. 281-298.

[77] It was announced on the inside cover of the books already published in the Collection "Art vivant." Gilles Hénault had already published "La question du primitivisme." *Le Quartier latin* (December 17, 1943): 3.

[78] Pierre Gélinas, *Combat*, (November 29, 1947), quoted by Marcel Fournier, *L'Entrée dans la modernité*, (Montreal: Éditions Saint-Martin), 1986, p. 194.

[79] Jean-Paul Mousseau, quoted in Madeleine Gariépy's "Mousseau et Riopelle." *Notre temps* (December 6, 1947): 5. When Gilles Hénault announced that Borduas' and his group's next exhibition would be under the auspices of the magazine *Combat*, the Automatists' refusal was immediate. Interview with Madeleine Arbour by Ray Ellenwood, Montreal, May 17, 1977, in Ray Ellenwood's *Egregore. The Montreal Automatist Movement*, (Toronto: Exile Editions), 1992, p. 84. This willing-

ness to distance oneself from the Communist movement will be found in the pages of *Refus global.*

80 This was naturally also the case for Catholic literature, as Cécile Vanderpelen-Diagre shows in *Mémoire d'y croire. Le monde catholique et la littérature au Québec (1920-1960)*, (Quebec: Nota Bene), 2007.

81 Henri Bremond, *La Poésie pure*, (Paris: Bernard Grasset), 1926, p. 16.

82 Jacques Maritain, *Frontières de la poésie*, (Paris: L. Rouart), 1935, pp. 29-30, quoted by Hélène Boily, "Entre la raison et l'expérience pour une approche des fondements intellectuels de la pensée artistique au Québec dans les années vingt." Doctoral thesis, Université du Québec à Montréal, 1998, p. 51. Apart from Hélène Boily's thesis, one can also see: "Intellectualisme et pensée artistique, 1915-1930," by the same author in *Peindre à Montréal, 1915-1930. Les peintres de la Montée Saint-Michel et leurs contemporains*, Laurier Lacroix (Dir.), (Montreal: Galerie de l'UQAM et Musée du Québec), 1996, pp. 108-120.

83 Jacques Maritain, *Art and Scholasticism and the Frontiers of Poetry*, translated by Joseph W. Evans (New York, Charles Scribner's Sons) 1943, p. 52.

84 Guy Sylvestre, "Confession de foi." *Le Droit* (April 11, 1942): 18.

85 Paul- Émile Borduas, "Quelques pensées sur l'oeuvre d'amour et de rêve de M. Ozias Leduc." [1953] *Écrits I*, p. 513.

86 Jean Éthier-Blais, *Autour de Borduas*, p. 55.

87 Ozias Leduc, quoted by Jean Éthier-Blais, *Autour de Borduas*, p. 73.

88 Marie-Alain Couturier, "Ce que nous devons à Denis." *L'Art sacré* (December 1937): 165-166.

89 Maurice Denis, "Pour l'art sacré." [1918], reproduced in *Du symbolisme au classicisme. Théories*, (Paris: Hermann), 1964, p. 78. See his famous definition of a painting: "Remember that a picture, before being a battle horse, a female nude, an anecdote or whatnot, is essentially a flat surface covered with colours assembled in a certain order."

90 Ibid.

91 Maurice Denis, in *Nouvelles théories sur l'art moderne, sur l'art sacré*, (Paris: Rouard et Watelin), 1922, quoted by Jacques Maritain, *Art and Scholasticism*, p. 204.

92 Claude Gauvreau, "Encore *Le Devoir!*" *Le Quartier latin* (March 19, 1946): 1-2.

93 "Indeed, for you ["young Canadian Automatists"], ever since the discovery of photography, the problem of exactly reproducing reality has been solved; we must advance, discover other pictorial problems, and solve them. It's fantastic." Maurice Gauthier, "Chers petits enfants sérieux d'automatistes." *Le Quartier latin* (January 30, 1948): 3. Borduas initiated himself to the art of photography in the 1930s. His

experimentations with the camera did not signal a will to surpass the immediacy of this medium, since they were most often the effect of chance. Artistic research was generally absent from what was still considered a hobby, an unpretentious amusement, even though the historian can discern certain groundbreaking aspects in Maurice Perron's images (spontaneity, movements, a fascination for childhood, etc). Serge Allaire, "Un photographe chez les automatistes. Entretien avec Maurice Perron." *Études françaises* 34. 2-3 (1998): 141-155. Gilles Lapointe and Raymond Montpetit, *Paul-Émile Borduas photographe. Un regard sur Percé, été 1938*, (Montreal: Fides), 1998.

[94] Maurice Gagnon, *Peinture moderne*, pp. 207-208.

[95] Marie-Alain Couturier, "Notes sur l'abstraction." [June 1945], *Art et liberté spirituelle*, (Paris: Éditions du Cerf), 1958, p. 66.

[96] Claude Gauvreau, "La grande querelle des peintres: réponse de Claude Gauvreau à l'inquiétude de Gabriel La Salle." *L'Autorité du peuple* (May 22, 1954): 6.

[97] Paul-Émile Borduas, "Manières de goûter une oeuvre d'art." p. 238.

[98] Ibid., p. 230.

[99] Paul-Émile Borduas, "Refus global." pp. 337-338.

[100] Paul-Émile Borduas, "Manières de goûter une oeuvre d'art." pp. 231-232.

[101] Postcard from Guy Courteau to Paul-Émile Borduas, March 15, 1943, quoted in *Écrits I*, p. 154. "As for me, it is thanks to Borduas that I have learned about Sacred Art and the grandeur of the Middle Ages." Guy Viau, "Les chrétiens et Borduas," *Maintenant* 2 (February 1962).

[102] [Anonymous], "Un nouveau Moyen Âge." *La Relève*, 8th cahier, 1st series, (1935): 212.

[103] Guy Sylvestre, "Poésie et métaphysique." *En avant!* (June 9, 1939): 3.

[104] Simone Aubry and Jacques de Tonnancour, "À propos de l'enseignement des beaux-arts." *Le Canada* (May 30, 1941): 2.

[105] Ibid.

[106] Marie-Alain Couturier, *Art et Catholicisme*, p. 43.

[107] Marie-Alain Couturier, "Problème d'un art religieux canadien." *Revue dominicaine* (June 1940): 283-284.

[108] Marie-Alain Couturier, *Art et Catholicisme*, pp. 67-68.

[109] Marie-Alain Couturier, "Abstract art has been a very important principle of freedom and perfection of forms." *Le Canada* (April 11, 1944): 12. He had communicated this same thought to Borduas in a letter dated July 1, 1941: "In the end, it is very difficult to do a six-week course, saying only one thing to people: 'There is

good painting and there is bad painting...and that's all!' But ultimately, that is all I know, in French and in English. And I hardly believe anything but that about art." Couturier Collection, Yale University, Ms 251, C-7C 31.

[110] "We knew very well that some of these artists were not strictly practicing Christians; that some were separated from us by serious divergences of a political as well as an intellectual order. Trusting in Providence, we told ourselves that a great artist is always a great spiritual being, each in his own manner..." Interview with Marie-Alain Couturier published in *Harper's Bazaar* (December 1947): 121-122.

[111] Maurice Gagnon, *Peinture moderne*, p. 178.

[112] Maurice Gagnon, "Borduas. Obscure puissance poétique!" *Amérique française* 6 (May 1942): 12.

[113] Maurice Gagnon, *Peinture moderne*, p. 108.

[114] Sabine de Lavergne, *Art sacré et modernité. Les grandes années de la revue L'Art sacré*, (Brussels: Éditions Lessius), 1992.

[115] [Anonymous], "Le peintre P.E. Borduas est reçu avec enthousiasme à Ottawa." *Arts et pensée* 2e année. 12 (November-December 1952): 170.

[116] Robert Élie, *Borduas*.

[117] François Hertel, *Cosmos*, (Montreal: Serge Brousseau), 1945, pp. 53-63.

[118] An earlier text can give us a taste of the opinions that Hertel seemed to express in his work: "Plaidoyer en faveur de l'art abstrait." *Amérique française* 2. 3 (November 1942): 8-16.

[119] François Hertel, *Journal philosophique et littéraire*, (Paris: Les Éditions de la Diaspora Française), 1961, p. 11. See Laurent-Michel Vacher's *Découvrons la philosophie avec François Hertel*, (Montreal: Liber), 1995.

[120] "Borduas, who was only able to attend the school in his village, had to invent his own language. He put the same passion and tenacity into this endeavour as he did in all the others; hence, everything that the language of shapes and colours taught him which is no less profound than that of words." Robert Élie, "Borduas à la recherche du présent," [1968] in *Oeuvres*, p. 610.

[121] Claude Gauvreau, "L'épopée automatiste vue par un cyclope." *La Barre du jour* 17-20 (January-August 1969): 68. Gauvreau is the author of a "monistic novel," *Beauté baroque*, started during the summer of 1952.

[122] "Let us stray as little as possible from the essential: the amplification of each one of us on a cosmic level—an increasingly intimate harmony with men, our brothers who may need us, and also with the mysteriously animated matter of the universe." Paul-Émile Borduas, "Communication intime à mes chers amis." [1950], *Écrits I*, p. 505.

[123] Letter from Paul-Émile Borduas to Claude Gauvreau, New York, March 25, 1954, *Écrits II. 2. Correspondance (1954-1960)*, p. 578.

[124] "In Borduas' mind, there is no rupture at all, from stone to the refined spirit: there is but a difference of degree in the refinement, in the sensible quality..." Jean Fisette "Troisième partie," *Écrits I*, p. 245.

[125] Letter from Paul-Émile Borduas to Robert Élie, end of October or beginning of November 1948, *Écrits II*, Vol. 1, p. 284.

[126] "Bergson is to contemporary art what Descartes was to classical art. One must follow his own time's line of thinking." Letter from François Hertel to Paul-Émile Borduas, January 9, 1942, quoted by Gilles Lapointe, *L'Envol des signes*, p. 66.

[127] Henri Bergson, *The Two Sources of Morality and Religion*, translated by R. Ashley Audra and Cloudesley Brereton, (New York: Doubleday Anchor), [1954], pp. 249-250.

[128] Lai-Kent Chew Orenduff, *The Transformation of Catholic Religious Art in the Twentieth Century*. Note that a monistic Catholicism is technically a contradiction of terms, and that it would be better to speak of monistic tendencies in Couturier's line of thinking, which remains fundamentally holistic, much like Teihard de Chardin's line of thinking, which dates from the same time.

[129] Marie-Alain Couturier, *Dieu et l'art dans une vie. Le père Marie-Alain Couturier de 1897-1945*, (Paris: Éditions du Cerf), 1965, p. 351.

[130] "This surrealism which fascinated them [Fernand Leduc, Pierre Gauvreau and their friends], one must understand it in a slightly distended way, in order to include Baudelaire's 'cursed' poems, Kafka's desperate fantasies, Sade's orgies and Bergson's 'vital impetus.'" Bernard Teyssèdre, "Fernand Leduc peintre et théoricien du surréalisme à Montréal." *La Barre du jour* 17-20 (January-August 1969): 229.

[131] Letter from Paul-Émile Borduas to Robert Élie, November 23, 1948, *Écrits II*, Vol. 1, p. 281.

[132] Jean Fisette, "Troisième Partie." p. 245. Fernand Leduc wrote: "[New] shapes conceived outside figurative recollections...where only the human connection with the diverse elements of the cosmos remains and is, consequently, exalted." Quoted in *La Revue moderne des arts et de la vie* (February 1, 1948): 10.

[133] Paul-Émile Borduas, "Refus global." p. 338.

[134] Paul-Émile Borduas, "Communication intime à mes chers amis." [1950], *Écrits I*, p. 506.

[135] André Breton, "Limites non frontières du surréalisme." *La Nouvelle Revue française* 281 (February 1, 1937): 207.

[136] "No one, who has not read the works of Pierre Mabille, will understand the intellectual posture of our revolutionary artists. The author of *Thérèse de Lisieux, Égrégores, Le Miroir du merveilleux*, has had a durable influence on the advanced Montreal milieu." Claude Gauvreau, "Douze articles." *Le Haut-Parleur* (April 7, 1951): 5. Pierre Gauvreau confirmed this by saying: "Among all the publications that we have read in this period, that Borduas read first, and then myself and my brother Claude, there was a book titled *Égrégore ou la Vie des civilisations*, by Pierre Mabille. This initiated the reflection that would lead to *Refus global*: the collapse of an identity reference." Pierre Gauvreau, "*Refus global*: l'effondrement d'un repère identitaire." in Jonathan Mayer's *Les Échos du Refus global*, (Montreal: Michel Brûlé), 2008, p. 48.

[137] Pierre Mabille, *Mirror of the Marvelous: The Classic Surrealist Work on Myth*, translated by Jody Gladding, (Rochester, Vermont: Inner Traditions), 1998, p.13.

[138] Rémy Laville, *Pierre Mabille: un compagnon du surréalisme*, (Clermont-Ferrand: Presses de l'Université de Clermont-Ferrand), 1983.

[139] Pierre Mabille quoted in Radovan Ivsic's "Pierre Mabille ou le refus du malheur." Preface to Pierre Mabille's *Égrégore ou la Vie des civilisations* [1938], (Paris: Le Sagittaire), 1977, p. 23.

[140] Pierre-Mabille, *Égrégore ou la Vie des civilisations*, pp. 120-121.

[141] André Breton, "Second manifeste du surréalisme," in *Qu'est-ce que le surréalisme*, (Brussels: Éditions René Henriquez), 1934, p. 21: *Oeuvres complètes*, Vol. 1, Gallimard, coll. "Bibliothèque de la Pléiade." (1988), p. 781.

[142] Robert Élie, "Borduas à la recherche du présent," in *Oeuvres*, p. 608.

[143] Fernand Leduc, "Vincent Van Gogh." *Le Quartier latin* (February 11, 1944): 5.

[144] Fernand Leduc, "Le surréalisme (notes)," [late 1946] in *Vers les îles de lumières. Écrits (1942-1980)*, (Montreal: Hurtubise HMH), 1981, p. 37.

[145] Jean Fisette, "Troisième partie." *Écrits I*, p. 273.

[146] Pierre Vadeboncoeur, "Les dessins de Gabriel Filion." [May 1947], *Liaison* 3. 22 (February 1949): 109.

[147] Pierre Vadeboncoeur, "Borduas ou la minute de vérité de notre histoire." *Cité Libre 2* (January 3, 1961): 29.

A PURE AND LIVING ART

[1] Henri Girard, "Des oeuvres vivantes." *Le Canada* (February 1, 1939): 2.

[2] Jacques G. de Tonnancour, "Pour un art canadien." *Le Quartier latin* (April 25, 1941): 9.

[3] Fernand Leduc, "L'artiste, un être anormal?" *Le Quartier latin* (December 3, 1943): 5.

[4] Fernand Leduc, "Borduas." *Le Quartier latin* (December 17, 1943): 4.

[5] Claude Gauvreau, "La peinture n'est pas un hochet de dilettante." [1946], *Écrits sur l'art*, p. 117.

[6] Bernard Morisset, "Nous sommes avec vous, Borduas!" *Le Canada* (October 2, 1948): 4.

[7] Paul-Émile Borduas, "[Variantes de "Parler d'art est difficile."]" [1942], *Écrits I*, p. 590.

[8] Paul-Émile Borduas, "Commentaires sur des mots courants." [1948], *Écrits I*, p. 301.

[9] Paul-Émile Borduas, "[Au printemps dernier]." [1942], *Écrits I*, p. 170.

[10] [Anonymous], "La meilleure peinture de la province." *Le Soleil* (April 26, 1941): 3.

[11] Marie-Alain Couturier, "Les Sagittaires." [Montreal, May 1, 1943], *Chroniques*, (Montreal: Éditions de l'Arbre), 1947, pp. 139-141.

[12] Letter from Marie-Alain Couturier to Jacques Maritain, Montreal, circa April 1941, Couturier Collection, Yale University, C-C 37a. From August 1940, Mgr. Joseph Charbonneau, considered more "liberal," was the Archbishop of Montreal. He was forced to resign in 1950.

[13] Maurice Gagnon, "Pensées sur l'art de tous les temps." *Le Quartier latin* (November 6, 1945): 3; (November 16, 1945): 5; (November 20, 1945): 3; (November 27, 1945): 3.

[14] Maurice Gagnon, *Pellan*, (Montreal: Éditions de l'Arbre), 1943, p. 34.

[15] Paul-Émile Borduas, "[Le retour]." [1947], *Écrits I*, p. 259.

[16] Paul-Émile Borduas, "[Ce destin, fatalement, s'accomplira]." [1942], *Écrits I*, p. 180.

[17] Ibid., p. 204.

[18] Paul-Émile Borduas, "Projections libérantes." [1949], *Écrits I*, p. 450.

[19] Claude Gauvreau, "La peinture n'est pas un hochet de dilettante." *Combat* 1. 5 (December 21, 1946): 3. Once again, there is nothing new about such statements. During the 1920s in Europe Jacques Guenne, founder and editor-in-chief of the French review *Art vivant*, repeated the same line. "Only the works of an artist who accepts the merciless struggle against the training of his mind, the force of his inspiration, the habits of his hand, against trends and dependency on a public, will stand the test of time. This desire to renew, which is the sound element of aes-

thetic questioning has never ceased to exalt the energy of the greats." Jacques Guenne, quoted by Hélène Boily, "Entre la raison et l'expérience pour une approche des fondements intellectuels de la pensée artistique au Québec dans les années vingt." Doctoral thesis, Université de Québec à Montréal, 1998, p. 161.

[20] Letter from Fernand Leduc to Paul-Émile Borduas, Paris, June 17, 1947, quoted by Thérèse Renaud, *Un passé recomposé: deux automatistes à Paris. Témoignages, 1946-1953*, (Quebec: Nota Bene), 2004, p. 56.

[21] Paul-Émile Borduas, "Projections libérantes." [1949], *Écrits I*, p. 428.

[22] Fernand Leduc, "L'artiste, un être anormal?" p. 5.

[23] Paul-Émile Borduas, "Manières de goûter une oeuvre d'art." [1943], *Écrits I*.

[24] Title inspired by Jacques de Tonnancour's "Pour un art canadien." *Le Quartier latin* (April 25, 1941): 9.

[25] Fernand Leduc, "Vincent Van Gogh." *Le Quartier latin* (February 11, 1944): 5.

[26] Robert Élie, "La vie la nuit." [1949], in *Oeuvres*, p. 667.

[27] Letter from Paul-Émile Borduas to Jacqueline Hambleton, [Mid-August 1948], *Écrits II*, Vol.1, p. 249.

[28] Jacques Maritain, *Art and Scholasticism and the Frontiers of Poetry*, translated by Joseph W. Evans, (New York: Charles Scribner's Sons), 1962, p. 50.

[29] Ibid., p. 215.

[30] Jean Bazaine, "Exposition surréaliste." *Esprit 66* (March 1938): 950-956.

[31] André-G. Bourassa, *Surréalisme et littérature québécoise. Histoire d'une révolution culturelle*, (Montreal: Typo), 1986, p. 140.

[32] Ibid., pp. 144-145. Gilles Hénault, *Interventions critiques*, pp. 155-158.

[33] Chantal Morelle, "Les années d'exil (1940-1944)." in Jean-Louis Crémieux-Brilhac and Jean-François Picard (Dir.), *Henri Laugier et son siècle* (Paris: CNRS Éditions), 1995, pp. 73-91.

[34] This preface has been reproduced under the title "Introduction à la peinture hermétique," in *Le Jour* (January 17, 1942): 7.

[35] Lucien Morin, interview with Gilles Marchand, "Lucien Morin dans la réflexion de son oeuvre." *Le Quartier latin* (October 17, 1947): 3.

[36] "Automatism is to art what personalism is to philosophy and pedagogy: a profound respect of the person, of his or her freedom." Marcel Fournier, *L'Entrée dans la modernité*, (Montreal: Éditions Saint-Martin), 1986, p. 218.

[37] Paul-Marie Lapointe, "Notes pour une poétique contemporaine," in Guy Robert's (Dir.), *Littérature du Québec*, Vol. 1, (Montreal: Déom), 1964, p. 88.

[38] This phenomenon is not particular to Quebec, as one can well imagine. See Daniel Belgrad's *The Culture of Spontaneity: Improvisation and the Arts in Postwar America*, (Chicago: University of Chicago Press), 1998.

[39] Marie-Alain Couturier, *Dieu et l'art dans une vie*, p. 338.

[40] [Anonymous], "L'abîme entre l'art et le grand public." *La Presse* (March 5, 1941): 15.

[41] [Anonymous], "La meilleure peinture de la province." *Le Soleil* (April 26, 1941): 8.

[42] Marie-Alain Couturier, *La Vérité blessée*, (Paris: Plon), 1984, p. 188.

[43] Marie-Alain Couturier, *Dieu et l'art dans une vie*, p. 342.

[44] Ibid., p. 351.

[45] "[Notes pour une conférence]" Couturier Collection, Yale University, Ms. 251.

[46] Jeffrey Mehlman, *Émigrés à New York: French Intellectuals in Wartime Manhattan, 1940-1944*, (Baltimore, Maryland: The Johns Hopkins University Press), 2000. Emmanuelle Loyer, *Paris à New York. Intellectuels et artistes français en exil (1940-1947)*, (Paris: Grasset), 2005. Colin Nettlebeck, *Forever French. Exile in the United States 1939-1945*, (Oxford: Berg), 1991. Serge Guilbaut, *How New York Stole the Idea of Modern Art: Abstract Expressionism, Freedom, and the Cold War*, (Chicago: University of Chicago Press), 1983.

[47] [Anonymous], "L'abîme entre l'art et le grand public." *La Presse* (March 5, 1941): 15.

[48] Marie-Alain Couturier, *Dieu et l'art dans une vie*, p. 256.

[49] Ibid., pp. 343-344.

[50] Maurice Gagnon, *Pellan*, p. 19.

[51] François-Marc Gagnon, "L'automatisme et le rêve," in Lise Gauvin (Dir.), *Les Automatistes à Paris. Actes d'un colloque*, (Montreal: Les 400 coups), 2000, pp. 41-55.

[52] Maurice Gagnon, *Pellan*, p. 20.

[53] Guy Sylvestre, "Art vivant." *Le Droit* (January 8, 1944): 8.

[54] Maurice Gagnon, Pellan, p. 34. "Our era has liquidated rationalism. There are only simple minds left to maintain that human reason is not a crude instrument." François Hertel, "Plaidoyer en faveur de l'art abstrait." *Amérique française* 2. 3 (November 1942): 14.

[55] Letter from François Hertel to Paul-Émile Borduas, January 9, 1942, quoted by Gilles Lapointe, *L'Envol des signes. Borduas et ses lettres*, (Montreal: Fides), 1996, p. 66. Gilles Lapointe is the first to insist on "the importance [...] of epistolary exchanges during this period between the painter and François Hertel, who

pushes the artist to pursue an investigation of his own interiority through an advanced discussion on philosophy and psychoanalysis. It is not by chance that this realization preceded the most defining experience in the artist-painter's career by only a few days, the production of 'gouaches' in the spring of 1942, which he revealed to the public shortly thereafter at the Ermitage." Gilles Lapointe, *L'Envol des signes*, p. 76. It is true that Hertel states in his letters that he is in favour of "instinctivism," the "magic of the trade," the impulse and inner dream, but these brief missives seem to me to have primarily fuelled a debate on art that began before these epistolary exchanges.

56 Letter from Paul-Émile Borduas to Josephine Hambleton, December 1946, *Écrits II*, Vol. 1, p. 186.

57 Claude Gauvreau, "L'automatisme ne vient pas de chez Hadès (deuxième partie)." *Notre temps* (December 13, 1947): 6.

58 Fernand Leduc, "La rythmique du dépassement et notre avènement à la peinture," [late 1946, early 1947], in *Vers les îles de lumières. Écrits (1942-1980)*, (Montreal: Hurtubise HMH), 1981, pp. 40-41.

59 Letter from Paul-Émile Borduas to Rolland Boulanger, March 27, 1950, *Écrits II*, Vol. 1, p. 392.

60 Guy Viau, "Avec l'énergie du désespoir Borduas a vécu ses rêves." *Cité Libre* 11. 26 (April 1960): 26.

61 Paul-Émile Borduas, "[Je n'ai aucune idée préconçue]." [1942], *Écrits I*, p. 638.

62 Letter from Paul-Émile Borduas to Josephine Hambleton, February 22, 1947, *Écrits II*, Vol. 1, p. 202.

63 "Once, when someone asked Borduas when he would return to figurative painting, he replied: 'We have just begun to explore the inner world of feeling and for this task we will need at least the rest of the century.'" Jacqueline Moore and Louis Jaques, "Young Montreal Painters Show That Their Objective Is Non-Objective." *Ottawa Citizen* (September 8, 1956): 51.

64 Paul-Émile Borduas, "Entrevue radiodiffusée à Radio-Canada." December 19, 1950, *Écrits I*, p. 618.

65 André Breton, *Le Surréalisme et la peinture*, (Paris: Gallimard), 1965.

66 Automatists, Leduc in particular, were greatly impressed by Matta's New York experiments. "The research that Matta was pursuing in New York at the same time stimulated [Leduc] and provided him with a revelation, that of a world with no horizon, of a space with neither floor nor ceiling." Guy Viau, "Reconnaissance de l'espace." *Notre temps* (July 12, 1947): 5.

67 The reported remarks date from 1953. "I don't think," he said, "my brush thinks for me, guided by instinct. My brush determines the composition, establishes what

I'm going to do.... No, I don't plan anything at the outset.... Let forms and colours grow out of the canvas." [S.A.], "Quebec's Own Version of French Surrealism." *Ottawa Citizen* (June 20, 1959): 18.

[68] Jean Le Moyne, "Signes de maturité dans les lettres canadiennes." *Le Canada* (October 12, 1943): 11.

[68] "The intention must first come from the work of art itself. Next, as an afterthought, psychology comes into play, no harm done." Jacques de Tonnancour, "Les beaux-arts. M. de Tonnancour écrit." *Le Devoir* (September 2, 1944): 9.

[70] Maurice Gagnon, *Peinture moderne*, p. 20. "Only the song of the work makes up its essential beauty." Paul-Émile Borduas, "[Je n'ai aucune idée préconçue]," p. 641. "The reasonable part of spiritual life, collective or individual, acquires, in a particular domain, the name of intellectual discipline." Paul-Émile Borduas, "Manières de goûter une oeuvre d'art." p. 212.

[71] Note that Leonardo da Vinci was the perfect model for the realist artist of the Renaissance, and that Paul Valéry, an inspiration for the collaborators of *Amérique française*, had written a small book entitled *Introduction à la méthode de Léonard de Vinci* praising Leonardo da Vinci. By twisting a passage on the Italian master to suit himself, Borduas was likely not insensitive to the fact that he was radically undermining the classical teaching that, until then, one had gleaned from Leonardo da Vinci's writings.

[72] *Mad Love* by André Breton. Translation by Mary Ann Caws. 1987. Lincoln, Nebraska. U of Nebraska Press (printed by Bison Books). pp. 86-87.

[73] Ibid.

[74] Henri Laugier, "Introduction à la peinture hermétique." *Le Jour* (January 17, 1942): 7.

[75] Marie-Alain Couturier, *Art et Catholicisme*, (Montreal: Éditions de l'Arbre), 1941, pp. 19-20.

[76] Jean Vallerand, "Borduas expose des gouaches à l'Ermitage." *Le Canada* (April 27, 1942): 3. Jean Ampleman also comes to Borduas' defense by drawing an analogy between the aesthetic gaze and listening to music. Jean Ampleman, "Des disciples au maître." *Notre temps* (April 27, 1946): 5.

[77] Henri Laugier, "Saison d'art à Montréal." *Amérique française* 1re année. 5 (April 1942): 6-11. "Thankfully," wrote one of Brébeuf's students, "the modern authors, craftsmen of the French music revival: Debussy, Ravel, Dukas, D'Indy, Fauré, are playing an increasingly important and well-deserved role in recitals and concerts in Quebec." Robert Ouellette, "Musique, s'il vous plaît." *Brébeuf* (February 16, 1935): 4.

[78] Maurice Gagnon, *Peinture moderne*, p. 15.

79 Maurice Gagnon, *Sur un état actuel de la peinture canadienne*, (Montreal: Société des Éditions Pascal), 1945, p. 41. "The sensibility inscribed within the painted matter, is for me the criteria of a work's authenticity." Pierre Gauvreau, interview with Tancrède Marsil, "Gauvreau automatiste." *Le Quartier latin* (November 28, 1947): 48. According to Fernand Leduc, the role of "signing his spiritual message in the matter," had always been incumbent upon the artist. Fernand Leduc, "À Monsieur Jean-Louis Roux." [Autumn 1945], in *Vers les îles de lumières*, p. 29.

80 Paul-Émile Borduas, "[Variantes de "Projections libérantes"], p. 575.

81 Ibid., pp. 578-579.

82 "From 1928 to 1932, [...] I go back to the first certainties of my childhood, without knowing where I am going. I discover the pleasures of love: Lulu and co., Saint Jean de la Croix, another marvel." Paul-Émile Borduas, "Projections libérantes." p. 410.

83 Max Milner, *Poésie et vie mystique chez saint Jean de la Croix*, (Paris: Seuil), pp. 95-97.

84 Madeleine Gariépy, "Surréalisme et automatisme. Ce qu'en dit Pierre Gauvreau." *Notre temps* (November 22, 1947): 3.

85 Paul-Émile Borduas, "Entrevue radiodiffusée à Radio-Canada." (December 21, 1950), *Écrits I*, p. 621. Having had the opportunity to listen to this interview at the Gaston Miron Research Centre, I have made very subtle modifications compared to the transcribed copy found in *Écrits I*.

86 Paul-Émile Borduas, "[Je n'ai aucune idée préconçue]." p. 640.

87 Claude Gauvreau, "La grande querelle des peintres: réponse de Claude Gauvreau à l'inquiétude de Gabriel La Salle." *L'Autorité du peuple* (May 22, 1954): 6.

88 Paul-Émile Borduas, quoted by Jean Éthier-Blais, "Conversation rue Rousselet." *Écrits I*, p. 675.

89 Paul-Émile Borduas, "Questions et réponses (réponses à une enquête de J.-R. Ostiguy." [1956], *Écrits I*, p. 533.

90 Paul-Émile Borduas, "Je n'ai aucune idée préconçue." p. 641.

91 Paul-Émile Borduas, "Entrevue radiodiffusée à Radio-Canada." p. 622.

92 Paul-Émile Borduas, "Je n'ai aucune idée préconçue." pp. 637-638.

93 Paul-Émile Borduas, "Parler d'art est difficile." p. 586.

94 Jacques Ferron, "Claude Gauvreau. From *Du fond de mon arrière-cuisine*" translated by Ray Ellenwood in *Exile, A Literary Quarterly*, 3. 2, (1976): 20-57.

95 Paul-Émile Borduas, "Parler d'art est difficile." p. 586.

96 Paul-Émile Borduas, quoted in Jean Éthier-Blais, "Conversation rue Rousselet." [1960] *Écrits I*, p. 674.

[97] Roland Giguère, "Au-delà." *Place publique* 1 (February 21, 1951): 19.

[98] Letter from Rémi-Paul Forgues to André Breton, July 27, 1945, Montreal, Bibliothèque littéraire Jacques-Doucet, Fonds André Breton, BRT C sup. 335. "Dear Mr. Breton. Perhaps you are unaware of the stance of Surrealists in Montreal? There are great painters here. Paul-Émile Borduas who has been working for many years. Fernand Leduc, a few youngsters [...]. But not one poet, not one review, not one book. We have problems you cannot imagine [*soupçon nez* – a play on the French verb 'soupçonner' (to suspect) and 'nose']. We have been subjugated by a bunch of monks, they are naturally the ones in charge of Instruction."

[99] Rémi-Paul Forgues, "Borduas." *Le Quartier latin* (February 9, 1945): 5.

THE CHARGE OF THE EXPORMIDABLE PAINTER

[1] The title is a reference to Claude Gauvreau's play, *La Charge de l'orignal épormyable*, 1956, (translated by Ray Ellenwood as *The Charge of the Exportmidable Moose*, Toronto: Exile Editions, 1996), in which Gauvreau describes a naive but strong poet struggling to overcome his society's cultural and normative straightjacket.

[2] L. Rolland La Rue, "L'étudiant des beaux-arts." *Le Quartier latin* (February 7, 1935): 10. The author was the president of la Masse, the student association at the École des Beaux-Arts.

[3] Quoted by René Doussin, "L'art de voir." *L'Action française* 20. 3 (September 1928): 183.

[4] Eddie Hamelin, "L'esthétique dans l'enseignement." *L'Action française* 20. 6 (December 1928): 361-366.

[5] Gilles Hénault, "La question du primitivisme." *Le Quartier latin* (December 17, 1943): 5.

[6] Paul-Émile Borduas, "Composition décorative." [1937], *Écrits I*, p. 118.

[7] Paul-Émile Borduas, "Je vous dois des explications (1)." [1942], *Écrits I*, p. 597.

[8] Breton expressed himself using "projections," that is to say, "spontaneous descriptions much more plastic than analytical." Claude Gauvreau and Jean-Claude Dussault, *Correspondance, 1949-1950*, (Montreal: L'Hexagone), 1993, p. 33.

[9] Franchette Lambert, "L'artisanat existe-t-il ? Un mouvement de renaissance paysanne." *En avant!* (December 23, 1938): 4.

[10] "So you spent the summer in the Gaspé with that metallic and golden sun, these open spaces of water and light. And to take inventories! Almighty gods, to what fate does the modern world subject its artists. One would think that we were in a coun-

try of refined penitence. [...] I imagine your torment. The silent disappointment pulsating in the depths of your soul." Letter from Carmel Brouillard to Paul-Émile Borduas, Ile Rousse, December 25, 1938, Fonds Paul-Émile Borduas, Documentation Centre, Musée d'art contemporain de Montréal, 184.11.1.

11 Maurice Gagnon, *Peinture moderne*, (Montreal: Éditions Bernard Valiquette), 1940, p. 152. Two pages further, Gagnon quotes a radio chat in which Gauvreau grants a certain value to Cubist experimentations.

12 Roland Dumais, "L'architecture dans l'art." *Le Quartier latin* (November 22, 1934): 3.

13 Irène Senécal, quoted by André-G. Bourassa, "Première partie," in Paul-Émile Borduas' *Écrits I*, p. 58.

14 Quoted by [Anonymous], "Ce que sera l'enseignement à l'École des beaux-arts." *Le Canada* (October 15, 1923): 8.

15 Robert Élie, "Au-delà du refus" [1949], *Oeuvres*, (Montreal: Hurtubise HMH), 1979, p. 588.

16 Maurice Gagnon, *Peinture moderne*, p. 39.

17 Maurice Gagnon, "Exposition au Collège Notre-Dame." *Le Collégien* [journal du Collège Notre-Dame] 5. 3 (1942): 8-11.

18 Reynald, "Les enfants, ces petits modernes." *La Presse* (October 29, 1938): 31.

19 Henri Girard, "Peintures d'enfants." *Le Canada* (October 25, 1938): 2.

20 Letter from François Hertel to Paul-Émile Borduas, Sudbury, February 15, 1942, Fonds Paul-Émile Borduas, Centre de documentation, Musée d'art contemporain de Montréal, 132.9.2.

21 Maurice Gagnon, *Pellan*, (Montreal: Éditions de l'Arbre), 1943, p. 35.

22 Maurice Gagnon, *Sur un état actuel de la peinture canadienne*, (Montreal: Société des Éditions Pascal), 1945, pp. 52-53.

23 Paul-Émile Borduas, "[Au printemps dernier]." [1942], *Écrits I*, p. 176.

24 Paul-Émile Borduas, "[Ce destin, fatalement, s'accomplira]." [1942], *Écrits I*, p. 187.

25 "There is still a moment in the life of every man when all he does is a work of art. It is unfortunately the moment when everything is forbidden, that of early childhood, on the condition that it be protected from our prejudices, our savoir-faire." Paul-Émile Borduas, "Parler d'art est difficile." [1942], *Écrits I*, p. 582.

26 Maurice Gagnon, *Sur un état actuel de la peinture canadienne*, p. 137.

27 Léon Bellefleur, "Plaidoyer pour l'enfant. Son message." *Les Ateliers d'arts graphiques 2* (1947).

28 Louis-Marie Régis, "Du consentement à la beauté." *Le Quartier latin* (December 7, 1944): 5.

29 Paul-Émile Borduas, "Projections libérantes." [1949], *Écrits I*, pp. 412-413.

30 Ibid., p. 412.

31 Paul-Émile Borduas, "Commentaires sur des mots courants." [1948], *Écrits I*, p. 312.

32 Olga Hazan, *La Culture artistique au Québec au seuil de la modernité. Jean-Baptiste Lagacé, fondateur de l'histoire de l'art au Canada*, (Quebec: Les Éditions du Septentrion), 2010, pp. 224-228.

33 Jérôme Paradis, "Beaux-Arts." *Le Collégien* (Christmas 1941): 4. Fonds du Frère Jérôme, Archives de l'UQAM, P12-010/1.

34 Testis, "Vernissage." August 1945. Fonds du Frère Jérôme, Archives de l'UQAM, P12-020/4.

35 Quoted by Marcel Huguet, "Le frère Jérôme s'est débarrassé des préjugés acquis pendant sa jeunesse." *Photo-Journal* (May 24-31, 1967): 4.

36 Paul Joyal, "Une expérience très concluante." *La Presse* (January 22, 1944): 26. The article summarizes the author's impression after a visit to the children's exhibition organized at the Collège Notre-Dame by Brother Jérôme.

37 Jérôme Paradis, "[Si je me remets à la tâche...]." Fonds du Frère Jérôme, Archives de l'UQAM, 12P.610/3.

38 Robert Élie, "Une exposition de travaux d'enfants: une nouvelle méthode d'enseignement de la peinture et du dessin a donné des résultats magnifiques au collège Notre-Dame." [1941], dans *Oeuvres*, (Montreal: Hurtubise HMH), 1979, p. 617.

39 Léon Bellefleur, "Plaidoyer pour l'enfant. Son message."

40 Maurice Gagnon, *Sur un état actuel de la peinture canadienne*, p. 56.

41 Ibid., p. 61.

42 Ibid., p. 116.

43 Maurice Gagnon, "L'enseignement des arts et le collège classique." *Le Quartier latin* (March 26, 1943): 8.

44 Marie-Alain Couturier, "Les artistes." *Le Quartier latin* (March 24, 1944): 10.

45 "I wish you would set up one of those free school projects that you've been toying with for so long." Letter from Bernard Morisset to Paul-Émile Borduas, September 22, 1948. Musée d'art contemporain de Montréal, Archives Borduas, Dossier 147.

46 Paul-Émile Borduas, Entrevue radiodiffusée à Radio-Canada, 1950, *Écrits I*, p. 619.

47 Guy Viau, "Borduas." *Arts et pensées* 3rd Year. 17 (May-June 1954): 133-134.

48 Paul-Émile Borduas, "Projections libérantes." p. 442.

49 Maurice Gagnon, "Exposition au Collège Notre-Dame," 1942, Fonds du Frère Jérôme, Archives de l'UQAM, 12P.010/1.

50 Claude Gauvreau, "L'automatisme ne vient pas de chez Hadès (deuxième partie)." *Notre temps* (December 13, 1947): 6.

51 Paul-Émile Borduas, "Projections libérantes." p. 448.

52 Ibid., p. 446.

53 Maurice Gagnon, *Pellan*, p. 33.

54 Maurice Gagnon, *Peinture moderne*, 1940, p. 39.

55 Éloi de Grandmont, "Reprise de la 'bataille d'Hernani' à la conférence Fernand Léger." *Le Canada* (May 14, 1945): 8.

56 Maurice Gagnon, *Peinture moderne*, p. 121.

57 Maurice Gagnon, "Exposition au Collège Notre-Dame."

58 Robert Élie, "Une exposition de travaux d'enfants." p. 618.

59 Claude Gauvreau, "L'automatisme ne vient pas de chez Hadès." p. 6.

60 Carolle Gagnon and Ninon Gauthier, *Marcel Barbeau. Le regard en fugue*, (Montreal: Éditions du Centre d'études et de communication sur l'art), 1990, p. 21.

61 Ninon Gauthier, "Échos et métamorphoses dans l'oeuvre de Marcel Barbeau." Paris: Doctoral thesis, Université de Paris IV-Sorbonne, March 2004.

62 Un Sportif, "En marge de l'exposition Pierre Gauvreau. Guy Beaugrand-Champagne, le père du découpantisme." *Le Quartier latin* (December 9, 1947): 3.

63 René Bergeron, *Art et Bolchevisme*, (Montreal: Fides), 1946, p. 30.

64 See Father Julien Déziel's speech given during the Sisters of Sainte-Anne Education Conference held in Lachine in September 1948. "Initiation artistique et art moderne." *Les Conférences pédagogiques* 5. 7 (1948-1949): 91-101. Also, Henri Girard, "Aspects de la peinture surréaliste," *La Nouvelle Relève*, 6. 5 (September 1948): 418-424.

65 Maurice Gagnon, *Sur un état actuel de la peinture canadienne*, p. 48.

66 Ibid., p. 61. "They tell me: 'It's anti-pedagogical, it's Rousseauism.' I answer that pedagogy can be wrong or right depending on its orientation. Life is neither good nor bad in itself, holding as much power to do evil as it has to do good. What pedagogy should be concerned about is primarily to preserve the life of the spirit, and then guide it toward the infinite of all things." Paul-Émile Borduas, "[Ce destin fatalement, s'accomplira]," p. 207. The accusation of Rousseauism is also found in

Maurice Gagnon's "L'enseignement des arts et le collège classique." *Le Quartier latin* (March 26, 1943): 8.

[67] "These two realities met one memorable evening. Claude Gauvreau was presenting his play *Bien-être*. Out of the crowd of friends there, barely five (outside our group) left remained with my admiration for them still intact. In addition to the emotion, specific to the epic drama taking place on the stage, I felt for the first time the dread of the upcoming and irremediable rupture. Aside from a small few, all those who were there and who had been so good to us in the past refused to go beyond the limits, which were well short of our present possibilities!" Paul-Émile Borduas, "Projections libérantes," p. 465.

[68] Claude Gauvreau, "L'épopée automatiste vue par un cyclope." *La Barre du jour* 17-20 (January-August 1969): 65.

[69] Jean-Paul Mousseau, "Claude Gauvreau," in Gilles Hénault's *Interventions critiques*, (Montreal: Les Éditions Sémaphores), 2008, p. 83.

[70] Jean-Marie Gauvreau, "1930-1935." *Technique* (November 1935): 449.

[71] René Chicoine, "L'École des Beaux-Arts." *La Nouvelle Relève* 6. 4 (May 1948): 331.

[72] Paul-Émile Borduas, "Projections libérantes." p. 439.

[73] "He told me that Paul-Émile Borduas had been hired originally to teach design to students studying furniture and industrial design. Instead of doing as directed, Borduas turned these classes into classes in painting! Borduas was warned that this was not in accordance with the director's wishes, but he paid no attention. 'One could not have this kind of professor, could one?'" quoted by Margaret Jean Vann, "A Bibliography and Selected Source Material for the Study of Paul-Émile Borduas and his Relationship to Other French-Canadian Automatists," Master's thesis, Winnipeg, University of Manitoba, 1964, pp. 50-51.

[74] Charles Maillard, "Le dessin." *La Revue moderne* 12 (October 1928): 6 and 12.

[75] Charles Maillard, *Vers un art canadien. Lettre aux Anciens à l'occasion du 20e anniversaire de fondation de l'École des beaux-arts de Montréal*, [no publisher], (Montreal), 1943, p. 9.

[76] Ibid.

[77] Bureau de l'enseignement en dessin, CÉCM, 1943, quoted by Francine Couture and Suzanne Lemerise, "Insertion sociale de l'École des Beaux-Arts de Montréal: 1923-1969" in Francine Couture et al., *Enseignement des arts au Québec*, (Montreal: UQAM), 1980, p. 30.

[78] Quoted in Éloi de Grandmont's "Les beaux-arts." *Le Devoir* (June 17, 1944): 7.

[79] Marie-Alain Couturier, "Art canadien." radio talk show, July 1949, Couturier Collection, Yale University, Ms 251.

[80] Jean Le Moyne, "Signes de maturité dans les lettres canadiennes." *Le Canada* (October 12, 1943): 11.

[81] Claude Gauvreau, "Révolution à la Société d'art contemporain." *Le Quartier latin* (December 3, 1946): 4.

[82] Charles Hamel, "Un peintre qui n'aimait pas l'art moribond!" *Le Jour* (June 16, 1945): 4.

[83] Marie-Alain Couturier, "Réponse à M. Maillard." *Le Canada* (May 24, 1941): 2.

[84] Marcel Parizeau, "Peinture libérée." *Le Canada* (May 28, 1941): 2.

[85] Simone Aubry and Jacques de Tonnancour, "À propos de l'enseignement des beaux-arts." *Le Canada* (May 30, 1941): 2.

[86] Maurice Gagnon, *Chronique du mouvement automatiste québécois*, pp. 117-122.

[87] Guy Robert, *Pellan, sa vie et son oeuvre / His Life and His Art*, (Montreal: Éditions du Centre de Psychologie et de Pédagogie), 1963, p. 42. See the stinging description of the spats between Pellan and Maillard in Hamel's "Un peintre qui n'aimait pas l'art moribond!" pp. 4-5.

[88] This same year, he had sent him a "manuscript of theatrical amusement" titled "La Vie, la Mort et l'Autre" to get his opinion. Letter from Pierre Gélinas to André Breton, November 23, 1944, Montreal, Bibliothèque littéraire Jacques-Doucet, Fonds André Breton, BRT C sup. 367.

[89] Pierre Gélinas, "Petite histoire de l'art." *Le Jour* (May 27 and June 3, 1944): 5.

[90] Éloi de Grandmont, "Reprise de la 'bataille d'Hernani' à la conférence Fernand Léger." *Le Canada* (May 14, 1945): 8.

[91] Alfred Pellan, "M. Pellan répond à M. Charles Maillard." *La Presse* (June 20, 1945): 9.

[92] Jean Verville [Éloi de Grandmont?] "Léger et Maillard." *Le Bloc* (May 30, 1945): 15.

[93] A. Berthiaume, "Les Bla...Bla...d'Éloi sur l'architecture." *Le Quartier latin* (November 20, 1945): 6. Jean-A. Gélinas, "Éloi le petit con récite un mauvais résumé de bonne lecture." *Le Quartier latin* (November 20, 1945): 6.

[94] Quoted by Jules Béliveau, "Trente ans sur la ligne de feu." *Photo-journal* (May 26 to June 2, 1965): 3.

[95] Gérard Petit, *L'Art vivant et nous*, (Montreal: Fides), 1946.

[96] Letter from Brother Jérôme Paradis to Brother Narcisse Meloche, Provincial Superior, 1949, quoted in Robert Rumilly's *Cent ans d'éducation. Le Collège Notre-Dame, 1869-1969*, (Montreal: Fides), 1969, p. 253.

[97] [Anonymous], "Refus global. M. Borduas proteste contre son renvoi." *La Patrie* (September 22, 1948): 6.

[98] Christopher Varley, *The Contemporary Arts Society, Montreal, 1939-1948: La Société d'art contemporain, 1939-1948*, (Edmonton, The Edmonton Art Gallery), 1980, p. 27.

[99] M.-J. O'Connor Lynch et al., "Influences regrettées." [Circa June 1944] in Fonds du Frère Jérôme, Archives de l'UQAM, 12P.010/2.

[100] Letter from Julien Hébert to Jacques de Tonnancour, Paris, December 13, 1947, Paris, Fonds Jacques de Tonnancour, Archives de l'UQAM, 170P-030/9.

[101] Maurice Gagnon, *Sur un état actuel de la peinture canadienne*, p. 110.

[102] "During the war, Pellan returned to Montreal and he, too, with his followers joined the Society. Thus, it became divided into two factions, each of which sought to prevail [...] I could not admit that the Society, oblivious of the purpose for which it was founded, namely, aesthetic liberty for all its members without distinction, should become an instrument of sectarian contention..." John Lyman, quoted in Evan H. Turner, John Lyman and Guy Viau's *Paul-Émile Borduas. 1905-1960*, exhibition catalogue, (Montreal: Musée des beaux-arts de Montréal), 1962, p. 41. In June 1947, Lyman wrote "I fear that the Society is dying. It would be a shame, for it could represent the group of independent artists, but their anarchy and jealousy seem to prevent them from agreeing on a collective action, which will enable official and unofficial organizations to control everything as they wish. The current state of affairs is total confusion." Letter from John Lyman to Marie-Alain Couturier, Montreal, June 9, 1947, Archives Couturier, Paris, Ms 251, C-9C 33a b.

[103] "Stopped by the stained glass and Sacred Art workshop, assessment by Maurice Denis. My drawing was the most criticized." Paul-Émile Borduas, "Journal." *Écrits II*, Vol. 1, p. 54.

[104] Interview with Pellan for the magazine, *Vie des arts*, quoted by Bernard Lecherbonnier, *La Chair du verbe. Histoire et poétique des surréalismes de langue française*, (Paris: Éditions Publisud), 1992, p. 83.

[105] Charles Hill, interview with Jacques de Tonnancour, September 19, 1973, National Gallery of Canada, Archives, Box 1523, p. 41.

[106] François Hertel, *Souvenirs, historiettes, réflexions*, (Paris: Éditions de la Diaspora Française), 1972, pp. 105-106.

WHEN MY DREAMS HEAD OFF TO WAR!

1 Title of one of Borduas' paintings dating from 1947.

2 Paul-Émile Borduas, "[Borduas parmi nous]." [1952], *Écrits I*, p. 652.

3 Claude Gauvreau, "L'épopée automatiste vue par un cyclope." p. 72.

4 Thérèse Renaud, *Un passé recomposé: deux automatistes à Paris. Témoignages, 1946-1953*, (Quebec: Éditions Nota Bene), 2004, p. 173.

5 Charles Hill, interview with Jacques de Tonnancour, September 19, 1973, Musée des beaux-arts de Montréal, Archives, Box 1523, p. 16. "From as far back as I can remember, relations with Borduas have been violent. How many times did I see him explode, criticizing everything and anything (sloppy wrapping, deficient heating, slow postage service) with a rage I found admirable." Pâquerette Villeneuve, "Une homme exemplaire." *Le Devoir* (February 27, 1960): 9. Borduas' wife did not hide her husband's often taciturn and occasionally disagreeable character, an "ultra-nervous" man who "smoked constantly" and "gulped down incredible quantities of coffee." "He asked and demanded a lot of others without getting it. As a result, this made him bitter and unpleasant." Gabrielle Borduas in Paul-Gilles Vaillancourt's "Paul-Émile Borduas. Sa vie, son oeuvre, son influence." April 2, 1964, Fonds Paul-Émile Borduas, p. 12, Centre de documentation, Musée d'art contemporain de Montréal, T277. "Ses sautes d'humeurs sont demeurées proverbiales." Gilles Hénault, "Profil de Borduas." *Le Nouveau Journal* (January 13, 1962): 21.

6 Did he not seem like the typical character from Robert Élie's novels? In Élie's novels, the hero, realizing his solitude after believing he had forged friendship with a small group of people, does not know how to back away from the abyss which stands before him. "Repelled by the lie of his entourage, he has woven a net of solitude around himself. Coldly, he accepts his fate, analyzes the world that is evolving around him up until the moment, characterized by extreme tension, where violence erupts. Everything ends with an explosion in Élie's works.") Marc Gagnon, *Robert Élie*, (Montreal: Fides), 1968, p. 18. To break the cage that holds him prisoner and hampers his pursuit of the absolute, the main character turns his back on his petty milieu and leaves friends and family without ever looking back. This way, he can taste the infinite, that is to say by diving into the most sensitive reality through the most complete austerity.

7 Denis Noiseaux, "Peinture moderne." *Le Quartier latin* (March 10, 1944): 5.

8 Joan Murray, *Impressionism in Canada 1895-1935*, (Toronto: Art Gallery of Ontario), 1973.

9 Paul-Émile Borduas, "[Au printemps dernier]." [1942], *Écrits I*, pp. 174-175.

[10] Bernard E. Bernard in Paul-Gilles Vaillancourt's "Paul-Émile Borduas. Sa vie, son oeuvre, son influence." (April 2, 1964), p.19, Fonds Paul-Émile Borduas, Centre de documentation, Musée d'art contemporain de Montréal, T277.

[11] Gilles Lapointe, *La Comète automatiste*, (Montreal: Fides), 2008, p. 19. Jeannette M. Bionti, *Pierre Gauvreau: le jeune homme en colère*, (Montreal: Lanctôt), 2003.

[12] François-Marc Gagnon mentioned how much the adherence to automatism was similar to a religious conversion. *Chronique du mouvement automatiste québécois, 1941-1954*, (Montreal: Lanctôt), 1998, p. 232.

[13] Letter from Fernand Leduc to Paul-Émile Borduas and Gabrielle Borduas, Montreal, June 14, 1942, in *Vers les îles de lumières. Écrits (1942-1980)*, (Montreal: Hurtubise HMH), 1981, p. 4.

[14] Thérèse Renaud, *Un passé recomposé*, p. 101. Dreaming of "a truly governmental and social theocracy" that could reestablish "the latent power of Christ," Leduc affirmed in January 1949, in a parlance inspired by Abellio's reading, that Borduas had "assumed Authority" in the midst of their "little society" and spoke of their group as if it were a phalanstery. Letter from Fernand Leduc to Paul-Émile Borduas, Clamart, January 10, 1949, in Fernand Leduc's *Vers les îles de lumières*, p. 106. In an interview given many years later, Leduc revealed: "I had abandoned a religion, I would even say an asceticism, a fervour, which I obviously had to replace." Fernand Leduc in Lise Gauvin's *Entretiens avec Fernand Leduc, suivis de Conversation avec Thérèse Renaud*, (Montreal: Liber), 1995, p. 63.

[15] Thérèse Renaud, *Une mémoire déchirée*, (Montreal: Hurtubise HMH/Éditions de l'Arbre), 1978, pp. 134-135.

[16] Interview with Ray Ellenwood, May 17, 1977, quoted in Ray Ellenwood's *Egregore: A History of the Montreal Automatist Movement*, (Toronto: Exile Editions), 1992, p. 61. "I told him [Jacques Dubuc] that I liked Borduas, but that I could no longer 'stand' his disciples. Those young people refuse the right for anyone other than their master to have an opinion and even the possibility of having some taste. In the long run, it is becoming intolerable. I can no longer subject myself to being 'bawled out' in public by some little girl who knows nothing about the problems that I have been studying for years. It is too embarrassing. It's useless. Other disciples, due to their stubbornness, pass off the one they follow for a visionary." Letter from François Hertel, Sudbury, February 1945, Fonds Paul-Émile Borduas, Musée d'art contemporain de Montréal, 132.25.2. Centre de documentation de Montréal, 132.25.2.

[17] Judith Ince, "The Vocabulary of Freedom in 1948: The Politics of the Montreal Avant-Garde." *The Journal of Canadian Art History* 6. 1 (1982): 36-54. Also see Rosalind E. Krauss' *The Originality of the Avant-Garde and Other Modernist Myths* (Cambridge: The MIT Press), 1983. Peter Bürger, *Theory of the Avant-Garde*,

(Minneapolis: University of Minnesota Press), 1984. Donald Kuspit, *The Cult of the Avant-Garde Artist*, (Cambridge: Cambridge UP), 1993.

[18] Paul-Émile Borduas, "Refus global." [1948], *Écrits I*, p. 344.

[19] Gérard de Cortanze, *Le Monde du surréalisme*, (Paris: Éditions Complexe), 2005, p. 292.

[20] Paul-Émile Borduas, "Manières de goûter une oeuvre d'art." [1943], *Écrits I*, p. 233.

[21] "Those who lovingly leafed through the quality art catalogues and reviews, such as "Verve," and "Le Minotaure" have familiarized themselves with the ingenious layout and the metallic confessions of this abstract sentimental: Fernand Léger." Charles Doyon, "Fernand Léger." *Le Jour* (June 12, 1943): 7.

[22] Claude Gauvreau, "L'épopée automatiste vue par un cyclope." *La Barre du jour* 17-20 (January-August 1969): 48.

[23] Charles Doyon, "Nos peintres de demain." *Le Jour* (May 15, 1943): 6.

[24] With Fernand Léger politely turning her away (he did not take on any students), she registered at the New School of Social Research to study under the stage director, Erwin Piscator. She abandoned her paintbrushes in 1944.

[25] We know, among other things, that in July 1941, Father Couturier showed some of Pellan's prints to Pierre Matisse. Archives Couturier, Paris, Ms 251.

[26] Claude Gauvreau, "L'épopée automatiste vue par un cyclope." p. 58.

[27] François-Marc Gagnon, "New York as Seen from Montreal by Paul-Émile Borduas and the Automatists, 1943-1953," in Serge Guilbaut's (Ed.), *Reconstructing Modernism: Art in New York, Paris and Montreal 1945-1964*, (Cambridge: The MIT Press), 1990, pp. 130-143.

[28] France Desmarais, "La présence de Fernand Léger sur la scène artistique montréalaise des années quarante." Master's thesis, UQAM, 1993.

[29] Marie-Alain Couturier, Maurice Gagnon, S. Giedion, et al., *Fernand Léger 1938-1944. La forme humaine dans l'espace*, (Montreal: Les Éditions de l'Arbre), 1945.

[30] "Borduas attended meetings animated by Laugier and Father (Couturier), which acquainted us with what was happening in New York." Louise Gadbois, quoted by Monique Brunet-Weinmann, "Le père Marie-Alain Couturier." *Parcours, l'informateur des arts* 4. 4 (Autumn 1998): 12.

[31] Letter from Henri Laugier to Marie-Alain Couturier, Montreal, 1943. Archives Couturier, Paris, Ms 251, A-3A 98.

[32] Guy Sylvestre, "Art Vivant." *Le Droit* (January 8, 1944): 8.

[33] Irène Legendre, *Petite Histoire de l'art moderne*, (Quebec: Soleil), 1947, p. 113.

[34] Jean-Charles Harvey, "L'Exposition Pellan." *Le Jour* (October 19, 1940): 7.

[35] Jean-Charles Harvey, "Cinquante dessins d'Alfred Pellan." *Le Jour* (February 23, 1946): 5.

[36] Guy Robert, *Pellan, sa vie et son oeuvre / His Life and His Art*, (Montreal: Éditions du Centre de Psychologie et de Pédagogie), 1963, p. 52. Pellan even claimed that it was he who, upon his return to France in 1940, had introduced Borduas to the surrealist way of thinking. "Alfred Pellan, peintre," *Gros plan* Television Program, Radio-Canada, August 5, 1970. Centre d'archives Gaston Miron, Université de Montréal.

[37] Marcel Parizeau, "Peinture canadienne d'aujourd'hui." *Amérique française* (November 1942): 17. "This return [of Pellan] liberated many imaginations and unshackled many. Immediately Paul Borduas appeared, and would be Pellan's emulator and his rival." Marie-Alain Couturier, "Art canadien." Radio, July 1949, Couturier Collection, Yale University, Ms 251.

[38] Claude Gauvreau, "Cézanne, la vérité et les vipères de bon ton." [1945], *Écrits sur l'art*, (Montreal: L'Hexagone), 1996, p. 100.

[39] "*Saint-Jean, Portrait de Mme B., Baigneuses, Portrait de Mme G., Femme à la mandoline, Paysage à la voie orangé-jaune, Ile fortifiée, Le Philosophe, Abstraction verte*, manifest the preoccupations of a painter who, through contact with the masters of the day, especially Renoir, Rouault, Matisse, Braque and Picasso, looks within himself in order to take possession of his being, to rediscover himself, to free himself." Maurice Gagnon, *Peinture moderne*, 1943, p. 106. "The gouaches of 1942 that we saw as Surrealist were merely Cubist. It took us five years to see it." Paul-Émile Borduas, "Questions et réponses (réponses à une enquête de Jean-René Ostiguy)." 1956, *Écrits I*, p. 531. The art exhibition at the Ermitage was called *Oeuvres surréalistes de Paul-Émile Borduas* (Surrealist Works of Paul-Émile Borduas).

[40] Clarence Gagnon, "L'immense blague de l'art moderniste." *Amérique française* 1. 1 (September 1948): 60-65; 1. 2 (December 1948): 44-48; 1. 3 (May 1949): 67-71 and 1. 4 (June 1949): 30-35. The talk, presented at the Pen and Pencil Club, dates from October 1942. Roy Kerwin, "Gagnon Lashes Out at False Values in Modernistic Art." *The Standard* (April 29, 1939): 22.

[41] F.R., "De la réalité à l'abstraction, avec Pellan." *La Presse* (October 12, 1940): 42.

[42] Jean-Paul Lemieux, "Aperçu sur la peinture contemporaine." *Le Jour* (June 18, 1938): 2.

[43] Reynald, "Sage peinture d'avant-garde." *La Presse* (November 6, 1937): 43.

[44] Quoted by Bernard Teyssèdre, "Fernand Leduc, peintre et théoricien du surréalisme à Montréal." *La Barre du jour* 17-20 (January-August 1969): 236. Marcel Rioux, "Notes sur le surréalisme." *Notre temps* (November 23, 1946): 6.

45 Claude Gauvreau and Jean-Claude Dusseault, *Correspondance, 1949-1950*, (Montreal: L'Hexagone), 1993, p. 137.

46 Guy Robert, *Pellan, sa vie et son oeuvre*, p. 46.

47 According to François Rozet, quoted in André-G. Bourassa's *Surréalisme et littérature québécoise. Histoire d'une révolution culturelle*, (Montreal: Typo), 1986, p. 117.

48 Paul Dumas, "Borduas." *Amérique française* 6 (June-July 1946): 40.

49 Paul-Émile Borduas, "Manières de goûter une oeuvre d'art." p. 237.

50 Bruno Cormier will evoke, and not without malice, the "Cubist pseudo experiences of 1948, [...] the moribund experimenters who stopped all pictorial experimentation at the Cubist stage" "eyeless painters" and "puppets born without strings, temporarily cluttering the stage." Bruno Cormier, "L'oeuvre picturale est une expérience," text included in *Refus global*.

51 Gabrielle Borduas quoted in Paul-Gilles Vaillancourt's "Paul-Émile Borduas. Sa vie, son oeuvre, son influence." April 2, 1964, p. 15, Fonds Paul-Émile Borduas, Centre de documentation, Musée d'art contemporain de Montréal, T277.

52 Pierre Bourgie, *Entretiens avec Jacques de Tonnancour. De l'art et de la nature*, (Montreal: Liber and musée d'art contemporain de Montréal), 1999, p. 56.

53 The anecdote was reported by Marie-Alain Couturier, Couturier Collection, Yale University, Ms 251.

54 "Plastic problems," he wrote, "no longer arise in terms of art, but in terms of the direction to follow in life." Paul-Émile Borduas, "[Parlons un peu peinture]" [1942], *Écrits I*, p. 291.

55 Jean-Paul Riopelle, quoted by Éloi de Grandmont, "Le groupe Borduas: Exposition à Paris de six jeunes peintres canadiens." *Le Canada* (July 16, 1947): 3.

56 François Gagnon, "Contribution à l'étude de la genèse de l'automatisme pictural chez Borduas." *La Barre du jour* 17-20 (January-August 1969): 206.

57 Letter from Paul-Émile Borduas to Fernand Leduc, Saint-Hilaire, January 21, 1948, *Écrits II*, Vol. 1, p. 228.

58 Albert Gleizes, *Vie et mort de l'Occident chrétien*, (Sablons (Isère): Éditions Moly-Sabata), 1930, p. 2.

59 Letter from Fernand and Thérèse Leduc to Paul-Émile Borduas, Paris, April 1 1948, in Fernand Leduc's *Vers les îles de lumières*, p. 88.

60 Bruno Cormier, "Pour une pensée moderne." *Le Quartier latin* (December 11, 1945): 3.

61 Claude Gauvreau and Jean-Claude Dussault, *Correspondance*, p. 361.

62 Fernand Leduc, "L'artiste, un être anormal?" *Le Quartier latin* (December 3, 1943): 5.

[63] Jean-Claude Dussault, "Présentation," in Claude Gauvreau and Jean-Claude Dussault's *Correspondance*, p. 14.

[64] Ibid.

[65] Letter from Fernand Leduc to Paul-Émile Borduas, in Fernand Leduc's *Vers les îles de lumières*, p. 87.

[66] Ibid.

[67] Letter from Paul-Émile Borduas to Fernand Leduc, *Écrits II*, p. 229.

[68] Claude Gauvreau and Jean-Claude Dussault, *Correspondance*, p. 127.

[69] Ibid., p. 80.

[70] Fernand Leduc, quoted by René Viau, "Le Refus global vu par ses signataires." *La Presse* (August 1, 1998): B3.

[71] Bruno Cormier, quoted by René Viau, Ibid.

[72] Jean-Paul Mousseau quoted by Viau, "Le Refus global vu par ses signataires." p. B3.

[73] Claude Gauvreau, "Lettre ouverte à M. Robert Cliche." *Le Canada* (February 22, 1949): 4.

[74] Letter from Paul-Émile Borduas to Claude Gauvreau, New York, September 16, 1954, *Écrits II*, Vol. 2, p. 640.

[75] See the anecdote that Jacques Ferron told in the humorous and caustic way for which he is famous. "Mousseau asks me: 'What time is it? – 10 o'clock.' Mousseau rubs his hands together: 'I know someone,' he says, 'who is having a bad time; we put our letter in the mail the day before yesterday; he probably received it this morning' – Who – Minister Barrette.'" It was in 1949. Automatism, which was meant to be cosmic, took sides in all instances; regarding the asbestos strike, in favour of the strikers, of course. Claude Gauvreau, the writer of the group, had written a clearly unfavourable and rather impolite letter to the government. This was the said letter. Mousseau in his naivety imagined that the Minister, going through his mail, was in the middle of reading it and was troubled, dismayed, eaten up with remorse. And Mousseau was not far from thinking: will he get over this letter? Jacques Ferron, "[Monsieur Borduas]," [196-], Fonds Jacques Ferron, Bibliothèque et archives nationales du Québec, MSS424.

[76] Quoted in François-Marc Gagnon's *Chronique du mouvement automatiste québécois*, p. 668.

[77] "I call Egregore, a word used long ago by Hermeticists, the human group endowed with a different personality than that of the individuals which make it up." Pierre Mabille, *Égrégores ou la Vie des civilisations* [1938], (Paris: Le Sagittaire), 1977, p. 64.

[78] Pierre Mabille, *Égrégores*, pp. 225-226.

[79] Pierre Mabille, *Conscience lumineuse et conscience picturale*, (Paris: José Corti), 1989, p. 100.

[80] Fernand Leduc, "Qu'on le veuille ou non" [1948], text included in *Refus global*.

[81] Letter from Paul-Émile Borduas to Jean-Paul Riopelle, Saint-Hilaire, February 21, 1947, *Écrits II*, Vol. 1, p. 196.

[82] Paul-Émile Borduas, "Refus global." pp. 348-349.

[83] Bernard Teyssèdre, "Au coeur des tensions." *La Presse* (October 26, 1968): 40.

[84] Paul-Émile Borduas, "Projections libérantes." [1949], *Écrits I*, p. 473.

[85] Julie Gaudreault, *Le Recueil écartelé. Étude de Refus global*, (Quebec: Nota Bene), 2007.

[86] René Viau, "Le Refus global vu par ses signataires." p. B3.

[87] Claude Gauvreau, "Débat sur la peinture des automatistes." [1967], *Écrits sur l'art*, p. 330.

[88] Fernand Leduc, quoted by René Viau, "Le Refus global vu par ses signataires." *La Presse* (August 1, 1998), p. B3.

[89] Thomas O'Meara, "'Raid on the Dominicans.' The Repression of 1954." *America* 170. 4 (February 4, 1994): 8-16.

[90] In 1947, the project to create an exhibition of paintings from avant-garde Quebecois painters in Paris, organized by Couturier, will fail, among other things, due to this hurdle.

[91] Letter from Jean-Marie Gauvreau to Maurice Gagnon, Montreal, April 21, 1947. Archives of l'École du Meuble, Cégep du Vieux Montréal, Fonds de l'École du meuble, Dossier, 5.2.9.15.

[92] Elzéar Soucy, quoted in [Anonymous], "Diplômes d'honneur à quatre artisans." *La Presse* (October 20, 1950): 49.

[93] Armand Filion, "Mise au point des 'Anciens des Beaux-Arts.'" *Le Devoir* (June 4, 1941): 6.

[94] Letter from Paul-Émile Borduas to Maurice Gagnon, Saint-Hilaire, February 13, 1948, *Écrits II*, Vol. 1, p. 232.

[95] François Hertel, *Souvenirs, historiettes, réflexions*, p. 30.

[96] "When my nomination was confirmed, I called Parizeau to tell him the news. He seemed very happy and offered me his congratulations. I then naturally thought of calling Borduas who, after a first few words, became violently angry. He wanted to hear nothing of it and said that I was switching sides, that I was going to play into Maillard's hands. I tried to explain that it wasn't so, as the following events

clearly showed, but he didn't listen to me. I even went to his home to clarify my position, but to no avail. Since dialogue had become impossible, I concluded that we had nothing left to say to each other." Germain Lefèbvre, *Pellan, sa vie, son art, son temps*, (La Prairie: Éditions Marcel Broquet), 1986, p. 110. Borduas was not the only one who Pellan failed to convince about the propriety of his decision. John Lyman concluded that Pellan "sold himself" when he accepted Maillard's proposition. Marian Scott in an interview with Christopher Varley, October 5, 1979, quoted in Christopher Varley's *The Contemporary Arts Society, 1939-1948*, (Edmonton: The Edmonton Art Gallery), 1980, p. 36.

[97] Gérard Petit, *L'Art vivant et nous*, (Montreal: Fides), 1946, pp. 197-200.

[98] Letter from Paul-Émile Borduas to Noël Lajoie, Paris, November 29, 1956, *Écrits II*, Vol. 2, p. 875.

[99] Jean-Éthier Blais, "Hertel, cet énigme." *L'incunable, bulletin de la Bibliothèque nationale du Québec* 20th year, 1 (March 1986): 20.

[100] Pierre Gauvreau, "L'effondrement d'un repère identitaire," in Jonathan Mayer's *Les Échos du Refus global*, (Montreal: Michel Brûlé), 2008, p. 51.

[101] Robert Élie, "Au-delà du refus." [1949], in *Oeuvres*, (Montreal: Hurtubise HMH), 1979, p. 589.

[102] [Anonymous], "Brièveté." *Montréal-Matin* (September 20, 1948): 4.

[103] Harry Bernard, "Le cas Borduas." *Le Courrier de Saint-Hyacinthe* (September 24, 1948): 1.

[104] Letter from Gustave Poisson to Jean-Marie Gauvreau, September 2, 1948, according to a copy in the archival collection of the École du meuble, Cégep du Vieux Montréal, quoted in *Écrits II*, Vol. 1, p.252.

[105] Claude Gauvreau, "La peinture n'est pas un hochet de dilettante." *Combat* 1. 5 (December 21, 1946): 3

[106] Letter from Jean-Marie Gauvreau to Paul-Émile Borduas, Montreal, August 19, 1948, according to a duplicate kept in the archival collection of the École du meuble, Cégep du Vieux Montréal, quoted in *Écrits II*, Vol. 1, p. 250.

[107] Gauvreau came to see "a dictator and a fanatic" in Borduas. Quoted in Margaret Jean Vann's "A Bibliography and Selected Source Material for the Study of Paul-Émile Borduas and his Relationship to Other French-Canadian Automatists." Master's thesis, Winnipeg, University of Manitoba, 1964, p. 51.

[108] Letter from Guy Viau to Borduas, Montreal, September 16, 1948, Musée d'art contemporain de Montréal, Archives Borduas, Dossier 166, quoted by François-Marc Gagnon, "Roger Duhamel, André Laurendeau et le *Refus global*." *L'Action nationale* 88. 7 (September 1998): 178.

109 Claude Gauvreau, "Le renvoi de M. Borduas." *Le Devoir* (September 28, 1948): 5.

110 Gloria Lesser, *École du meuble, 1930-1950. La décoration intérieure et les arts décoratifs à Montréal*, (Montreal: Musée des arts décoratifs de Montréal), 1989 p. 42. Andrée-Anne de Sève, *Hommage à Jean-Marie Gauvreau. Étude ethno-historique*, (Montreal: Conseil des Métiers d'Art du Québec), 1995.

111 Letter from Jean-Marie Gauvreau to Paul-Émile Borduas, Montreal, September 4, 1948, quoted in François-Marc Gagnon's *Paul-Émile Borduas*, pp. 256-257.

112 It seems that Gauvreau was disappointed by the turn of events, but did nothing to save Borduas' position. He knew all too well that his fate was sealed (one did not mess with the Union Nationale in those years). His personal relationship with Borduas had deteriorated in an irremediable way. Still, he hired Guy Viau, one of Borduas' disciples to succeed him. "I am very sad to see what has happened," he wrote to Borduas. "It is overwhelming, but there is absolutely nothing I can do about it." Letter from Jean-Marie Gauvreau to Paul-Émile Borduas, Montréal, September 4, 1948, Fonds Paul-Émile Borduas, Centre de documentations, Musée d'art contemporain de Montréal, 232.18.

113 Lise Gauvin, *Entretiens avec Fernand Leduc*, p. 30

114 René Viau, "Le Refus global vu par ses signataires." p. B3. "We had not foreseen the wall of hate and rejection that came to stand before us." Marcel Barbeau, interview with Ninon Gauthier, "À propos de *Refus global.*" *L'Action nationale*, 88. 7 (September 1998): 154. In a letter to her brother, Marcelle Ferron expressed concern about Borduas' dismissal and was frightened by the possible imprisonment of the signatories, although this last fear seems more a figure of speech than anything else.

115 Henri Tranquille, in 1978, quoted by René Viau, "Le Refus global vu par ses signataires." p. B3

116 Paul-Émile Borduas, quoted in Jean-Éthier Blais, "Conversation rue Rousselet." *Vie des arts* 5.19 (Summer 1960), *Écrits I*, p. 674.

117 Jacques Dubuc, "La peau du lion et l'âne (en marge de "Refus global," et de ses piètres défenseurs)." *Le Devoir* (December 4, 1948): 13

118 Letter from Brother Jérôme to Paul-Émile Borduas, Montreal, November 20, 1958, Fonds Paul-Émile Borduas, Centre de documentation, Musée d'art contemporain de Montréal, T135-A.

119 Pierre Gélinas, "La querelle des peintres devient une querelle de mots." *L'Autorité du peuple* (June 12, 1954): 6.

120 Marcel Fournier, *Les Générations d'artistes*, (Quebec: Institut québécois de recherche sur la culture, (IQRC)), 1986, pp. 48-50

CÉZANNE'S ONIONS

[1] Henri Girard, "Aspects de la peinture surréaliste." *La Nouvelle Relève* 6. 5 (September 1948): 418-424. Hyacinthe-Marie Robillard, "L'automatisme surrationnel et la nostalgie du jardin d'Éden." *Amérique française* 4: 217.

[2] Jean Gilles Flynn, "Entrevue sur la peinture moderne," *Brébeuf* (October 1943): 4.

[3] Charles Doyon, "Nos peintres de demain." *Le Jour* (May 15, 1943): 6

[4] Marie-Alain Couturier, *Art et Catholicisme*, (Montreal, Éditions de l'Arbre), 1941, p. 19

[5] André Rousseaux, "Consécration d'André Breton." [1948], *Littérature du vingtième siècle*, (Paris: Albin Michel), 1949, p. 147.

[6] René Bergeron, *Art et Bolchevisme*, (Montreal: Fides), 1946, p. 10.

[7] René Bergeron, *L'Art et sa spiritualité*, (Quebec: Éditions du Pelican), 1961. Paul Gladu admits having experienced a similar change of opinion. "One can never forget that these [Borduas'] audacious experiments and these seemingly gratuitous games end up being part of daily life. You get up one fine morning and you notice that the ads in your newspaper are influenced by this new style, that your dress or your tie bears patterns you used to find weird and that the joys of the solitary artist have imposed themselves on the world due to their originality!" Paul Gladu, "Un peintre canadien à Paris. Paul-Émile Borduas a brûlé ce qu'il adorait." *Le Petit Journal* (October 6, 1957): 84.

[8] Marie-Alain Couturier, *Se garder libre*, (Paris: Cerf), 1962, p. 25.

[9] Pierre Vallières, *White Niggers of America: The Precocious Autobiography of a Quebec Terrorist*, translated by Joan Pinkham, (Toronto: McClelland and Stewart), 1971, p. 159.

[10] Ibid, p. 160.

[11] Guy Viau, "Les chrétiens et Borduas." *Maintenant* 2 (February 1962).

[12] "God's presence in the midst of our life is far from being a self-evident reality. Our God is a hidden God." Jacques Lavigne, *L'Inquiétude humaine*, (Paris: Montaigne), 1953.

[13] Letter from Paul-Émile Borduas to Josephine Hambleton, [mid-August 1948], *Écrits II*, Vol. 1, p. 248.

[14] Ibid.

[15] Letter from Borduas to Robert Élie, [end of October or beginning of November 1948], *Écrits II*, Vol. 1, p. 282.

[16] Paul-Émile Borduas, "[Le Retour]." [1947], *Écrits I*, p. 263.

17 Respectively from Paul-Émile Borduas, "[Le Retour]." [1947], *Écrits I*, p. 261; letter to Fernand Leduc, Saint-Hilaire, January 4, 1949, *Écrits II*, Vol. 1, p. 298; Paul-Émile Borduas, "[Approximations]." [1958], *Écrits I*, p. 540-541.

18 Letter from Paul-Émile Borduas to Noël Lajoie, Paris, March 10, 1956, *Écrits II*, Vol. 2, pp. 824-825.

19 Letter from Paul-Émile Borduas to Claude Gauvreau, Paris, December 24, 1957, *Écrits II*, Vol. 2, p. 955.

20 Letter from Paul-Émile Borduas to Claude Gauvreau, Paris, December 22, 1956, *Écrits II*, Vol. 2, p. 889.

21 Paul-Émile Borduas, "Objectivation ultime ou délirante." [1955], in *Écrits I*, p. 523.

22 Ibid.

23 André Malraux, "Voix du silence," in *Oeuvres complètes*, Vol. 4, (Paris: Gallimard, coll. "Bibliothèque de la Pléiade"), 2004, p. 392.

ACKNOWLEDGEMENTS

This book has benefitted from comments and advice from many people. I must first and foremost thank Christian Roy, without whom this book would not exist. Hired on as a research assistant, his erudition helped me to clarify my initial hypothesis. Karim Larose read a first version of the manuscript with his usual finesse and, through his agreements and disagreements, allowed me to untangle ambiguous passages. His contribution to the final version of this manuscript cannot be overstated, and I could not express without some embarrassment the debt I owe him. One of the evaluators of the Awards to Scholarly Publications Program, Michel Biron, also generously agreed to share his remarks and critiques with me. I thank them all for their support. I would finally like to extend my thanks to Steven Urquhart for his rigorous translation and Ray Ellenwood for his generous preface. The translation has benefitted from a Canada Council for the Arts translation grant and financial support from Concordia University.

I thank Jasmine Pocock who provided the cover photo by Philip Pocock: Paul-Émile Borduas in his Paris studio on rue Rousselet (Paris 1957). Silver gelatin print, Archives of the Musée d'art contemporain de Montréal.

The paintings are reproduced courtesy of the Art Gallery of Ontario, the Montreal Museum of Fine Arts, the Musée d'art contemporain de Montréal, the Musée d'art de Joliette, and the National Gallery of Canada. The photographs are reproduced courtesy of the Archives de la province dominicaine de France, Concordia University, the Maurice Perron family, the Musée national des beaux-arts du Québec, and the Société d'histoire de Beloeil–Mont-Saint-Hilaire.

Jean-Philippe Warren

I would like to acknowledge the Canada Council for the Arts for their support of my translation. I would also like to thank Jean-Philippe Warren, Ray Ellenwood, Marsha Bolton and Nina Callaghan for their guidance and advice with respect to this translation.

Steven Urquhart